CONTENTS

Introduction and Overview

The combinations of things we eat affect our health significantly. The ketogenic diet has proved to be significant not only for epileptic patients but also has been known to be an effective weight loss method. It stimulates the brain and helps to reduce seizures. It is also high in fat content which contradicts with the common belief that fats are bad for the human body. In this diet, ketones are produced which help the body to use fats rather than using glucose to gain energy.

Keto diet is not for everyone however, it can be tried. It can be hard to maintain and not everyone's body may be able to cope up with the changes. Try to keep the diet simple and straightforward. Install a tracker on your phone to keep a check on the number of carb consumption. Generally, 70% fat is in this diet whilst only 5% carb intake is there. Don't forget to hydrate as this is a key to stabilize the body. Supplement the diet with a multi-vitamin, this will be helpful in the long run as well. Add milk, nuts, and porridge to breakfast. Adding exercise to this diet will significantly help in the weight reduction. Buying an instant pot and using slow cooker recipes can significantly help with the diet plan. Some side effects of this diet can be cramps, constipation, increased heartbeat level, and reduced physical performance. In such cases, it is best to seek medical advice and see if any changes can be made to the diet.

Ketogenic Diet

What is ketogenic Diet?

The ketogenic diet has gained immense popularity due to the amazing health benefits it brings with it. while cutting down the carbohydrates intake and increasing the amount of the fat in the diet, keto dietary approach allows the body to harness the extra energy through the breakdown of fats. It makes our body fat dependent while turning it less carb dependent. This results in great health advantages like loosing of body fat deposits, maintenance of blood sugar levels, etc. There are many other perks of switching to a keto diet. The word ketogenic is basically derived from ketosis which is a metabolic process of breaking down fats in the absence of carbohydrates to produce energy and ketones. In the absence of sugars or carbs, the body stays free from harmful radicals and works more efficiently.

Switching to a Ketogenic Diet:

Ketogenic is not simply a diet; it is a whole lifestyle unlike many misinterpret. Being a lifestyle means that you just not need some dietary changes to get to the perks of the ketosis, you also need to turn your whole routine according to those changes, meaning, keto meal along with routine exercise, hydration, and proper sleep. A combination of all these changes will result in the keto oriented health effects.

When a person switches to a ketogenic diet, he or she goes through three important phases:

1. Induction Phase:

Entering into the world of ketogenic diet require more of the mental strength than physical. It is important to prepare your mind for it and then act on it. Thus, the first phase is all about preparing yourself for this special diet. An easy way to do that is by removing all the possible high carb food items from your groceries and opting for more clean carbs. Do your research and plan things out for yourself. Be steadier and more gradual to have a more lasting impact. Start limiting the number of carbs and keep track of the fat's intake. Habit and discipline are most important while surviving through this phase. Loss of will means loss of efforts, so start sticking to the routine.

2. Adjustment Phase:

Now that the induction phase has passed, the adjustment phase allows a person to add more variety to the diet using a variety of keto friendly fruits and vegetables. It is safe to add more fats to the diet through cream, cheeses or vegetable oils. In this phase, the body goes through slight changes in terms of energy levels and health. This adjustment in the diet is important to keep up with the pace of those changes.

3: Fitness Phase:

The last phase is the fitness phase. By this time, the routine for the keto diet must be well developed. However, the body still needs a kick start to burn more fat than glucose. A little exercise is recommended at this stage to help achieve the aim. Such exercise may range from light intensity aerobics to high-intensity exercises. Physical exercises together with a planned ketogenic diet are the road to a healthy and active life. The keto diet triggers the production of ketones inside the body. These ketone masses are then used as an energy source instead of glucose. The 'keto' part of the ketogenic diet plan is extracted from this. The ketones act as energy sources while the amount of sugar in the body is low.

Carbohydrates intake is inversely proportional to the production of the ketones in the body, meaning the lesser the carb intake, the higher the ketones production. Ketones are not directly produced through food breakdown rather, the processing of fat results in the ketonic production. These ketones are essential for vital brain functions. This is the reason that the first ketogenic diet was used only to cure patients of epilepsy and other brain-related diseases. That is why switching to a ketogenic diet quickly results in better mental health.

Carbohydrates may provide energy instantly, but that amount is not lasting that is why a sugary meal can make your energy levels drain within an hour or so, whereas keto diet provides energy through fat processing and consumption, which is long lasting and much higher than provided through the same amount of carbs.

When Ketogenic Diet is Right for You?

Being safe and healthy, the Ketogenic diet plan is now being followed by millions of users. It helps to prevent many diseases without the use of medications. It strengthens the body both mentally and physically. However, for every diet specific plan, it is important to always consult the physician before opting it. Many people suffer from internal weaknesses or special health complications which may render ketogenic diet more destruction than beneficial. These conditions include:

• People having type 1 diabetes or taking insulin medications. Ketogenic diet in such cases can cause ketoacidosis which is quite harmful and even fatal.

• People having Blood Pressure complications should also ask a professional before opting for ketogenic lifestyle.

• Breastfeeding mothers.

Signs that you are on a ketogenic diet:

Many individuals ask when actually the sign of ketosis appears? Having to know it tells you that you are in the right direction and following the diet correctly. Since this diet benefits us more internally than externally for normal people, it is hard to witness the changes easily. There are however certain related signs which help us predict the direction correctly, and those are:

- **Dry Mouth and Constant Thirst:**

Right from the induction phase, ketosis can render more dehydration and requires more water intake than usual. This is why, when a person switches to the diet it gives a constant feeling of thirst. Making your body fat dependent is a major shift, which can cause a temporary electrolyte imbalance as the body molds to adopt it. That is why try to drink as much water as to can on a daily basis.

- **Increased Urination**:

Acetoacetate is the compound which is a ketosis byproduct. It ends up in the urine and produces a constant urge of urination. Moreover, more water intake in the diet also adds up to the frequent urination. These two reasons together can cause an increased rate of urination. Which is a healthy sign as it allows the toxins to release out of the body more frequently?

- **Ketogenic breath**:

It will be interesting to know for many that when we switch to a ketogenic diet, it also affects our breath and render is smell more fruiter like a nail polish remover. It is mainly because acetone is released out of the body through the mouth. It happens of quite a few days after starting the ketogenic diet whereas it disappears with time. The same smell can be sensed through the body sweat.

- **High Energy Level:**

The most visible sign of a keto diet is elevated levels of energy. The concentration level increases and a person can feel a spark in the body. Such positive energy can last throughout the day both physically and mentally.

- **Lower Need to Eat:**

This happens because the body has shifted from glucose to fats as energy sources. Keto followers are satisfied with eating once or twice a day, and this leads to unconscious intermittent fasting. This aids a lot in losing weight and is very tie saving apart from its financial feasibility.

What are the Perks of a Keto Diet?

The ketogenic diet has numerous advantages due to the selective approach it has. Every meal that we eat is an energy booster that is equally healthy. This is the secret behind the popularity of the keto plan. It has outpaced all other dietary plans in the race due to its rich and healthy content. Let's find out more of its pros before switching to the plan.

1. **Fat Burn**

The main objective of a keto diet is to consume fats as a source of energy instead of carbohydrates. Therefore, when a person is on a keto diet, more fats present in the body are burnt which consequently reduced weight and prevents obesity.

2. Lower Cholesterol:

Consumption of fats in the energy-producing process means reduced cholesterol levels in the blood. This is particularly important for patients suffering from cardiovascular diseases and higher cholesterol levels.

3. Lower Blood Sugar:

Diabetes or high blood sugar level is caused due to zero or minimum production of insulin hormone in the body. People suffering from such disorder cannot regulate their blood sugar levels naturally, therefore, they need a diet low on sugars, and ketogenic is one best option for such individuals.

4. Increased Energy:

A single fats molecule can produce three times more energy than a carbohydrate when broken down. This is the reason that the use of the ketogenic diet gives us an instant and long-lasting boost of energy after a meal.

5. Vitality:

Though scientists are still trying to bring out direct evidence of the effects of ketogenic diet on the increased vitality of a person, they are however sure to say that keto food improves health in the longer run, aides an active metabolism and detoxifies the body regularly, which all can lead to increased vitality.

6. Mental focus:

While it is true that the ketogenic diet originally came to use for the treatment of mental illnesses like epilepsy and Alzheimer etc. it is also true that lesser consumption of carbohydrates and more availability of ketones in the body, detoxify the blood and nourished neural cells.

7. Reduce obesity:

There is a huge misconception that intake of more fats can cause obesity. It is true when you take fats along with excessive carbohydrates. Along with fats like that in keto diet does not cause obesity instead it reduces it by consuming all the deposited fats in the body.

8. Metabolism:

Increased energy production through ketosis leads to better metabolism. Due to the presence of fat molecules in the food, the bodywork rigorously during and after the digestion to generate energy.

9. Additional Benefits:
- It is great for the skin and helps it fight against the acne problems.
- Reduces the sensation of heart burning.
- It aids the body to fight against brain cancer.
- Reduces the rate of migraine attacks.
- Lowers the level of sugar in the blood and prevents its addiction.
- Treats Alzheimer's disease.

What to Eat on a Ketogenic Diet?

To make things simple and easier, let's break it down a little and try to understand the Keto vegetarian diet plan as a chart explaining what to have and what not to have. Down below is a brief list of all the items which can be used on a Ketogenic vegetarian diet.

- **All Meats:**

All types of meat are free from carbohydrates, so it is always safe to use meat in the ketogenic diet. However, processed meat which may contain high traces of carbohydrates should be avoided.

- **Selective Vegetables:**

Keep this in mind that not all vegetables are low on carbs. There are some who are full of starch, and they need to be avoided. A simple technique to access the suitability of the vegetables for a keto diet is to check if they are 'grown above the ground' or 'below it.' All vegetables which are grown underground are a no go for Keto whereas vegetables which are grown above are best for keto and these mainly include cauliflower, broccoli, zucchini, etc. Among the vegetables, all the leafy green vegetables can be added to this diet which includes spinach, kale, parsley, cilantro, etc.

- **Dry Nuts and Seeds etc.:**

Nuts and seeds like sunflower seeds, pistachios, pumpkin seeds, almonds, etc. can all be used on a ketogenic diet.

- **Selective Dairy:**

Not every dairy product is allowed on a keto diet. For example, milk is a no-go for keto whereas hard cheeses, high fat cream, butter, eggs, etc. can all be used.

- **Keto friendly Fruits:**

Not all berries are Keto friendly, only choose blackberries or raspberries, and other low carb berries. Similarly, not all fruits can be taken on a keto diet, avocado, coconut, etc. are keto friendly whereas orange, apples, and pineapple, etc. are high in carbohydrates.

- **All Fats:**

Ghee, butter, plant oils, animal fats all forms of fats can be used on a ketogenic diet.

- **Keto substitute:**

As sugar is strictly forbidden for a ketogenic diet, may it be brown or white there is a certain substitute which can be used like:

1. Stevia
2. Erythritol
3. Swerve
4. monk fruit,

5.   Natvia
6.   other low-carb sweeteners

What to Avoid on Keto Diet?

Avoiding carbohydrate is the main aim of a ketogenic diet. Most of the daily items we use contain a high amount of carbohydrates in the form of sugars or starch. In fact, any amount these items drastically increase the carbohydrate value of your meal. So, it is best to avoid their use completely.

1. All Grains including Rice and Wheat:

All types of grains are high in carbohydrates, whether its rice or corn or wheat. And product extracting out them is equally high in carbs, like corn flour, wheat flour or rice flour. So, while you need to avoid these grains for keto, their flours should also be avoided. Coconut and almond flours can be used as a good substitute.

2. All Legumes including lentils and beans:

Legumes are also the underground parts of the plants; thus, they are highly rich in carbohydrates. Make no mistake of using them in your diet. These include all sorts of beans, from Lima to chickpeas, Garbanzo, black, white, red beans, etc. cross all of them off your grocery list if you are about to go keto. All types of lentils are also not allowed on a keto diet.

3. Every natural and synthetic Sugar:

Besides white and brown sugar there are other forms of it which are also not keto friendly, this list includes honey, agave, molasses, maple syrup, etc. Also, avoid chocolates which are high in sugar. Use special sweeteners and sugar-free chocolates only.

4. High Carb Fruits:

Certain fruits need to be avoided while on a keto diet. Apples, bananas, oranges, pineapple, etc. all fall into that category. Do not use them in any form. Avoid using their flesh, juice, and mash to keep your meal carb free.

5. Underground Tubers:

Tubers are basically underground vegetables, and some of them are rich in carbs including potatoes, yams, sweet potatoes, beets, etc.

6. Animal Milk:

As stated above, not all dairy product can be freely used on a ketogenic diet. Animal milk should be strictly avoided.

Benefits of Keto Diet

Body Shape:
Most people tend to go on this diet because it helps weight loss. Studies have shown that it is a faster method of weight reduction than the traditional dieting.

Cholesterol and Sugar Control:
It also helps to decrease cholesterol levels and type-2 diabetes. It has proved to be such an effective method to control sugar.

Mental Capability:
Ketones tend to be a good source of fuel for the mind. Without carbohydrates, there are lesser chances of increments in sugar which help concentration.

A cure for Seizures:
It has proved to be a great source to help reduce seizures especially in children and this can be done alongside minimal medications.

Controlling Blood Pressure:
It is known to help cholesterol and blood pressure as it helps improve triglyceride levels.

Help with Skin Problems:
A significant difference reduction in acne has been seen in people who try this diet. Excessive amounts of carbs can be a leading cause of skin problems. The ketogenic diet has helped this problem.

Health issues regarding Ketogenic Diets

There are a few complications regarding the intake of ketogenic diets. The most common are the following:

Cramps:
Cramps can be caused due to the lack of magnesium in the body. The most common cramp is the leg cramps which happen on the beginning of starting a ketogenic diet. This usually happens in the mornings or nights and is the result of lacking minerals like magnesium in the body. Fluid intake and magnesium supplements help in overcoming this issue.

Constipation:
The main reason for constipation is lack of fluid or more commonly known as dehydration. This can be overcome by increasing fluid consumption to almost one gallon per day and with non-starchy vegetables having fibers.

Heart Palpitations
It is also common to note that while converting on a ketogenic diet, a person's heart rate is faster and harder than normal. Normally high fluid intake and sufficient salt consumption will overcome the problem, if it doesn't then potassium supplements will help in overcoming the issue,

Effects on Physical Performance:

A person's physical performance may reduce while converting on a ketogenic diet. This is because the body is getting adjusted to using fat for the body needs. Once it gets adjusted, everything will be fine, else cycling carbs before a workout may help.

What is Meal Prepping?

In simpler words, meal prepping is actually preparing your whole or a few foods and meals prior to consuming them. In other words, it is just like you are having those fancy TV recipes that you're going buy from the store, except for the fact that you will be preparing them yourself, with much healthier, unprocessed and better ingredients.

It is not only time saving (which is what everyone wants these days due to their busy lifestyles), but it assists in ensuring the fact that you are consuming proper and healthier food in the right amount time to time instead of opting for canned, packaged and processed foods which are having harmful ingredients and are high in calories.

The main agenda behind this whole 'meal prepping' operation is that when you already have healthy cooked food, you won't find a reason to opt for foods which are having harmful ingredients, and this idea actually works!

How to Get Started?

This should be strictly kept in mind that you should not overwhelm yourself with different ideas in the beginner stage. It is a common phenomenon that most people are too caught up in every detail while they can do really good by just following the basic guidelines.

Never try introducing and then accomplishing too many innovative steps altogether. For example, never ever opt for meal prepping with recipes you haven't prepared previously. Always initiate with prepping those recipes which you know well and then with the pace of tie, depending upon your comfort level, opt for fresh recipes. Meal prepping requires doing small from to time and that is the technique for making it successfully accomplished. For an effective meal prepping plan, the following steps should be noted and followed:

Select a Day:

The very first thing is that you should accomplish is to select a day for preparing your foods. Generally, the best day for preparing your meals is Sunday, as it is a holiday so one can also take help from other family members in preparing the food and it will be very time-saving as compared to working days.

Almost every experienced meal preppers usually select both Sunday and Wednesday to prepare their foods, this helps them dividing the foods prepping in two days for every half of the week. In the initial stages, almost nobody opts for preparing foods for the whole week; rather they focus on 2-3 meals in the beginning. Using a simple calendar for meal prepping will benefit a lot in practically applying the meal prepping plan.

Select the Meals:

It is critical to decide which meal you want to prepare first. In case of having a family, preparing the dinner will be your first priority while if you are single, lunch and breakfast will be n top of your priority list for meal prepping. After this, the next task will be selecting the recipes you want to prepare. The recipes should be balancing in their ingredients and for this, you can use a kitchen scale.

Use Appropriate Jars & Containers:

Perfect and proper storage containers are literally the very foundation of the whole meal prepping process. The method of how do you store your prepared food really affects meal prepping a lot. For beginners, opt for airtight jars and containers which are having airtight compartments, this single aspect will keep your food fresh, crispy and better than having it stored in a normal container. Following is the list of the most suitable and proper containers:

- Freezer Safe
- Microwaveable
- Reusable
- BPA Free
- Dishwasher Safe
- Stackable

What to Do In the Kitchen?

As stated earlier, always start with small and fewer meals. It is not recommended to opt for preparing a meal for the entire week in the beginning. You may do it later, once you are having full command and confidence over yourself, but till then, start building your stamina for food prepping. Always start from doing small and then gradually go for the hardest meals keeping in view your capabilities and capacity.

When it comes to being in the kitchen for food prep, the following things are necessary to be followed and kept in mind for better and effective execution of the plan:

Aim on prepping simpler meals:

The main agenda while food prepping is to ensure preparing simpler recipes. The reason for 'chicken' being the favorite among notably experienced meal preppers is that it can be prepared in an infinite number of methods while it is really convenient to freeze and store. Just by using chicken and some veggies, one can easily prepare 2-3 entirely different meals.

Be a good multitasker:

You can cook different meals at one without wasting much time. Utilize your oven space at its full, either use different oven trays or go for aluminum foiling to create divisions on a single tray and prepare different meals together. Try preferring recipes which can be prepared in this manner. Whenever planning the very first shopping trip for your food prep, do consider if you have sufficient utensils, aluminum foils, and oven trays etc.

Fruits:

Fruits are one of the most beneficial and integral parts of food prep. They can be easily cut into different sizes and stored just like any other meals that you can prepare. They can be used for preparing smoothies and fruit-salads which can be used alongside the prepped meals or even you can initiate with having only fruits as prepped meals.

The InstantPot:
This is the most important and critical portion of the entire food prepping plan but usually many people ignore it. The InstantPot has taken the world by storm due to its convenience and easy cooking methods. It is very time saving and is without a doubt the best option for food preppers. Use it at its full and prepare one of the most delicious and healthy meals within no time and then store them as you like.

Types of equipment Needed For Meal Prepping

Cutting Board and Storage Containers (Quriky's):
The most ideal and suitable chopping block for meal prepping is the Quirky's cutting board having storage containers in it. Simply chop and store your veggies into any of three drawers below the board and here you go, no worries till the next recipe!

Electric food Chopper (Black & Decker's 3-Cup):
The last preferred thing while meal prepping is dicing. The Black & Decker's choppers will do all the dicing for you just by tossing your vegetables into it. This will save you time for the next step of your recipes.

Heavy Duty 3-Egg Slicer (New Star's):
It doesn't matter if you are cutting strawberries for morning cereal, dicing mushroom for a dinner recipe or slicing eggs for a salad in lunch, the New Star's Heavy Duty 3-Egg Slicer is there to do all this mess for you without any worries.

2-Speed Hand Blender (Cuisinart's):
Soups are the dream of every meal prepper. Cuisinart's 2-Speed Hand Blender is very useful for recipes which need puréeing. It prevents soup blending in portions in a complicated blender; this blender is single handed and also means that you won't have to wash more.

Silicon Baking Sheet (Silpat's Nonstick):
There will be a lot of roasted veggies in your recipes if you are meal prepping. You can go eco and money friendly by getting the less parchment paper called the Silpat's Nonstick Silicon Baking Sheet.

Silicon Muffin Pan (Wilton's):
A stellar muffin tin is required irrespective of if you are baking a tray of egg muffins or blueberries. The Wilton's Silicon Muffin Pan is stain resistant and easy to wash.

Instant Pot (Pressure Cooker):
It is the advanced form of a slow cooker and can cook anything that you want ranging from oatmeal, stew, meat, preparing yogurt and much more in very less time. It is most suited for meal prepping as it prepares a large quantity of food in a faster time.

Stackable Lunch Box (Bentgo's):
The Bengto Stackable Lunch Box is preferred after you have prepped your entire week and now you want to store it properly. These storage boxes are manufactured with plastic flatware which is built-in.

What Are the Benefits Of Meal Prepping?

There are numerous benefits of meal prepping including better nutrition and regulated metabolism. Some of them are as detailed as follows:

Time-Saving:

It is very time-saving to prepare meals for an entire week than cooking every single day. Meal prepping knocks off wasting time on cooking every day or even the time wasted in waiting for getting services at a diner or a restaurant.

Financially Feasible & Money Saving:

One of the most attractive advantages of meal prepping is that it is very beneficial economically. Eating at restaurants is very expensive as compared to cooking your own food at an average. The recipes in this cookbook cost very low as compared to having expensive meals at restaurants and diners. If you try calculating the amount of money you spend on eating out and compare it to expenditure on cooking at home, you will clearly find the difference.

Keeps you focused on healthy a diet:

If you have prepared healthy food for the entire week beforehand, it is without a doubt a noted fact that you will be less likely to opt for foods and snacks having harmful ingredients in them over the food you cooked at home. This will not only help you financially but also keep your health sound and perfect.

Regulated Metabolism:

Whenever you feel hungry, you will be having already prepared food and thus resulting in your metabolism getting stronger. Consuming snacks at regular intervals will avoid your body getting into a catabolic state. This will stop you from having loss of lean body tissues which also includes muscles and improve your metabolism.

There are a few disadvantages of food prepping too alongside its numerous benefits. A few of them are explained as follows:

Lesser variety:

There is a chance that you might be eating the same food every for the whole week which is highly dependent on your meal prepping plan. It can be overcome by using different food items.

Time Demanding:

It surely saves time but also requires time for preparing a meal and the cleanup for an entire week. With time, the prepping time decreases and one can also select more than a single day for meal prepping.

Reasons Why You Should Meal Prep on Keto

Following are the reasons why you should always go for meal prepping while following a ketogenic diet plan.

1. The keto plan will be hard to follow without meal prepping because it follows a certain breaking down of calories i.e. 5% carbohydrates, 20% proteins and 75% fats.

2. Planning for an entire week relives you from stressing and panicking about what to eat every day. It doesn't let you start from scratch daily and saves you much time.
3. Although the keto plan is not expensive it may become a financial burden if you are repeatedly forgetting items from the store, wasting food due in the fridge and getting takeouts. Meal prepping prevents you from this and makes your plan financially feasible.

The Basics of Meal Planning

Meal planning or in other words 'menu planning' is the basis of meal prep. Instead of getting worried every day for what to have for the next meal, one can easily plan his meal plan and then prepare them beforehand. It is very time and money-saving alongside it ensures that you eat healthy, nutritious and a balanced diet depending on your body needs.

What differentiates Meal Prepping and Meal Planning?

Both, meal prep and meal planning work synchronously to serve a single purpose, giving you food that is healthy and nutritious in a convenient way. Mea planning is the procedure which ponders and answers the question 'what is for the next meal?' by selecting recipes as per your needs and requirements. Meal prepping, on the other hand, is a step in the meal planning procedure. It is basically putting all you're planning into action and executing the plan by gathering all the required ingredients for the recipes you want to prepare for the coming days or the entire week.

Advantages of Menu Planning

There are numerous benefits of menu planning. Some of them are stated as follows:

Health benefits:
Just by preparing your food and eating homemade food, one can ensure guaranteed sound health if your meal planning is based on a balanced and nutritious diet.

Financial Benefits:
Menu planning helps you understand the nature of your meals and lets you draft your shopping list in a befitting and feasible manner and avoids market visits for one or two items. It also helps in knocking off impulsive purchases.

The Basics of Menu Planning

This isn't that complicated as it is framed to be. Simply write down whatever meals and recipes you like and go for them. If you are prepping and planning for the entire family, do take suggestions and input from them while planning the menu. With so much content available online, there are numerous menu planning portals and applications available online.

For efficient and befitting menu planning, plan for an entire week at a single time. Do take into consideration the inclusion of secondary dishes alongside desserts and other entrees too. After the successful completion of menu planning, draft a shopping list of all the ingredients you will need as per your drafted menu plan. To draft an effective menu plan with a proper strategic approach, the following things should be kept in mind:

Keep in view 'Dates and Days':
Keep a check of which days or nights will be free enough to give you time for food prepping and which days or nights will be busy enough to make you opt for reheating the already prepped food. Always draft the menu planning in accordance with your schedule ahead for the time span you want to draft the menu for.

Always keep an eye for 'sales':
Keep an eye for sales and discount offers in different superstores, grocery stores, and markets for timely availing them. It will really help a lot in financially improving your menu plans and food prepping planning.

Keep in mind the 'season':
Always have knowledge about which foods will be available fresh at this time of the year. This will result in the availability of the most nutritious and balanced meal with fresh ingredients right in your plate.

Blend different food categories:
It is recommended to keep your menu colorful and versatile by blending in different food categories, planning various meat-free meals and even interchanging meals from breakfast to lunch and dinner. You can also replace new recipes with your previously liked recipes and keep on doing this cycling of bringing in new recipes from time to time.

Imagine your plate:
The most integral part of meal planning for any occasion is to picture your plate efficiently. It is recommended that for each meal you plan, half of your plate should be filled with fruits and veggies, a quarter with lean proteins and the rest of the quarter with preferably whole grains.

How to Master Menu Planning?
Just like any ordinary habit, menu planning gets better and better with practice and time. As soon as you spend more time on menu planning, you will realize different strategies and methods which will make the process work for you in an easy way. To plan the menu in the most convenient way possible there are some tips explained below:

Devise themes for days:
To make your menu colorful and versatile, decide different foods for different days and try new recipes as you get experienced.

Reuse Leftovers:
Reuse leftover food in different ways you like. For example, a leftover chicken can be used in a soup or with salad on any other day.

Recycling the plan:
Don't just throw off the menu plan after its completion. It can be used later on entirely or a portion of it can be utilized.

Flexibility in the menu:
You can alter your menu plan if desired. You can easily swap between recipes without much hindrance and it can keep your menu colorful without altering its nutrition and balancing.

Common Mistakes for Meal Prepping Beginners

Though meal prepping isn't that complicated, yet there are certain common mistakes committed by beginners which should be avoided while following the plan.

Insufficient Ingredients:
Once you have devised your menu plan, go for writing down a shopping list on the basis of the menu plan. It should be having all the ingredients which are included in the menu plan so that when it comes to prepping the food, everything is on available with you.

Preparing too much of a meal:
With the help of meal prep, the desire to order take away food can be resisted easily. But if you are preparing too much of your favorite meal regularly, you will soon get fed up of it. Try devising a menu plan which includes food from almost every category so that it remains versatile and gives you different options for every meal.

Insufficient containers:
Food prepping clearly requires a lot of containers and storage jars for storing the food. There are different container qualities and designs available at supermarkets which can be utilized according to the storage space and requirements of the user. Freeze the food the way it suits your requirements. Snacks can also be frozen but they have to be snap freeze first with the aid of items like slices or bliss balls placed on a lined chopping board and then freezing them individually. They can be afterward placed in a ziplock bag without the fear of them clumping together.

Insufficient freezer storage:
A lot of food is feared to be wasted when you have prepared food which is filling 30 containers and your freezer's max storage space is just 20 containers. Try freeing as much storage as you can in your freezer and alongside it some of the prepped food can be stored in the refrigerator too.

Not giving sufficient time to meal prep:
Meal prepping requires a lot of time and is not an hour game. Give yourself sufficient time to properly shop the ingredients, unpack them, chop and cook them properly and then place them in containers in the fridge after labeling them properly.

Forgetting to label the containers:
In order to avoid any unwanted surprises, properly name and label the containers before storing them in the freezer. Devise a proper format having the meal name, cooking date, portion numbers etc for your convenience. You can also add details about defrosting and heating instructions too.

Tips

For better and efficient meal prepping, the following tips will prove to be very beneficial and helpful.

Master Your Multitasking Skills:
Instead of preparing different meals and foods separately, try preparing them at once. Simply put ingredients in the oven or the InstantPot and then go for preparing the rest of the food without much worry. For microwaving and freezing, the glass snap-lid storage containers can be used due to their high safety measures.

Prepare 1-2 Meals Maximum:
Too much variety of food will not only confuse you but will also be very time consuming to prepare too. To avoid this prepare one or two meals at maximum and this for sure doesn't mean that the menu shouldn't be bought at all.

Regularly Update List of Available Items:
Keep yourself updated about the availability of ingredients in your pantry at regular intervals. This will help you decide when to shop, what to shop and how much to shop, resulting not only in time-saving but also giving you a financial check about your plan.

Take & Devise Strategic Shortcuts:
If you are too short ion time or too caught up in your busy schedule, there is no harm at all in going for certain beneficial and convenient things from the grocery store like pre-cut veggies etc. This will still be very good on economic and health as compared to take away.

Cut-short the Recipes:
Recipes usually involve complicated and time-consuming steps to cut them short and prepare food according to your need and requirements. Try focusing on simple foods like veggies and roasted chickens, low-maintenance soups, slices veggies, and boiled eggs etc.

Take Suggestions In the Menu:
If you are prepping for the entire family, try taking suggestions and input from the entire family before menu planning so that the entire family can have a proper food without any dominance from a single person's choices.

Entertain Yourself While Prepping:
Prepping doesn't require you to be silent; you can listen to audiobooks, podcasts, and music etc. while prepping food.

Keto Meal Prep Recipes

Day 1

Breakfast: Keto Bacon Eggs
Serves: 15 /Prep Time: 5 minutes

Ingredients:

- 12 eggs
- salt and pepper, to taste
- 4 oz. cooked bacon

Directions

1. Adjust your oven to 400 degrees F (200°C).
2. Line a muffin tray with cupcake liners.
3. Crack one egg into each liner and top it with bacon.
4. Drizzle some salt and pepper on top.
5. Bake for 15 minutes.
6. Serve warm.

Nutrition Calories: 211 Carbs: 0.5g Fats: 18.5g Proteins: 11.5g Sodium: 280g Sugar: 0.3g

Lunch: Chicken Enchilada Bowl
Prep Time: 10 mins/Serves: 4

Ingredients:

- 2-3 chicken breasts
- 3/4 cups red enchilada sauce
- 1/4 cup water
- 1/4 cup onion
- 1 4 oz. can green chile
- 1 (12oz) steam bag cauliflower rice
- Preferred toppings- avocado, jalapeno, cheese, and Roma tomatoes
- Seasoning, to taste

Directions

1. Heat a greased skillet and sear chicken breasts until golden brown from both the sides.
2. Stir in enchilada sauce, onions, chile and water. Reduce the heat and cover the lid.
3. Cook until chicken is completely cooked.
4. Remove the chicken and shred it with fork.
5. Return the chicken to the skillet and cook for 10 minutes.
6. Serve on top of cauliflower rice along with desired toppings.

Nutrition *Calories: 182; Carbs: 11.1g; Fats: 1.4g; Proteins: 22.2g; Sodium: 560mg; Sugar: 2.1g*

Dinner: Zoodles with Avocado Sauce
Serves: 15 /Prep Time: 5 minutes

Ingredients

- 3 cups yellow and red cherry tomatoes

avocado sauce:

- 1 avocado
- 1/4 cup olive oil
- 1/2 teaspoon salt
- 1/2 cup fresh flat leaf parsley

- 3 zucchinis, spiralized
- Parmesan for topping

- 3-4 green onions (green parts)
- 1 garlic clove
- juice of 1 lemon
- freshly ground pepper to taste

Directions

1. For sauce add everything to a blender and blend until smooth.
2. Take a skillet and heat a drizzle of oil in it.
3. Add tomatoes and sauté until soft. Keep these tomatoes aside.
4. Now add zucchini to the same skillet and sauté for 2 minutes.
5. Toss sautéed zucchini with tomatoes and avocado sauce.
6. Top this mixture with cheese.
7. Serve.

Nutrition *Calories: 109 Carbs: 6.2g Fats: 9.6g Proteins: 0.9g Sodium: 227mg Sugar: 1.8g*

Day 2

Breakfast: **Breakfast Biscuits with Sausage and Cheese**
Serves: 6 /Prep Time: 8 minutes

Ingredients:

- 2 ounces cream cheese
- 2 cups mozzarella, shredded
- 2 eggs, beaten
- 1 cup almond flour

- pinch salt & pepper
- 2 ounces Colby jack cheese, thin cubes
- 6 breakfast sausage patties, pre-cooked

Directions

1. Add cream cheese and mozzarella to a bowl and microwave for 30 seconds. Mix well.
2. Beat egg with almond flour in the mixer then add cream cheese mixture. Blend well.
3. Knead the dough on a lightly floured surface. Wrap it a plastic sheet then refrigerate until firm.
4. Cut the dough ball into six 3inch balls.
5. Flatten each dough ball and place the sausage on each.
6. Top the sausages with cheese then wrap the dough around the sausage.
7. Place stuffed dough in a greased baking tray.
8. Bake for 15 minutes until golden brown.
9. Top with mozzarella and serve warm.

Nutrition *Calories: 489 Carbs: 5g Fats: 43.6g Proteins: 0.9g Sodium: 662mg Sugar: 0.1g*

Lunch: Zucchini Noodles with Spicy Pepita Gremolata
Serves: 4/Prep Time: 8 minutes

Ingredients

Gremolata

- 1/4 cup pepitas, roughly chopped
- zest of one lemon
- 1/3 cup Italian flat-leaf parsley, chopped

Noodle

- 2 large zucchinis, peeled
- 2-3 T olive oil

- 1 tsp fresh garlic, finely minced
- a dash of cayenne pepper, to taste
- a big pinch of salt

- salt, to taste

Directions

1. For gremolata mix everything in a bowl and set it aside.
2. Process zucchinis through a spiralizer to get its noodles.
3. Take a wok and heat a drizzle of oil in it on medium heat.
4. Add zucchini noodles and sauté for 7 minutes. (in batches if needed)
5. Sprinkle salt over these noodles and sauté.
6. Top the noodles with gremolata.
7. Serve.

Nutrition Calories: 109 Carbs: 6.2g Fats: 9.6g Proteins: 0.9g Sodium: 227mg Sugar: 1.8g

Dinner: Bacon, Chicken & Tomato Stuffed Avocado
Serves: 3/Prep Time: 10mins

Ingredients:

- 2 Chicken Breasts grilled
- 3 pieces bacon cooked and chopped
- 2 Avocado, pitted, peeled and sliced

- 1/3 cup Grape Tomatoes chopped
- 1/3 cup mayo paleo
- Additional seasonings to taste

Directions

1. Season chicken with salt and pepper. Grill over medium heat until tender.
2. Add bacon strips to the grill and cook until crispy.
3. Cut the chicken into cubes and transfer it to a bowl.
4. Add bacon, onions, and tomatoes.
5. Stir in mayo along with seasoning.
6. Top the mixture with avocado slices.
7. Serve.

Nutrition Calories: 487; Carbs: 10.6g; Fats: 37.4g; Proteins: 28.1g; Sodium: 501mg; Sugar: 1.2g

Day 3

Breakfast: **Greek Egg Bake**
Serves: 10/Prep Time: 5 minutes

Ingredients:

- 12 Eggs
- 1 cup Chopped Kale
- 1/4 cup Sun-dried tomatoes
- 1/2 cup Feta
- 1/2 teaspoon Oregano
- Salt & pepper, to taste

Directions

1. Adjust your oven to 350 degrees F.
2. Whisk eggs in a glass bowl then stir in all the remaining ingredients.
3. Line a baking pan with a parchment paper.
4. Grease the pan with non-stick cooking spray.
5. Bake for 25 minutes in the oven
6. Slice and serve.

Nutrition Calories: 139; Carbs: 2.3g; Fats: 10.1g; Proteins: 10.9g; Sodium: 238mg; Sugar: 1.5g

Lunch: **South Western Chicken**
Serves: 1/Prep Time: 10 mins

Ingredients:

- 1 boneless Chicken Breasts (boneless)
- 2 teaspoon Olive Oil (extra virgin optional)
- 1 whole Lemon - zested and juices
- 1/2 teaspoon Red chili powder
- 1/2 teaspoon Cumin
- 1 teaspoon Oregano dried
- 3 cloves Garlic minced
- 1 teaspoon Onion powder
- 1/2 teaspoon Salt
- 1/2 teaspoon Black pepper freshly ground

Directions

1. Mix everything in a large bowl.
2. Cover the bowl and marinate for 1 hour in the refrigerator.
3. Meanwhile, Adjust a grill pan over low heat for 4 minutes.
4. Add a tsp olive oil and add the marinated chicken.
5. Cook for 7 minutes per side on medium heat.
6. Serve warm.

Nutrition *Calories: 355; Carbs: 11.8g; Fats: 15g; Proteins: 44.2g; Sodium: 971mg; Sugar: 2.5g*

Dinner: **Thai Quinoa Salad**
Serves: 1 /Prep Time: 15 minutes

Ingredients

For the Salad

- ½ cup cooked quinoa
- 3 tbsp grated carrot
- 2 tbsp red pepper, finely chopped
- 3 tbsp cucumber, finely chopped
- ½ cup edamame (thawed)

- 2 scallions, finely chopped
- ¼ cup red cabbage, finely sliced
- 1 tbsp cilantro, finely chopped
- 2 tbsp roasted peanuts, chopped
- to taste salt

Thai Peanut Dressing:

- 1 tbsp creamy natural peanut butter
- 2 tsp low sodium soy sauce
- 1 tsp rice vinegar
- ½ tsp sesame oil
- 1 tsp sriracha sauce (optional)

- 1 garlic clove, finely minced
- ½ tsp grated ginger
- 1 tsp lemon juice
- ½ tsp agave nectar (or honey)

Directions:

1. For salad dressing mix everything in a small bowl.
2. Toss the salad ingredients in a large bowl.
3. Pour in the prepared dressing and mix well.
4. Serve

Nutrition *Calories: 109 Carbs: 6.2g Fats: 9.6g Proteins: 0.9g Sodium: 227mg Sugar: 1.8g*

Day 4

Breakfast: **Turmeric Scrambled Egg**
Serves: 2 /Prep Time: 5 minutes

Ingredients

- 4 large eggs
- 2 tablespoons coconut milk
- 2 teaspoons dried turmeric
- ½ teaspoon. dried parsley

- salt & black pepper to taste
- steamed veggie of choice
- pre-cooked sausage of choice

Directions

1. Grease a small frying pan with nonstick cooking spray and place it on medium heat.
2. Whisk eggs with milk, parsley, salt, pepper and turmeric in a bowl.
3. Pour this eggs mixture into the greased pan and cook for 3 minutes with constant stirring.
4. Flip and cook for another 3 minutes.
5. Transfer the scramble to the meal prep containers.
6. Serve with sautéed vegetables and sausage.

Nutrition *Calories: 231; Carbs: 3.1g; Fats: 17.6g; Proteins: 15.7g; Sodium: 244mg; Sugar: 1.3g*

Lasagna Stuffed Portobello Mushrooms
Serves: 4/Prep Time: 5 minutes

Ingredients

- 4 large portobello mushrooms
- 1-2 tablespoons olive oil
- 1 cup marinara sauce
- 1 1/2 cups light ricotta
- 1/4 teaspoon salt
- 1 egg
- 1 1/2 cup chopped spinach
- 1/2 cup basil chopped
- 1 cup shredded mozzarella

Directions

1. Adjust your oven to 400 degrees F. Layer a baking sheet with parchment paper.

2. Clean the mushrooms by removing the gills and stem then wash them.

3. Layer the mushrooms with olive oil inside out.

4. Add ¼ cup marinara sauce into each mushroom cap.

5. Add ricotta, spinach, basil, egg, and salt to a bowl and toss well.

6. Divide this mixture into the four mushrooms.

7. Top each mushroom cup with ¼ cup mozzarella.

8. Place the stuffed mushrooms in the baking sheet.

9. Bake for 20 minutes.

10. Serve.

Nutrition *Calories: 261 Carbs: 11g Fats: 16g Proteins: 21g Sodium: 457mg Sugar: 5g*

Chicken Pesto
Serves: 1/Prep Time: 10 minutes

Ingredients:

- 1 chicken breasts (boneless)
- 3 tablespoons olive oil extra virgin
- ¼ cup almonds, chopped
- 2 garlic cloves, minced
- 1 cup basil leaves
- 1/2 cup coriander leaves
- 1/2 teaspoon salt each
- 1/2 teaspoon black pepper freshly crushed

Directions

1. Add everything to a food processor except chicken.

3. Mix the marinade with chicken in a bowl.
4. Cover the bowl and marinate for 1 hour in the refrigerator.
5. Meanwhile, Adjust a grill pan over low heat for 4 minutes.
6. Add a tsp olive oil and add the marinated chicken.
7. Cook for 7 minutes per side on medium heat.
8. Serve warm.

Nutrition *Calories: 455; Carbs: 10.8g; Fats: 34.4g; Proteins: 10.9g; Sodium: 227mg; Sugar: 1.8g*

Day 5

Breakfast: Cauliflower Cheddar Pancakes
Serves: 4/Prep Time: 10 minutes

Ingredients

- 1 small head grated cauliflower
- 1 large Egg
- 3/4 cup Shredded Cheddar Cheese
- 1/4 teaspoon Cayenne Pepper
- 1/4 teaspoon garlic powder
- 1/2 teaspoon Pink Salt
- 1/8 teaspoon black pepper

Directions

1. Add grated cauliflower to a bowl and microwave for 3 minutes.
2. Transfer the cauliflower to the cheesecloth and drain excess water.
3. Mix the drained cauliflower with all the remaining ingredients in a bowl.
4. Divide the batter into six squares arrange on a greased baking tray.
5. Bake for 15 to 20 minutes at 400 degrees F.
6. Serve warm.

Nutrition Calories: 111; Carbs: 1.9g; Fats: 8.3g; Proteins: 7.4g; Sodium: 896mg; Sugar: 0.8g

Lunch: Chicken Vegetable Stew
Serves: 10/Prep Time: 10 minutes

Ingredients:

- 3.5 pounds chicken thighs, bone & skin on
- 1 large yellow onion, chopped
- 4 medium-size carrots, diced
- 4 stalks celery, diced
- 10 ounces cremini mushrooms, sliced
- ½ teaspoon dried thyme
- 3 cloves garlic, minced
- ½ cup frozen peas
- 1-2 cups low sodium chicken broth
- 2 tablespoons Xanthan gum
- Olive oil
- Kosher salt
- Fresh cracked pepper

Directions

1. Adjust your oven to 400 degrees F.
2. Rub the chicken with pepper and salt then place it on a baking sheet.

4. Bake for 1 hour then allow it to cool for 10 minutes.
5. Pull the meat then cut it into small pieces.
6. Heat oil in a saucepan over medium heat and add celery, carrots, onion, mushrooms, thyme, salt, and pepper.
7. Sauté for 12 minutes then add garlic to cook for another 7 minutes.
8. Add chicken shred, peas and stock to the pan and cook for 10 minutes.
9. Mix xanthan gum with water in a small bowl and pour the mixture into the pan.
10. Stir cook for 10 minutes.
11. Serve warm.

Nutrition *Calories: 364 Carbs: 10.8g Fats: 13.6g Proteins: 47.9g Sodium: 227mg Sugar: 2.8g*

Dinner: Enchilada Stuffed Eggplants
Serves: 4/Prep Time: 5 minutes

Ingredients

- 2 medium eggplants
- 1/2 cup enchilada sauce
- 1/4 tsp salt
- 1/4 teaspoon chili powder
- 1/8 teaspoon ground cumin
- 1.5 cups shredded cheese
- Serve with avocado salsa and/or sour cream

Directions

1. Adjust your oven to 400 degrees F.
2. Prepare eggplant by scrubbing them gently and poke some holes using a fork.
3. Place these prepared potatoes in the baking sheet.
4. Bake them for 50 mins until they are soft.
5. Slice each eggplant into half lengthwise.
6. Scoop out the flesh from the center while leaving some with the skins.
7. Mash this scooped out flesh in a bowl and add cumin, chili powder, salt, enchilada sauce, corn, beans, and ¾ cup cheese.
8. Mix well then divide the mixture into the eggplant skins.
9. Top each with the remaining cheese.
10. Bake the eggplant for 15 minutes.
11. Serve warm.

Nutrition *Calories: 359 Carbs: 11 g Fats: 9.6g Proteins: 0.9g Sodium: 227mg Sugar: 1.8g*

Day 6

Breakfast: Strawberry Pancake Bites
Serves: 8/Prep Time: 10 minutes

Ingredients:

- 4 large eggs
- 1/4 cup Swerve Sweetener
- 1/2 teaspoon vanilla extract
- 1/2 cup coconut flour

- 1/4 cup butter melted
- 1 teaspoon baking powder
- 1/2 teaspoon salt
- 1/4 teaspoon cinnamon
- 1/3 to 1/2 cup water
- 1/2 cup strawberry, chopped

Directions

1. Adjust your oven to 325 degrees F and grease a muffin tray.
2. Blend eggs with vanilla extract, the sweetener in a blender.
3. Stir in melted butter, coconut flour, salt, cinnamon, and baking powder. Blend well until smooth.
4. Add 1/3 cup water to the mixture and blend again.
5. Divide the batter into each muffin cups and top it with few blueberries.
6. Press the blueberries gently and bake for 20 to 25 minutes.
7. Serve warm.

Nutrition *Calories: 121 Carbs: 13.8g Fats: 9g Proteins: 4.3g Sodium: 184mg Sugar: 8.2g*

Lunch: **Broccoli Quinoa Casserole**
Serves: 5/Prep Time: 10 minutes

Ingredients:

- 2 1/2 cup uncooked quinoa
- 4 1/2 cup low-sodium vegetable stock, or water
- 2 tbsp pesto sauce
- 1/2 tsp Celtic salt
- 2 tsp arrowroot powder, or cornstarch
- 2 cups fresh organic spinach
- 12 oz skim mozzarella cheese, I used 16oz
- 1/3 cup parmesan cheese
- 12 oz fresh broccoli florets
- 3 green onions, chopped

Directions

12. Adjust the oven to 400 degrees F.
13. Spread green onions and quinoa in a 9x13 baking sheet.
14. Add broccoli to a glass bowl and heat it for 5 minutes on high temperature.
15. Now whisk vegetable stock with salt, arrowroot, and pesto in a saucepan.
16. Heat the stock mixture until it boils.
17. Pour the stock over quinoa in the baking pan.
18. Top it with spinach, ¾ mozzarella cheese, and parmesan.
19. Bake it for 35 minutes.
20. Add in broccoli and top the casserole with remaining cheese.
21. Bake for another 5 minutes.
22. Serve warm.

Nutrition *Calories: 109 Carbs: 6.2g Fats: 9.6g Proteins: 0.9g Sodium: 227mg Sugar: 1.8g*

Meal Prep Chicken Fajitas
Serves: 4/Prep Time: 10 minutes

Ingredients:

Rub:

- 1 tablespoon erythritol
- 3/4 teaspoon salt
- 1 tablespoon chili powder
- 1.5 teaspoon cumin

Fajitas

- 1.5 teaspoon paprika
- 1/2 teaspoon garlic powder
- 1/2 teaspoon onion powder
- 1/8-1/4 teaspoon cayenne optional

- 2 large chicken breasts sliced into 1/2-inch-thick strips
- 6 cups mixed veggies sliced into strips
- -bell peppers

To Serve

- -zucchini
- -red onion
- -mushrooms
- juice from 1 lime
- 1 tablespoon olive oil

- Tortillas or tortilla bowls
- Salsa & Greek yogurt

- Fresh avocado

Directions

1. Adjust oven to 425 degrees F.
2. Mix chicken with all the vegetables, lime juice and olive oil in a bowl.
3. Gradually add the rub with continuous mixing.
4. Spread the chicken and vegetables on two large sheet pans.
5. Roast for 10 minutes then flip. Roast for another 10 minutes.
6. Transfer the roasted chicken and veggies to the meal prep containers.
7. Store up to 4 days in the refrigerator.
8. Reheat and serve with salsa.

Nutrition *Calories: 202 Carbs: 11.5g Fats: 9.6g Proteins: 22g Sodium: 526mg Sugar: 1.5g*

Day 7

Low Carb Bagels
Serves: 14/Prep Time: 5 minutes

Ingredients:
- 2 cups almond flour
- 1 tablespoon baking powder
- 1 teaspoon garlic powder
- 1 teaspoon onion powder
- 1 teaspoon dried Italian seasoning

- 3 large eggs, divided
- 3 cups shredded low moisture mozzarella cheese
- 5 tablespoons cream cheese

- 3 tablespoons Everything Bagel Seasoning

Directions
1. Adjust the oven to 425 degrees F.
2. Layer a rimmed baking sheet with wax paper.
3. Mix almond flour with garlic powder, baking powder, onion powder and Italian seasoning in a mixing bowl.
4. Whisk 1 egg in a bowl and set it aside.
5. Add cream cheese with mozzarella to a bowl and heat for 1.5 minutes in the microwave.
6. Whisk 2 eggs with the almond flour mixture in a mixing bowl.
7. Stir in cream cheese mixture and mix well.
8. Divide the dough into 6 pieces and shape them into smooth balls.
9. Press your finger through the center of each ball to make a ring. Stretch the ring into a bagel.
10. Place all the bagels on the baking sheet.
11. Brush each bagel with egg wash and Everything bagel seasoning.
12. Bake for 14 minutes until golden brown.

Nutrition *Calories: 207 Carbs: 5.4g Fats: 15g Proteins: 11.1g Sodium: 252mg Sugar: 0.2g*

Lunch: **Fiesta Lime Chicken Chowder**
Serves: 4/Prep Time: 10 minutes

Ingredients:
- 1 pound of chicken thighs, skinless and boneless
- 8 oz. cream cheese
- 1 cup of chicken broth
- 1 can of diced tomatoes
- 1 small onion, diced
- 1 jalapeno, diced
- 1 lime, juiced
- 2 tablespoons of cilantro, chopped
- 1 clove of garlic, chopped
- a few dashes of liquid smoke
- 1 teaspoon of salt
- 1 tablespoon of pepper
- Garnish with shredded cheddar cheese
- lime wedge
- fresh cilantro

Directions
1. Add all the ingredients to a slow cooker.
2. Cover the lid and cook on low for 6 hours.
3. Use two forks to shred the chicken.
4. Garnish with cheddar cheese, lime wedges, and cilantro.
5. Serve.

Nutrition *Calories: 449; Carbs: 8.4g; Fats: 28.7g; Proteins: 39.3g; Sodium: 1044mg; Sugar: 2.6g*

Dinner: **Butter Chicken**
Serves: 6/Prep Time: 10 minutes

Ingredients

- 1-pound boneless skinless chicken breast cut into bite-size chunks
- 1/2 onion finely minced
- 2 tablespoons butter
- 3 cloves garlic minced or grated
- 1 tablespoon freshly grated ginger
- 2 teaspoons curry powder
- 1-2 teaspoons Thai red curry paste
- 2 tablespoons garam masala
- 1/2-1 teaspoon turmeric
- 1 teaspoon cayenne pepper
- 1/4 teaspoon salt
- 1 (6 ounces) can tomato paste
- 1 (14 ounces) can coconut milk
- 1/2 cup Greek yogurt
- 1/4 cup half and half cream
- cooked white rice for serving
- Fresh homemade naan for scooping

Directions

23. Mix coconut milk, cream and Greek yogurt in a glass bowl.
24. Add garlic, ginger, all the spices, and tomato paste. Mix until well combined.
25. Layer the bowl of the crockpot with olive oil.
26. Add onion, chicken, and coconut milk mixture to the crockpot.
27. Top the mixture with butter and seal the lid.
28. Cook on the high-temperature setting for 4 hours.
29. Adjust seasoning with salt and pepper.
30. Serve warm.

Nutrition *Calories: 109 Carbs: 6.2g Fats: 9.6g Proteins: 0.9g Sodium: 227mg Sugar: 1.8g*

Day 8

Breakfast: **Bacon and Mushroom Casserole**
Serves: 8/Prep Time: 10 minutes

Ingredients:

- 6 oz. mushrooms, trimmed and quartered
- 10 oz. bacon, diced
- 2 oz. butter
- 8 eggs
- 1 cup heavy whipping cream
- 5 oz. shredded cheddar cheese
- 1 teaspoon onion powder
- salt and pepper

Directions

1. Adjust your oven to 400 degrees F (200°C).
2. Heat butter in a skillet over medium-high heat and add bacon and mushrooms to sauté until golden brown.
3. Season the mixture with salt and pepper. Add it to a greased baking dish.
4. Mix all the remaining ingredients in a bowl along with salt and pepper.
5. Pour this mixture over the mushrooms and bake for 30 to 40 minutes.
6. Add remaining ingredients to a medium bowl and whisk to combine.
7. Serve warm.

Nutrition *Calories: 434 Carbs: 2.5g Fats: 36.4g Proteins: 24.9g Sodium: 1038mg Sugar: 0.9g*

Lunch: **Mixed Cauliflower Rice**
Serves: 8/Prep Time: 10 minutes

Ingredients

- 2 Eggs
- Salt and Pepper to taste
- 1 tbsp. Vegetable Oil Divided
- 1/2 Yellow Onion Diced
- 1 cup Frozen Peas and Carrots

- 1/2 Cup Frozen Corn
- 5 cups Fresh Minced/Crumbled Cauliflower
- 1 tsp. Sesame Oil
- 2 Green Onions Chopped

Sauce:

- 4 tbsp. Soy Sauce Low Sodium
- 3 Garlic Cloves Minced

- 2 tsp. Sesame Oil

Directions

31. Whisk eggs in a bowl and add pepper and salt.
32. Mix soy sauce with 1 tsp. sesame oil and garlic in a bowl.
33. Use a large skillet and add ½ tbsp oil.
34. After heating the oil add onion and all the frozen vegetables.
35. Sauté them for 5 minutes while adding salt and pepper to taste.
36. Stir in remaining vegetable oil, cauliflower rice, and soy sauce mixture.
37. Sauté for 6 minutes.
38. Keep this mixture on one side of the pan and reduce the heat.
39. Pour 1 tsp sesame oil to empty side and pour the whisked egg into it.
40. Cook the egg scramble for 2-3 minutes.
41. Sauté with the cauliflower mixture.
42. Garnish with green onions and serve.

Nutrition *Calories: 109 Carbs: 6.2g Fats: 9.6g Proteins: 0.9g Sodium: 227mg Sugar: 1.8g*

Dinner: **Turkey Zucchini Noodles in Romesco Sauce**
Serves: 4/Prep Time: 10 minutes

Ingredients:

Romesco Sauce:

- 1 jar roasted red peppers drained
- 1/2 cup cherry tomatoes
- 1 clove garlic
- 1/4 cup almonds

- 2 tablespoons red wine vinegar
- 1/4 cup olive oil
- 1/2 teaspoon salt
- 1/4 teaspoon smoked paprika

Ground Turkey Pasta:

- 1 lb. lean ground turkey
- 2 large zucchini spiralized (approx. 4-6 cups)
- Parmesan cheese to taste

Directions

1. Add all the ingredients for Romesco sauce to a blender and blend until smooth.
2. Heat a skillet and add ground turkey to sauté until it is no longer pink.
3. Stir in spiralized zucchini and cook for 3 minutes.
4. Add Romesco sauce and toss everything together.
5. Serve.

Nutrition Calories: 225 Carbs: 11.3g Fats: 17.7g Proteins: 7.9g Sodium: 386mg Sugar: 2.3g

Day 9

Breakfast: **Turkey Edamame Bowl**
Serves: 4/Prep Time: 10 mins

Ingredients:

- 1 cup turkey, thinly sliced
- 3/4 cups red enchilada sauce
- 1/4 cup water
- 1/4 cup onion
- 1 4 oz. can green chile
- 1 12oz steamed edamame
- Preferred toppings- avocado, jalapeno, cheese, and Roma tomatoes
- Seasoning, to taste

Directions

1. Heat a greased skillet and sauté turkey until golden brown.
2. Stir in enchilada sauce, onions, chile and water. Reduce the heat and cover the lid.
3. Cook until turkey is completely cooked.
4. Remove the turkey and shred it with a fork.
5. Return the chicken to the skillet and cook for 10 minutes.
6. Serve on top of edamame along with desired toppings.

Nutrition *Calories: 182; Carbs: 11.1g; Fats: 4.6g; Proteins: 22.2g; Sodium: 560mg; Sugar: 2.1g*

Lunch: **Caribbean Shrimp**
Serves: 4/Prep Time: 10mins

Ingredients:

- 10 oz. large shrimp, peeled and deveined
- 2 tablespoons olive oil
- 2 tablespoons red wine vinegar
- 2 tablespoons freshly squeezed lemon juice
- 1 tablespoon erythritol
- 1 tablespoon coconut aminos

- 2 tablespoons green onions, chopped
- 1 tablespoon jalapeño, seeded and finely chopped
- Lime wedges, if desired

Directions

1. Gently mix all the ingredients for shrimps in a bowl.
2. Cover and marinate for 30 minutes in the refrigerator.
3. Adjust the grill over medium heat.
4. Thread the marinated shrimp onto the skewers.
5. Place the skewers on the grill . Cook, it covered for 6 minutes over indirect heat.
6. Pour the remaining marinade into a saucepan and boil.
7. Decrease the heat to low then let it simmer for 10 minutes.
8. Pour the sauce over the shrimps and serve.

Nutrition *Calories: 132; Carbs: 8.2g; Fats: 9.6g; Proteins: 13.9g; Sodium: 94mg; Sugar: 1.9g*

Dinner: **Broccoli Stir Fry Recipe**
Serves: 4/Prep Time: 10mins

Ingredients

- 1 tbsp. Vegetable Oil
- 1/2 Red Onion thinly sliced
- 1 Orange Bell Pepper thinly sliced
- 12 oz Broccoli Florets Fresh
- Salt and Pepper to taste

Sauce:

- 5 Garlic Cloves minced
- 2 tsp. Sesame Oil
- 1/4 Cup Soy Sauce Low Sodium
- 1/2 cup Vegetable Broth

- 1 cup Sugar Snap Peas
- 1 Green Onion chopped
- 1 tbsp. Sesame Seeds
- Juice of half a lime

- 2 tsp. Maple Syrup
- Salt and Pepper to taste
- 2 tsp. Corn Starch

Directions

1. Add garlic, sesame oil, broth, cornstarch, maple starch and soy sauce in a bowl and mix.
2. Take a pan and add vegetable oil.
3. Add bell pepper, broccoli florets, and onions. Sauté for 7 minutes.
4. Add salt and pepper for seasoning.
5. Decrease the heat then add soy sauce mixture and sugar snap peas.
6. Stir cook for 3 minutes until it thickens.
7. Add green onion, sesame seeds, and lime juice.
8. Serve warm.

Nutrition *Calories: 109 Carbs: 6.2g Fats: 9.6g Proteins: 0.9g Sodium: 227mg Sugar: 1.8g*

Day 10

Chicken Avocado Bowl
Serves: 3/Prep Time: 10mins

Ingredients:

- 2 Chicken Breasts grilled
- 3 pieces bacon cooked and chopped
- 2 Avocado, pitted, peeled and diced
- 1/3 cup Grape Tomatoes chopped
- 1/3 cup mayo paleo
- Additional seasonings to taste

Directions

1. Season chicken with salt and pepper. Grill over medium heat until tender.
2. Add bacon strips to the grill and cook until crispy.
3. Cut the chicken into cubes and transfer it to a bowl.
4. Add bacon, onions, and tomatoes.
5. Stir in mayo along with seasoning.
6. Toss in avocado cubes and mix.
7. Serve.

Nutrition *Calories: 487; Carbs: 12.6g; Fats: 37.4g; Proteins: 28.1g; Sodium: 501mg; Sugar: 1.2g*

Lunch: **Instant Pot Pulled Pork**
Serves: 4/Prep Time: 10 minutes

Ingredients:

- 2 tablespoons olive oil
- 3-4 lbs. boneless pork shoulder cut into 3-4 pieces
- 2 cups barbecue sauce
- 1 1/2 cups beer of choice or water or chicken broth
- 2 tablespoons molasses

Directions

1. Select sauté function on the pressure cooker.
2. Add oil to the cooking pot along with pork. Cook for 3 minutes per side.
3. Transfer the seared pork to a plate.
4. Stir in 1 cup BBQ sauce, 1 cup beer and molasses to the cooking pot.
5. Return the beef to the pot.
6. Secure the lid and cook for 90 mins on high pressure.
7. Allow the pressure to release naturally for 20 minutes.
8. Shred the pork using two forks.
9. Return the shredded pork to the pot along with all the remaining ingredients.
10. Serve.

Nutrition *Calories: 392; Carbs: 7.2g; Fats: 40.4g; Proteins: 21g; Sodium: 423mg; Sugar: 3g*

Stuffed Salmon Rolls with Lemon Sauce
Serves: 4/Prep Time: 10 minutes

Ingredients:

- 4 (5 ounces) salmon fillets, skins removed
- salt and pepper to taste
- 1 (12 ounces) container ricotta
- 1/2 cup Parmigiano Reggiano (parmesan), grated
- 2 tablespoons basil, chopped

- 2 teaspoons lemon zest
- 1/2-pound asparagus, trimmed
- 1 tablespoon butter
- 1/2 cup chicken broth
- 2 tablespoons lemon juice
- 2 teaspoons xanthan gum

Directions

1. Season the fillets with salt and pepper.
2. Spread them on a surface with their skin side up.
3. Top each fillet with ricotta, parmesan, lemon zest, basil, salt, pepper, and asparagus.
4. Roll each fillet and place on a baking sheet with its seam side down.
5. Bake for 15 to 20 minutes at 425 F in a preheated oven.
6. Heat butter on medium flame in a small saucepan.
7. Pour in broth mixture, lemon juice, and xanthan gum to the pan and stir cook for 5 minutes.
8. Pour this sauce over the baked rolls and serve with basil and lemon zest on top.
9. Serve the salmon rolls topped with the lemon sauce and optionally garnish with more basil and lemon zest.

Nutrition *Calories: 394 Carbs: 8.3g Fats: 21.7g Proteins: 43.2g Sodium: 384mg Sugar: 1.6g*

Day 11

Teriyaki Beef Zoodles
Serves: 4/Prep Time: 10 minutes

Ingredients:

- 1/4 cup coconut aminos
- 2-3 tablespoons erythritol
- 3 tablespoons rice vinegar
- 2 garlic cloves minced

For the zoodles

- 8 ounces flank steak sliced against the grain into 1/4-inch thick slices
- 1 teaspoon sesame oil

- 1/2 teaspoon grated ginger
- 1 tablespoon xanthan gum
- 2 tablespoons water

- Salt and black pepper to taste
- 5-6 medium zucchini cut into noodles
- 3 tablespoons olive oil divided
- Salt and black pepper, to taste
- Red chili flakes to taste

Directions

1. Mix all the ingredients for sauce in a container without water.
2. Rub the steak with salt, pepper, sesame oil, and 2 tablespoons sauce.
3. Let it marinate at room temperature.
4. Heat 2 tablespoons in a large flat pan over medium flame.
5. Add beef to cook for 1 minute per side.
6. Transfer the beef to a plate.
7. Heat remaining oil in a skillet and stir in beef along with the sauce.
8. Cook until the sauce thickens and add the water.
9. Stir in zucchini noodles to the pan and cook for 2 minutes.
10. Garnish with green onions and sesame seeds.
11. Serve.

Nutrition *Calories: 406 Carbs: 10g Fats: 40.4g Proteins: 2.2g Sodium: 406mg Sugar: 4.8g*

Lunch: **Tuscan Baked Salmon and Veggies**
Serves: 4/Prep Time: 10 mins

Ingredients:

For the Topping and Salmon:

- 1/4 cup tomato paste
- 2 tablespoons olive oil
- 1 teaspoon mustard
- 1 tablespoon dried Italian herb

- 1 teaspoon ground paprika
- 1/ teaspoon salt
- Pepper to taste
- 1 1/2-pound salmon fillet skin on

For the Vegetables:

- 2 large red peppers , sliced
- 1-2 large zucchini sliced
- 1 tablespoon dried Italian herb

- 1 tablespoon olive oil
- Salt and pepper to taste
- 1/2-pound cherry tomatoes

Directions

1. Adjust the oven to 400 degrees F. Line a baking tray with a parchment sheet.
2. Mix all topping ingredients in a bowl.
3. Spread the salmon fillet on the baking sheet and top it with the topping evenly.
4. Toss peppers with zucchini, herbs, 1 tablespoon olive oil, salt, and pepper in a large bowl.
5. Place this mixture around the salmon fillets along with cherry tomatoes.
6. Bake for 15 to 20 minutes.
7. Serve.

Nutrition *Calories: 336 Carbs: 10.6g Fats: 18.3g Proteins: 35.9g Sodium: 104mg Sugar: 6.1g*

Dinner: Parmesan-Dijon Crusted Pork Chops
Serves: 2/Prep Time: 10 minutes

Ingredients:

- 4 boneless pork loin chops
- 1/4 teaspoon sea salt
- 1/4 teaspoon black pepper
- 1/4 cup Dijon mustard
- 2 tablespoons spicy brown mustard
- 2 tablespoons olive oil
- 1/2 teaspoon garlic powder
- 1/2 teaspoon dried thyme
- 1/4 teaspoon onion powder
- 1/4 teaspoon dried oregano
- 1/4 teaspoon dried basil
- 1/4 teaspoon Italian seasoning
- 1 cup grated Parmesan cheese

Directions
1. Adjust the oven to 400 degrees F.
2. Keep a wire rack on a baking sheet.
3. Place the pork chops on the wire rack and bake until crispy.
4. Season the chops with salt and pepper.
5. Mix spicy mustard, olive oil, thyme, garlic powder, onion powder, basil, oregano and Italian seasoning in a mixing bowl.
6. Dip the chops in the mustard the mixture and mix well to coat.
7. Coat the chops with a thin layer of Parmesan cheese.
8. Place the pork chops over the wire rack in the baking sheet.
9. Bake for 20 minutes.
10. Broil it for 4 minutes until golden brown.

Nutrition *Calories: 349 Carbs: 23.1g Fats: 6.6g Proteins: 11g Sodium: 237mg Sugar: 1.4g*

Day 12

Breakfast: Butter Pecan Fat Bombs
Prep Time: 10mins /Serves: 12

Ingredients:

- 1/2 cup pecans
- 1/4 cup coconut butter
- 1/4 cup ghee or butter
- 1/4 cup coconut oil
- 1/2 teaspoon vanilla extract
- 1/8 teaspoon sea salt

Directions

1. Heat a frying pan over medium heat.
2. Add pecans to the pan and toast until dark brown.
3. Coarsely chop the roasted pecan. Set them aside.

5. Mix coconut butter with ghee and coconut oil in a saucepan. Let it simmer over low heat.
6. Stir in sea salt and vanilla extract. Mix well.
7. Transfer the chopped pecan into the silicon mold having 12 mini cubes.
8. Pour the butter mixture over the pecans
9. Refrigerate for 30 mins.
10. Serve.

Nutrition *Calories: 145; Carbs: 2g; Fats: 16g; Proteins: 1g; Sodium: 111mg; Sugar: 1g*

Lunch: **Creamy Mustard Pork Loin**
Serves: 4/Prep Time: 10 minutes

Ingredients:
Pork Loins

- 4 4 oz. pork loins
- 1 tablespoon pink Himalayan sea salt
- 1 teaspoon black pepper

Mustard Sauce

- 1/2 cup chicken broth
- 1/4 cup heavy cream
- 1 teaspoon apple cider vinegar
- 1/2 lemon

- 1 teaspoon paprika
- 1 teaspoon thyme

- 1 tablespoon mustard
- Suggested Side
- 2 cups green beans

Directions
1. Pat dry the pork loins with salt, pepper, paprika, and thyme.
2. Heat a large pan and brown the pork in it for 3 minutes per side. Set them aside.
3. Add apple cider vinegar, chicken broth and ¼ cup heavy cream to a skillet.
4. Bring the mixture to a simmer.
5. Add lemon juice and mustard. Mix well.
6. Return the pork to the sauce and combine well.
7. Let it cook for 10 minutes.
8. Serve with sautéed green beans.

Nutrition *Calories: 269 Carbs: 8.6g Fats: 11.9g Proteins: 15g Sodium: 437mg Sugar: 1.2g*

Dinner: **Avocado Tuna Salad**
Serves: 10/Prep Time: 10mins

Ingredients:

- 15 oz. tuna in oil, drained
- 1 English cucumber, sliced
- 2 large avocados peeled, sliced

- 1 small/medium red onion thinly sliced
- 1/4 cup cilantro

- 2 tablespoons lemon juice freshly squeezed
- 2 tablespoons extra virgin olive oil

- 1 teaspoon sea salt or to taste
- 1/8 teaspoon black pepper

Directions

1. Add all the vegetables and drained tune to a large bowl.
2. Mix all the remaining ingredients in a bowl to prepare the dressing.
3. Pour the dressing over the vegetables.
4. Toss well and serve.

Nutrition *Calories: 304; Carbs: 9g; Fats: 20g; Proteins: 22g; Sodium: 645mg; Sugar: 2g*

Day 13

Breakfast: **Avocado Brownies**
Serves: 12/Prep Time: 10 minutes

Ingredients:

- 2 avocados, pitted and peeled
- 1/2 teaspoon vanilla
- 4 tablespoons cocoa powder
- 1 teaspoon stevia powder

Dry Ingredients

- 1/3 blanched almond flour
- 1/4 teaspoon baking soda
- 1 teaspoon baking powder

- 3 tablespoons refined coconut oil
- 2 eggs
- 1/2 cup lily's dark chocolate melted

- 1/4 teaspoon salt
- 1/4 cup erythritol

Directions

1. Adjust the oven to 350 degrees F.
2. Blend the avocado flesh in a blender until smooth.
3. Add all the remaining ingredients to the food processor.
4. Blend well until smooth.
5. Line a baking dish with wax paper and pour the batter into the dish.
6. Bake for 35 minutes. Allow it to cool for 10 minutes.
7. Slice the cake into 12 pieces.
8. Serve.

Nutrition *Calories: 158 Carbs: 9.1g Fats: 14.2g Proteins: 3.8g Sodium: 243mg Sugar: 1.1g*

Lunch: **Sesame Salmon with Bok Choy**
Serves: 4/Prep Time: 10 minutes

Ingredients:
Main Dish

- 4 each 4-6 oz. salmon fillet
- 2 each Portobello mushroom caps, sliced
- 4 each baby bok choy, trimmed and halved
- 1 tablespoon toasted sesame seeds
- 1 green onion, chopped

Marinade

- 1 tablespoon olive oil
- 1 teaspoon sesame oil
- 1 tablespoon Coconut Aminos
- 1/2-inch Ginger grated (approx. 1 teaspoon.)
- 1/2 lemon juice
- 1/2 teaspoon Salt
- 1/2 teaspoon black pepper

Directions
1. Mix all the marinade ingredients in a container.
2. Pour half of this marinade over the salmon and mix well to coat.
3. Cover the fish and marinate for 1 hour in the refrigerator.
4. Adjust the oven to 400 degrees F.
5. Mix the remaining half of the marinade with all the vegetables in a bowl.
6. Spread the veggies mixture over the baking sheet lined with parchment paper.
7. Place the marinated fillets on the baking sheet as well and bake for 20 minutes.
8. Garnish with green onions and sesame seeds
9. Serve.

Nutrition *Calories: 294 Carbs: 1.1g Fats: 16.4g Proteins: 35g Sodium: 343mg Sugar: 0.1g*

Dinner: **Spiced lamb shoulder chops**
Serves: 4/Prep Time: 10 minutes

Ingredients:
For the lamb

- 5-10 lamb shoulder chops
- 1.5 teaspoons smoked paprika
- 1.5 teaspoons ground cumin
- ½ teaspoon dried oregano

For the yogurt dipping sauce:

- ½ cup whole fat Greek-style yogurt
- Zest & juice of half a lemon
- 2 teaspoons freshly chopped dill

For the green beans

- 1-pound green beans
- 2 tablespoons sunflower seeds & pumpkin seeds

- ½ teaspoon cayenne pepper
- ¼ teaspoon ground cinnamon
- Olive oil
- Kosher salt

- 1 teaspoon extra virgin olive oil
- ¼ teaspoon kosher salt
- Couple cracks of fresh black pepper

- ¼ cup pitted Kalamata olives, sliced
- 1 small red-hot chili or jalapeno pepper, thinly sliced
- ½ cup orange peppers, diced
- ½ cup cherry tomatoes quartered lengthwise
- ¼ cup crumbled feta cheese
- Kosher salt
- Fresh cracked black pepper

Directions

1. Season the lamb chops with all the ingredients for lamb in a bowl.
2. Let it marinate for 20 minutes at room temperature.
3. Add 2 teaspoons salt to a pot filled with water. Bring the water to a boil.
4. Add green beans to boiling water and let them soak for about 2 ½ minutes.
5. Immediately transfer the beans to an ice bath and strain. Let it set aside.
6. Mix pumpkin and sunflower seeds in a bowl along with all the remaining ingredients for green beans.
7. Heat oil in a skillet and brown the chops for 6 minutes per side.
8. Allow them rest for 5 to 7 minutes.
9. Mix all the ingredients for yogurt sauce in a bowl.
10. Serve the lamb with green beans and yogurt sauce.

Nutrition *Calories: 376 Carbs: 12.1g Fats: 21.9g Proteins: 33.2g Sodium: 227mg Sugar: 1.2g*

Day 14

Breakfast: **Cloud Bread**
Serves: 4/Prep time: 15minutes

Ingredients

- 3 eggs
- 4¼ oz. cream cheese
- 1 pinch salt

- ½ tbsp ground psyllium husk powder
- ½ tsp baking powder
- ¼ tsp cream of tartar (optional)

Toppings

- 8 tbsp mayonnaise
- 5 oz. bacon
- 2 oz. lettuce

- 1 tomato, thinly sliced
- fresh basil (optional)

Directions

1. Adjust your oven to 300 degrees F.
2. Separate egg yolks from egg whites.
3. Whisk egg whites with salt until foamy using a hand-held blender.
4. Mix egg yolks with cream cheese, baking powder, and psyllium husk.
5. Stir in egg white foam and fold in gently.

7.   Mix well and divide the dough into 8 pieces on a baking sheet, lined with parchment paper.
8.   Bake for 25 minutes until golden brown.
9.   Serve with your favorite toppings.

Nutrition *Calories: 109 Carbs: 6.2g Fats: 9.6g Proteins: 0.9g Sodium: 227mg Sugar: 1.8g*

Lunch: Harissa Portobello Mushroom
Serves: 6/Prep Time: 10mins

Ingredients:

Portobello Mushrooms

- 1-pound Portobello mushrooms stem removed and rinsed
- 1/4 cup spicy harissa
- 3 tablespoons olive oil, divided

Guacamole

- 2 medium ripe avocados
- 2 tablespoons chopped tomatoes
- 2 tablespoons chopped red onion

Optional Toppings

- cashew cream
- chopped tomatoes

- 1 teaspoon ground cumin
- 1 teaspoon onion powder
- 6 collard green leaves

- 1 1/2 lemon juice
- 1 pinch of salt
- 1 tablespoon chopped cilantro

- chopped cilantro

Directions

1.   Combine harissa with cumin, 1 1/2 tablespoons olive oil and onion powder in a bowl.
2.   Coat each mushroom with harissa mixture and let them marinate for 15 minutes.
3.   Meanwhile, mash avocados in a bowl and add all the ingredients for guacamole to the bowl.
4.   Heat remaining olive oil in a frying pan.
5.   Stir in marinated mushrooms and cook for 3 minutes per side.
6.   Turn off the heat and for 3 mins, let them rest.
7.   Slice the mushrooms and serve with guacamole and collard green.
8.   Add desired toppings.

Nutrition *Calories: 131 Carbs: 9.1g Fats: 10.4g Proteins: 2.3g Sodium: 106mg Sugar: 0.5g*

Lemon Pepper Sheet Pan Salmon
Serves: 4/Prep Time: 10 minutes

Ingredients:

- 16 oz. salmon cut into four portions
- 12 oz. green beans, trimmed
- 1 bunch asparagus ends trimmed

Lemon Dill Yogurt

- 3/4 cup yogurt
- 1 clove garlic minced
- 1/4 teaspoon salt

- 1 lemon sliced into rounds
- 1 tablespoon olive oil
- 1 1/2 tablespoons lemon herb seasoning

- 1/2 teaspoon dill
- 1 tablespoon lemon zest

Directions

1. Adjust the oven to 425 degrees F.
2. Mix green beans with asparagus, olive oil, and 1 tablespoon lemon herb seasoning.
3. Spread this mixture over a baking sheet with lemon slices.
4. Place the salmon pieces in the asparagus mixture and drizzle the remaining herb seasoning on top.
5. Place lemon slices over the fish and bake for 15 minutes.
6. Meanwhile, mix all the ingredients for dill yogurt in a bowl.
7. Serve the roasted fish and veggies with dill yogurt.

Nutrition *Calories: 202 Carbs: 10g Fats: 6g Proteins: 25g Sodium: 141mg Sugar: 7g*

Day 15

Frittata with fresh spinach
Serves: 4/Prep Time: 10 minutes

Ingredients

- 5 oz. diced bacon or chorizo
- 2 tbsp butter, for frying
- 8 oz. fresh spinach
- 8 eggs

- 1 cup heavy whipping cream
- 5 oz. shredded cheese
- salt and pepper

Directions

1. Adjust the oven to 350 degrees F.
2. Grease a skillet with butter and sauté bacon on medium heat until crispy.
3. Add spinach and cook for 2 to 3 minutes until wilted.
4. Beat eggs with cream in a bowl and pour the mixture into a 9x9inch baking dish.
5. Top this mixture with spinach, bacon, and cheese.
6. Bake for 30 minutes until golden brown.

8.   Slice and serve.

Nutrition *Calories: 109; Carbs: 6.2g; Fats: 9.6g; Proteins: 0.9g; Sodium: 227mg; Sugar: 1.8g*

Lunch: Shrimp Zucchini Noodles
Serves: 4/Prep Time: 10 minutes

Ingredients:

- 4 medium zucchinis, spiralized
- 1 tablespoon olive oil
Sauce
- 1/4 cup 2 tablespoons fat-free plain Greek yogurt
- 1/4 cup 2 tablespoons light mayonnaise
- 1/4 cup 2 tablespoons Thai sweet chili sauce

- 1/2 lb. Shrimps
- 1 1/2 tablespoons liquid erythritol
- 1 1/2 teaspoon Sriracha sauce
- 2 teaspoon lime juice

Directions

1.   Heat a greased skillet and add shrimp to sauté until well cooked.
2.   Season the shrimps with salt and pepper then set them aside.
3.   Heat olive oil in a large skillet and add zucchini noodles.
4.   Cook until zucchini noodles are just cooked.
5.   Turn off the heat and let them rest for 10 mins.
6.   Drain the excess water out of zucchini and set it aside.
7.   Mix all the ingredients for sauce in a small bowl.
8.   Divide the sauce into 4 meal prep containers and top it with zucchini noodles and sautéed shrimp.
9.   Serve or refrigerate up to 3 days.
10. Toss well before each serving.

Nutrition *Calories: 135 Carbs: 3.1g Fats: .9g Proteins: 8.6g Sodium: 10mg Sugar: 3.4g*

Dinner: One Pot Zucchini Pasta
Serves: 4/Prep Time: 10mins

Ingredients:

- 2 pounds zucchini (approx. 4-5 large zucchini), spiralized
- 1-pint cherry tomatoes halved
- 1 large red onion, thinly sliced

- 4 garlic cloves, minced
- 1/4 cup extra-virgin olive oil
- 1/2 cup fresh basil
- salt & pepper to taste

- 1/2 teaspoon crushed red pepper
- shredded parmesan for topping

Directions

1. Heat olive oil in a saucepan over medium heat.
2. Add garlic and onion to sauté for 3 minutes.
3. Stir in zucchini noodles along with salt and pepper.
4. Cover the lid and cook for 2 mins. With occasional stirring.
5. Stir in tomatoes and cook for 4 minutes with constant stirring.
6. Add red pepper, parmesan cheese, and fresh basil.
7. Garnish with basil and serve.

Nutrition *Calories: 204; Carbs: 10.7g; Fats: 15.6g; Proteins: 6.3g; Sodium: 141mg; Sugar: 3.4g*

Day 16

Breakfast: **Coconut Porridge**
Serves: 4/Prep Time: 10mins

Ingredients

- 1 oz. butter or coconut oil
- 1 egg
- 1 tbsp coconut flour
- 1 pinch ground psyllium husk powder
- 4 tbsp coconut cream
- 1 pinch salt

Directions

1. Add everything to a cooking pot and cook on low heat until it reaches desired consistency.
2. Pour a splash of cream or coconut milk.
3. Top with frozen berries.
4. Serve.

Nutrition *Calories: 109; Carbs: 6.2g; Fats: 9.6g; Proteins: 0.9g; Sodium: 227mg; Sugar: 1.8g*

Lunch: **Sesame Pork Tenderloin**
Serves: 4/Prep Time: 10 mins

Ingredients:

- 1/2 cup hoisin sauce
- 2 teaspoons coconut aminos
- 1 teaspoon sesame oil
- Two 1- to 1 1/4-pound pork tenderloins, trimmed
- 2 pounds carrots, cut diagonally into 1/4-in. slices
- 1 tablespoon olive oil
- 3 scallions, thinly sliced
- 1 1/2 teaspoons toasted sesame seeds

Directions

1. Preheat the oven to 500 degrees F.
2. Mix coconut aminos, hoisin sauce and sesame oil in a bowl.
3. Spread the pork on a rimmed baking sheet and pour the hoisin mixture over the pork.
4. Arrange the carrots around the pork and drizzle the sesame seeds and scallions on top
5. Roast for 25 minutes then let it rest for 10 minutes.
6. Slice the pork and serve with carrots.

Nutrition *Calories: 234; Carbs: 10.1g; Fats: 23.4g; Proteins: 2.3g; Sodium: 10mg; Sugar: 12.7g*

Dinner: **Zucchini Scallops Scampi**
Serves: 4/Prep Time: 10 minutes

Ingredients:

- 2 tablespoons unsalted butter
- 1-pound scallops
- 3 cloves garlic, minced
- 1/2 teaspoon red pepper flakes
- 1/4 cup chicken stock
- Juice of 1 lemon
- Kosher salt and black pepper, to taste
- 1 1/2 pounds (4 medium-sized) zucchini, spiralized
- 2 tablespoons freshly grated Parmesan
- 2 tablespoons chopped fresh parsley leaves

Directions

1. Heat butter in large skillet over medium flame.
2. Stir in scallops, garlic, and red pepper flakes.
3. Cook for 2 to 3 minutes then adds chicken stock, lemon juice, salt, and pepper.
4. Bring the mixture to a simmer and add zucchini noodles.
5. Cook for 3 minutes then garnish with Parmesan and parsley.
6. Serve.

Nutrition *Calories: 154 Carbs: 3.4g Fats: 10.4g Proteins: 6.7g Sodium: 156mg Sugar: 0.9g*

Day 17

Breakfast: **Keto mushroom omelet**
Serves: 4/Prep Time: 10 mins

Ingredients

- 3 eggs
- 1 oz. butter, for frying
- 1 oz. shredded cheese
- 1⁄5 yellow onion
- 3 mushrooms
- salt and pepper

Directions

1. Take a bowl and beat eggs with salt and pepper in it.
2. Take a frying pan and melt butter in it.
3. Pour the egg mixture into it and cook for 2 mins until firm.
4. Top the egg with onion, mushrooms, and cheese.
5. Flip the egg and cook for 1 minute.
6. Serve.

Nutrition *Calories: 109; Carbs: 6.2g; Fats: 9.6g; Proteins: 0.9g; Sodium: 227mg; Sugar: 1.8g*

Lunch: **Skinny Lemon Garlic Shrimp Caesar Salad**
Serves: 2/Prep Time: 10 minutes

Ingredients:

- 1/4 cup cubed almond flour bread
- 1-pound large raw shrimp (prawns), peeled and deveined, tails intact
- Juice of 1/2 a large lemon
- 1 tablespoon minced garlic
- Pinch of salt
- Cracked pepper, to taste
Dressing:
- 1/4 cup plain, nonfat Greek yogurt
- 1 tablespoon whole egg mayo
- 1/2 tablespoon olive oil
- 1 garlic clove, crushed

- ¼ cup nonfat diced bacon
- 1 egg, soft boiled (or poached)
- 4 cups Romaine (Cos) lettuce, leaves washed and dried
- 1/2 an avocado, sliced
- 1/4 cup shaved parmesan cheese

- 1 anchovy fillet, finely chopped or minced
- 1 tablespoon lemon juice
- 1 1/2 tablespoons parmesan cheese, freshly grated
- Salt and pepper for seasoning

Directions

1. Adjust the oven to medium-high heat on grill settings.
2. Spread the bread cubes on a baking tray and drizzle olive oil on top.
3. Bake for 5 to 10 minutes until crispy.
4. Mix shrimp with lemon juice, salt, pepper and garlic in a small bowl. Set it aside.
5. Heat a lightly greased grill pan over medium heat and add shrimp.
6. Cook for 3 minutes per side then set them aside.
7. Blend yogurt with garlic, oil, mayo, lemon juice, anchovies and parmesan in a blender.
8. Season the mixture with salt and pepper.

10. Toss lettuce with shrimp, bacon, bread cubes, parmesan cheese and avocado slices in a large bowl.
11. Pour the dressing on top and mix.
12. Top the salad with boiled egg and serve.

Nutrition *Calories: 199; Carbs: 9.9g; Fats: 17.4g; Proteins: 2.4g; Sodium: 296mg; Sugar: 5.5g*

Roasted Tofu
Serves: 4/Prep Time: 10mins

Ingredients:

- 2 (14 ounces) packages extra-firm, water-packed tofu, drained
- ⅔ cup coconut aminos
- ⅔ cup lime juice
- 6 tablespoons toasted sesame oil

Directions

1. Pat dry the tofu and slice into half inch cubes.
2. Mix all the remaining ingredients in a small bowl.
3. Marinate for 1 to 4 hours in the refrigerator.
4. Adjust the oven to 450 degrees F.
5. Spread the marinated tofu on a baking sheet and bake for 20 minutes.
6. Serve.

Nutrition *Calories: 104 Carbs: 6.7g Fats: 3.6g Proteins: 5.4g Sodium: 141mg Sugar: 1.4g*

Day 18

Cauliflower hash browns
Serves: 4/Prep Time: 10mins

Ingredients

- 15 oz. cauliflower
- 3 eggs
- ½ yellow onion, grated
- 1 tsp salt
- 2 pinches pepper
- 4 oz. butter, for frying

Directions

1. Grate the cauliflower in a food processor grinder to get fine rice.
2. Mix the cauliflower with all the remaining ingredients in a bowl. Let it sit for 10 minutes.
3. Take a large skillet and heat butter.
4. Spread a dollop of the cauliflower into the skillet to get a 4-inch round.

6. Cook for 3 minutes per side.
7. Use the entire batter to cook more hash browns.
8. Serve and enjoy.

Nutrition *Calories: 109; Carbs: 6.2g; Fats: 9.6g; Proteins: 0.9g; Sodium: 227mg; Sugar: 1.8g*

Lunch: **Colorful Roasted Sheet-Pan Veggies**
Serves: 4/Prep Time: 5 minutes

Ingredients:

- 3 cups cubed carrots (1-inch)
- 3 tablespoons extra-virgin olive oil, divided
- 4 cups broccoli florets
- 2 red bell peppers, cut into squares
- 1 large red onion, diced
- 2 teaspoons Italian seasoning
- 1 teaspoon coarse kosher salt
- ¼ teaspoon pepper
- 1 tablespoon best-quality balsamic vinegar

Directions

1. Adjust the oven to 425 degrees F.
2. Toss carrots with oil and spread them on a baking sheet.
3. Roast for 5 minutes.
4. Toss all the remaining ingredients in a large bowl.
5. Stir in roasted carrots and spread the mixture on the baking sheet.
6. Bake for 5 to 7 minutes.
7. Serve.

Nutrition *Calories: 124; Carbs: 6.4g; Fats: 13.4g; Proteins: 4.2g; Sodium: 136mg; Sugar: 2.1g*

Dinner: **Korean Beef Brisket**
Serves: 3/Prep Time: 10 minutes

Ingredients:

- 4 to 5 pounds beef brisket, diced into chunks
- 1 tablespoon sweet paprika
- ½ teaspoon red chili flakes
- 2½ teaspoon kosher salt
- ½ teaspoon freshly ground black pepper
- 1 to 3 tablespoons peanut oil, as needed
- 1 large onion, diced
- 4 garlic cloves, minced
- 1 tablespoon grated peeled fresh ginger
- 1 cup water
- ¼ cup Gochujang (Korean chili paste)
- 2 tablespoons sugar-free ketchup
- 2 tablespoons soy sauce
- 2 teaspoon Asian fish sauce
- 1 teaspoon toasted sesame oil

Directions

1. Season the beef pieces with paprika, chili flakes, salt, and pepper.
2. Heat oil in a large skillet and add beef to sear for 2 minutes per side.
3. Transfer the beef to a plate.
4. Add ginger, garlic, and onion to the skillet and sauté for 3 to 5 minutes.
5. Add ketchup, soy sauce, fish sauce, sesame oil, water and water to the pan.
6. Transfer the mixture to an electric pressure cooker along with the sautéed meat.
7. Cover the lid and cook on high pressure for 90 minutes.
8. Release the pressure naturally for 20 minutes
9. Transfer the beef to a cutting surface and place a foil sheet on top.
10. Cook the remaining mixture in the cooker for 15 to 20 minutes on sauté settings.
11. Serve the beef with prepared sauce on top.

Nutrition *Calories: 196 Carbs: 13.4g Fats: 10.4g Proteins: 14.3g Sodium: 226mg Sugar: 1g*

Day 19

Breakfast: **Keto Mexican scrambled eggs**
Serves: 4/Prep Time: 10mins

Ingredients

- 6 eggs
- 1 scallion, chopped
- 2 pickled jalapeños, finely chopped
- 1 tomato, finely chopped
- 3 oz. shredded cheese
- 2 tbsp butter, for frying
- salt and pepper

Directions

1. Take a skillet and heat butter in the skillet.
2. Add scallions, tomatoes, and jalapenos. Sauté for 3 minutes.
3. Whisk eggs with salt and pepper.
4. Pour them into the skillet and cook for 2 minutes while scrambling it.
5. Top with cheese and serve.

Nutrition *Calories: 109; Carbs: 6.2g; Fats: 9.6g; Proteins: 0.9g; Sodium: 227mg; Sugar: 1.8g*

Lunch: **Sheet Pan Chipotle Eye Round Roast**
Serves: 6/Prep Time: 10 minutes

Ingredients:

- 1 tablespoon erythritol
- 1 tablespoon ground chipotle chile pepper
- 1 tablespoon paprika
- 1 tablespoon cumin powder
- Salt and pepper
- 1 (2.5-pound) eye round roast
- 3 tablespoons olive oil
- 1 white onion, chopped
- 1-pound Brussels sprouts halved

Directions

1. Adjust the oven to 425 degrees F. Layer a baking sheet with parchment paper.
2. Mix erythritol with paprika, cumin powder, and chipotle chile pepper in a small bowl.
3. Season the round roast with salt.
4. Toss Brussels sprouts with onion, salt, black pepper and 1 tablespoon oil in a large bowl.
5. Heat remaining 2 tablespoons oil in a flat skillet.
6. Place roast in the skillet and cook for 8 minutes until golden brown.
7. Transfer the roast to the baking sheet and top it with chipotle mixture.
8. Spread the vegetables around the roast in the baking sheet.
9. Bake for 25 minutes until al dente.
10. Spread the vegetables onto the same baking tray around the roast.
11. Slice the roast and serve.

Nutrition *Calories: 266 Carbs: 5.4g Fats: 26.4g Proteins: 0.6g Sodium: 455mg Sugar: 2g*

Dinner: Roasted Veggie Mason jar Salad
Serves: 1/Prep Time: 10mins

Ingredients:

- 2 tablespoons Creamy Vegan Cashew Sauce
- 1 cup roasted tofu
- 1 tablespoon pumpkin seeds
- 1 cup roasted vegetables
- 2 cups mixed greens

Directions

1. Layer a 4-cup jar with tofu, pumpkin seeds, vegetables, cashew sauce, and greens.
2. Cover the lid tightly.
3. Refrigerate up to 5 days.
4. Toss well before serving.

Nutrition *Calories: 191 Carbs: 7.1g Fats: 8.4g Proteins: 6.3g Sodium: 226mg Sugar: 0.1g*

Day 20

Breakfast: Low-carb baked eggs
Serves: 4/Prep Time: 10mins

Ingredients

- 3 oz. ground beef
- 2 eggs
- 2 oz. shredded cheese
- Salt and pepper, to taste

Directions

1. Adjust the oven to 400 degrees F.

3. Spread the beef in a baking dish and poke two holes using a spoon.
4. Crack one egg into each hole.
5. Sprinkle salt, pepper, and cheese on top.
6. Bake for 15 minutes.
7. Serve warm.

Nutrition *Calories: 109; Carbs: 6.2g; Fats: 9.6g; Proteins: 0.9g; Sodium: 227mg; Sugar: 1.8g*

Lunch: **Lamb Shanks, Cauliflower Mash & Beans**
Serves: 6/Prep Time: 10 minutes

Ingredients:
Lamb Shanks

- 6 Lamb Shanks
- 1 tablespoon olive oil
- 2 teaspoons salt
- 2 teaspoons pepper
- 2 carrots, roughly chopped
- 2 stalks celery, roughly chopped
- 1 brown onion, roughly chopped

- 1 tablespoon dried oregano
- 1 cup red wine
- 1.5 cups chicken stock
- 1.5 tablespoons rosemary
- 1 400gram can have crushed tomatoes
- 3 Bay leaves

Cauliflower Mash

- 1 head cauliflower, broken into small florets
- 4 tablespoons salted butter
- 4 tablespoons heavy cream
- 1 teaspoon salt and pepper

Green Beans

- 300 grams green beans, ends trimmed
- 1 tablespoon olive oil
- 1/2 teaspoon salt and pepper
- 1/2 teaspoon crushed garlic

Directions
1. Heat olive oil in a skillet over medium flame.
2. Sear the lamb shanks until brown from both the sides.
3. Season the lamb with salt and pepper. Set them aside.
4. Add vegetables to the same pan and sauté for 5 minutes.
5. Stir in red wine and bring the mixture to a boil then reduce the heat to low.
6. Let it simmer for 1 minute then transfer them to the slow cooker.
7. Add chicken stock, tomatoes, spices, and lamb shanks to the slow cooker.
8. Pour the prepared sauce over the shanks.
9. Cover the lid and cook for 4 hours on low settings.
10. Add cauliflower to a bowl along with a splash of water.
11. Microwave the cauliflower chunks for 9 minutes.

13. Blend all the ingredients for cauliflower mash along with cooked cauliflowers in a blender.
14. Meanwhile, sauté green beans in a skillet along with all the remaining ingredients.
15. Serve the lamb shanks with green beans and cauliflower mash.

Nutrition *Calories: 369; Carbs: 13.8g; Fats: 24.9g; Proteins: 31.9g; Sodium: 537mg; Sugar: 1.4g*

Dinner: Edamame Vegetable Bowl
Serves: 1/Prep Time: 10mins

Ingredients:

- ½ cup cooked cauliflower rice
- 1 cup roasted vegetables
- ¼ cup edamame
- ¼ avocado, diced
- 2 tablespoons sliced scallions
- 2 tablespoons chopped fresh cilantro
- 2 tablespoons Citrus-Lime Vinaigrette

Directions

1. Add cauliflower rice to the meal prep container or a bowl.
2. Top the rice with roasted veggies and edamame.
3. Add avocado slices, scallions and cilantro to the container.
4. Pour the vinaigrette over the vegetables.
5. Serve.

Nutrition *Calories: 142; Carbs: 3.4g; Fats: 8.4g; Proteins: 4.1g; Sodium: 346mg; Sugar: 1g*

Day 21

Breakfast: Keto western omelet
Serves: 4/Prep Time: 10mins

Ingredients

- 6 eggs
- 2 tbsp heavy whipping cream
- salt and peppers, to taste
- 3 oz. shredded cheese
- 2 oz. butter
- ½ yellow onion, finely chopped
- ½ green bell pepper, finely chopped
- 5 oz. smoked deli ham, diced

Directions

1. Beat eggs with cream, salt, and pepper until fluffy in a bowl.
2. Stir in half of the cheese and combine gently.
3. Take a frying pan and melt butter in it.
4. Add onion, ham, and pepper. Sauté for 4-5 minutes.
5. Pour in egg mixture and cook eggs until set.
6. Top the egg with remaining cheese then fold the omelet.
7. Serve warm.

Nutrition *Calories: 109; Carbs: 6.2g; Fats: 9.6g; Proteins: 0.9g; Sodium: 227mg; Sugar: 1.8g*

Lunch: Garlic and Sage Rubbed Pork Tenderloin
Serves: 4/Prep Time: 10 minutes

Ingredients:

- One 2-pound pork loin
- 2 cloves garlic, minced
- Zest of 1 lemon
- 2 tablespoons fresh sage, finely chopped
- 2 teaspoons Dijon mustard
- 2 teaspoon olive oil
- 1/2 teaspoon salt
- 1/4 teaspoon pepper
- Lemon slices

Directions

1. Adjust the oven to 375 degrees F.
2. Bake dry the paper towels and set it aside on a baking sheet.
3. Mix garlic with lemon zest, Dijon mustard, salt, oil, pepper and sage in a mixing bowl.
4. Rub the pork loin with mustard mixture.
5. Place the loin on the baking sheet and top it with lemon slices.
6. Roast for 30 to 35 minutes.
7. Turn the oven to broil setting on high temperature and broil for 3 minutes.
8. Transfer the pork to the cutting board and let it rest for 10 minutes.
9. Slice the pork into half inch slices.
10. Serve.

Nutrition *Calories: 213 Carbs: 4.5g Fats: 23.4g Proteins: 33.2g Sodium: 86mg Sugar: 2.1g*

Dinner: Citrus Lime Tofu Salad
Prep Time: 10 minutes/Serves: 3

Ingredients:

- 1 cup roasted vegetables, chopped
- 1 cup roasted tofu, cubed
- 1 tablespoon pumpkin seeds
- 2 tablespoons Citrus-Lime Vinaigrette

Directions

1. Add all the ingredients to a bowl.
2. Mix well.
3. Serve or refrigerate up to 5 days.

Nutrition *Calories: 79 Carbs: 5.8g Fats: 4.8g Proteins: 5g Sodium: 24mg Sugar: 2.3g*

Breakfast Recipes

Morning Hash

Serves: 2/Prep Time: 30 mins

Ingredients

- ½ teaspoon dried thyme, crushed
- ½ small onion, chopped
- 1 tablespoon butter
- ½ cup cauliflower florets, boiled
- ¼ cup heavy cream
- Salt and black pepper, to taste
- ½ pound cooked turkey meat, chopped

Directions

1. Blend the cauliflower florets in a chopper and keep aside.
2. Put butter and onions in a skillet and sauté for about 3 minutes.
3. Add chopped cauliflower and sauté for about 3 more minutes.
4. Add turkey and cook for about 6 minutes.
5. Stir in heavy cream and cook for about 2 minutes, stirring constantly.
6. Dish out to serve or refrigerate it for about 3 days for meal prep. You just have to heat it in the microwave while reusing it.

Nutrition Calories per serving: 309 Carbohydrates: 3.6g Protein: 34.3g Fat: 17.1g Sugar: 1.4g Sodium: 134mg

Spanish Scramble

Serves: 2/Prep Time: 20 mins

Ingredients

- 3 tablespoons butter
- 2 tablespoons scallions, sliced thinly
- 4 large organic eggs
- 1 Serrano chili pepper
- ¼ cup heavy cream
- 2 tablespoons cilantro, chopped finely
- 1 small tomato, chopped
- Salt and black pepper, to taste

Directions

1. Combine together cream, eggs, cilantro, salt and black pepper in a medium bowl.
2. Put butter, tomatoes and Serrano pepper in a pan on medium heat and sauté for about 2 minutes.
3. Add egg mixture in the pan and cook for about 4 minutes, continuously stirring.
4. Garnish with scallions and dish out to immediately serve.
5. You can refrigerate this scramble for about 2 days for meal prepping and reuse by heating it in microwave oven.

Nutrition Calories per serving: 180 Carbohydrates: 2g Protein: 6.8g Fat: 16.5g Sugar: 1.1g Sodium: 231mg

Cheese Waffles

Serves: 2/Prep Time: 20 mins

Ingredients

- ½ cup Parmesan cheese, shredded
- 2 organic eggs, beaten

- 1 teaspoon onion powder
- 1 cup mozzarella cheese, shredded
- 1 tablespoon chives, minced
- ½ teaspoon ground black pepper
- 1 cup cauliflower
- 1 teaspoon garlic powder

Directions
1. Combine all the ingredients in a bowl and keep aside.
2. Grease a waffle iron and heat it.
3. Pour half of the mixture into the waffle iron and cook until golden brown.
4. Repeat with the remaining half mixture and dish out to serve.
5. You can refrigerate these waffles up to 4 days for longer use for meal prepping. Place the waffles in a container and slide wax paper between each waffle.

Nutrition Calories per serving: 149 Carbohydrates: 6.1g Protein: 13.3g Fat: 8.5g Sugar: 2.3g Sodium: 228mg

Spinach Frittata

Serves: 2/Prep Time: 45 mins
Ingredients
- 1½ ounce dried bacon
- 2 ounce spinach, fresh
- 1½ ounce shredded cheese
- ½ tablespoon butter
- ¼ cup heavy whipped cream
- 2 eggs
- Salt and black pepper, to taste

Directions
1. Preheat the oven to 360 degrees F and grease a baking dish.
2. Heat butter in a skillet and add bacons.
3. Cook until they become crispy and add spinach.
4. Stir thoroughly and keep aside.
5. Whisk together eggs and cream in a bowl and pour it in the baking dish.
6. Add bacon spinach mixture on to the baking dish and transfer in the oven.
7. Bake for about 30 minutes and remove from the oven to serve.
8. You can refrigerate this frittata for about 2 days for meal prepping and reuse by heating it in microwave oven.

Nutrition Calories per serving: 592 Carbohydrates: 3.9g Protein: 39.1g Fat: 46.7g Sugar: 1.1g Sodium: 1533mg

Keto Oatmeal

Serves: 2/Prep Time: 20 mins
Ingredients
- 2 tablespoons flaxseeds
- 2 tablespoons sunflower seeds
- 2 cups coconut milk
- 2 tablespoons chia seeds
- 2 pinches of salt

Directions
1. Put all the ingredients in a saucepan and mix well.
2. Bring it to boil and allow it to simmer for about 7 minutes.
3. Dish out in a bowl and serve warm.
4. For meal prepping, you can put all the seeds in a jar and mix them well, so it would be quicker for you to make your oatmeal.

Nutrition Calories per serving: 337 Carbohydrates: 7.8g Protein: 4.9g Fat: 32.6g Sugar: 4.1g Sodium: 98mg

Cheese Rolls

Serves: 2/Prep Time: 20 mins
Ingredients
- 2 ounce butter, thinly sliced
- 8 ounce cheddar cheese slices

Directions
1. Arrange the cheese slices on a board and cover each slice of cheese with butter.
2. Roll it up and serve as a nutritious breakfast.
3. You can cover these cheese rolls with a plastic wrap and freeze for meal prepping. Heat them in a microwave to reuse them.

Nutrition Calories per serving: 330 Carbohydrates: 0.7g Protein: 14.2g Fat: 30.3g Sugar: 0.3g Sodium: 434mg

Buttered Eggs

Serves: 2/Prep Time: 30 mins
Ingredients
- ¼ teaspoon black pepper, ground
- 2 eggs
- 2½ ounces butter
- ¼ teaspoon salt

Directions
1. Boil the eggs in a pot and allow them to simmer for about 7 minutes.
2. Remove the eggs from the pot, peel and chop them.
3. Add butter and season with salt and black pepper.
4. Mix well and serve to enjoy.
5. For meal prepping, you can add different herbs and chili flakes to add a good taste.

Nutrition Calories per serving: 635 Carbohydrates: 0.9g Protein: 11.7g Fat: 66.2g Sugar: 0.7g Sodium: 1113mg

Baked Eggs

Serves: 2/Prep Time: 10 mins
Ingredients
- 2 eggs
- 3 ounce ground beef, cooked
- 2 ounce cheddar cheese, shredded

Directions
1. Preheat the oven to 390 degrees F and grease a baking dish.
2. Arrange the cooked ground beef in a baking dish.
3. Make two holes in the ground beef and crack eggs in them.
4. Top with cheddar cheese and transfer the baking dish in the oven.
5. Bake for about 20 minutes and remove from the oven.
6. Allow it to cool for a bit and serve to enjoy.
7. For meal prepping, you can refrigerate these baked eggs for about 2 days wrapped in a foil.

Nutrition Calories per serving: 512 Carbohydrates: 1.4g Protein: 51g Fat: 32.8g Sugar: 1g Sodium: 531mg

Blueberry Smoothie

Serves: 2/Prep Time: 15 mins
Ingredients
- 1 cup fresh blueberries
- 1 teaspoon vanilla extract
- 28 ounce coconut milk
- 2 tablespoons lemon juice

Directions
1. Drop all the ingredients in a blender and blend until smooth.
2. Pour it in the glasses to serve and enjoy.
3. Meal prep tip: If you want more filling smoothie you can add more coconut milk in it. You can also use yogurt. If you want it to be more liquid add some water in it.

Nutrition Calories per serving: 152 Carbohydrates: 6.9g Protein: 1.5g Fat: 13.1g Sugar: 4.5g Sodium: 1mg

Quick Keto Pancakes

Serves: 2/Prep Time: 30 mins
Ingredients
- 3 ounce cottage cheese
- 2 eggs
- ½ tablespoon psyllium husk powder, ground
- ½ cup whipped cream
- 1 ounce butter

Directions
1. Mix together all the ingredients in a bowl except whipped cream and keep aside.
2. Heat butter in the frying pan and pour half of the mixture.
3. Cook for about 3 minutes on each side and dish out in a serving platter.
4. Add whipped cream in another bowl and whisk until smooth.
5. Top the pancakes with whipped cream on them.
6. Meal Prep Tip: These keto pancakes can also be used as a snack. They taste awesome when serve cold.

Nutrition Calories per serving: 298 Carbohydrates: 4.8g Protein: 12.2g Fat: 26g Sugar: 0.5g Sodium: 326mg

Spinach Quiche

Serves: 2/Prep Time: 15 mins
Ingredients
- 1½ cups Monterey Jack cheese, shredded
- ½ tablespoon butter, melted
- 5-ounce frozen spinach, thawed
- Salt and freshly ground black pepper, to taste
- 2 organic eggs, beaten

Directions
1. Preheat the oven to 350 degrees F and grease a 9-inch pie dish lightly.
2. Heat butter on medium-low heat in a large skillet and add spinach.
3. Cook for about 3 minutes and keep aside.
4. Mix together Monterey Jack cheese, eggs, spinach, salt and black pepper in a bowl.

6. Transfer the mixture into prepared pie dish and place in the oven.
7. Bake for about 30 minutes and dish out to serve by cutting into equal sized wedges.
8. Meal Prep Tip: You can take spinach quiche as your lunch when you are going to work.

Nutrition Calories per serving: 349 Carbohydrates: 3.2g Protein: 23g Fat: 27.8g Sugar: 1.3g Sodium: 532mg

Cream Crepes

Serves: 2/Prep Time: 25 mins
Ingredients

- 1 teaspoon Splenda
- 2 tablespoons coconut flour
- 2 tablespoons coconut oil, melted and divided
- 2 organic eggs
- ½ cup heavy cream

Directions

1. Put 1 tablespoon of coconut oil, eggs, Splenda and salt in a bowl and beat until well combined.
2. Sift in the coconut flour slowly and beat constantly.
3. Stir in the heavy cream and continuously beat until the mixture is well combined.
4. Heat a non-stick pan and pour half of the mixture in it.
5. Cook for about 2 minutes on each side and repeat with the remaining mixture.
6. Dish out to serve and enjoy.
7. For meal prepping, wrap each cream crepe into wax paper pieces and place into a resealable bag. Freeze for up to 3 days and remove from the freezer. Microwave for about 2 minutes to serve.

Nutrition Calories per serving: 298 Carbohydrates: 8g Protein: 7g Fat: 27.1g Sugar: 2.4g Sodium: 70mg

Smoothie Bowl

Serves: 2/Prep Time: 15 mins
Ingredients

- ¼ cup unsweetened almond milk
- 1 cup frozen strawberries
- ½ cup fat-free plain Greek yogurt
- 1 tablespoon walnuts, chopped
- ½ tablespoon unsweetened whey protein powder

Directions

1. Put the strawberries in a blender and pulse until smooth.
2. Add almond milk, Greek yogurt and whey protein powder in the blender and pulse for about 2 minutes.
3. Transfer the mixture evenly into and top with walnuts to serve.
4. You can wrap the bowls with plastic wrap and refrigerate for 2 days for meal prepping. Add 2 tablespoons of unsweetened almond milk and walnuts before serving.

Nutrition Calories per serving: 71 Fat: 19g Carbohydrates: 6.3g Protein: 6.8g Sugar: 0.7g Sodium: 65mg

Pumpkin Pancakes

Serves: 2/Prep Time: 20 mins
Ingredients
- 6 tablespoons pumpkin filling
- ¼ teaspoon cinnamon
- 2 squares puff pastry
- 2 small eggs, beaten

Directions
1. Preheat the Airfryer to 30 degrees F and grease a baking dish.
2. Roll out a square of puff pastry and stuff with pumpkin filling.
3. Leave ¼-inch space around the edges and cut it up into equal sized square pieces.
4. Cover the gaps with beaten egg and place the squares into a baking dish.
5. Cook for about 12 minutes and sprinkle cinnamon to serve.
6. You can wrap these pumpkin pancakes in a plastic sheet and freeze for up to 2 days. Warm for about 1 minute in the microwave before serving.

Nutrition Calories per serving: 51 Carbs: 5g Fats: 2.5g Proteins: 2.4g Sugar: 0.5g Sodium: 48mg

Devilish Pancakes

Serves: 2/Prep Time: 25 mins
Ingredients
- 2-ounce cream cheese, softened
- ½ packet stevia
- 2 organic eggs
- ½ teaspoon ground cinnamon

Directions
1. Blend all ingredients in a blender until smooth and keep aside for about 3 minutes.
2. Heat a skillet over medium heat and half of the mixture, spreading evenly.
3. Cook for about 2 minutes on each side until it becomes golden brown.
4. Repeat with the remaining mixture and dish out to serve.
5. For meal prepping, you can refrigerate these pancakes for about 4 days. Place them in a container and place wax paper between each pancake.

Nutrition Calories per serving: 163 Fat: 14.3g Carbohydrates: 1.6g Protein: 7.7g Sugar: 0.6 g Sodium: 324mg

Cheesy Muffins

Serves: 2/Prep Time: 45 mins
Ingredients
- ¼ cup raw hemp seeds
- ¼ teaspoon baking powder
- 1/8 cup nutritional yeast flakes
- ¼ cup Parmesan cheese, grated finely
- 3 organic eggs, beaten
- ¼ cup almond meal
- 1/8 cup flax seeds meal
- Salt, to taste
- ¼ cup low-fat cottage cheese
- ¼ cup scallion, sliced thinly

Directions
1. Preheat oven to 360 degrees F and grease 2 muffin cups.
2. Combine almond meal, flax seeds, hemp seeds, baking powder and salt in a bowl and mix well.
3. Mix together cottage cheese, parmesan cheese, nutritional yeast flakes and egg in another bowl.

5. Combine the cheese and almond mixture and mix until well combined.
6. Fold in the scallions and pour this mixture into the greased muffin cups.
7. Transfer into the oven and bake for about 30 minutes.
8. Dish out to serve warm immediately or for meal prepping, you can refrigerate muffins in the refrigerator for 3-4 days, by covering them with paper towel and heat again before use.

Nutrition Calories per serving: 179 Fat: 10.9g Carbohydrates: 6.9g Protein: 15.4g Sugar: 2.3g Sodium: 311mg

Scrambled Eggs

Serves: 2/Prep Time: 25 mins
Ingredients
- 1 tablespoon butter
- 4 eggs
- Salt and black pepper, to taste

Directions
1. Combine together eggs, salt and black pepper in a bowl and keep aside.
2. Heat butter in a pan over medium-low heat and slowly add the whisked eggs.
3. Stir the eggs continuously in the pan with the help of a fork for about 4 minutes.
4. Dish out in a plate and serve immediately.
5. You can refrigerate this scramble for about 2 days for meal prepping and reuse by heating it in microwave oven.

Nutrition Calories per serving: 151 Fat: 11.6g Carbohydrates: 0.7g Protein: 11.1g Sodium: 144mg Sugar: 0.7g

Bacon Veggies Combo

Serves: 2/Prep Time: 35 mins
Ingredients
- ½ green bell pepper, seeded and chopped
- 2 bacon slices
- ¼ cup Parmesan Cheese
- ½ tablespoon mayonnaise
- 1 scallion, chopped

Directions
1. Preheat the oven to 375 degrees F and grease a baking dish.
2. Place bacon slices on the baking dish and top with mayonnaise, bell peppers, scallions and Parmesan Cheese.
3. Transfer in the oven and bake for about 25 minutes.
4. Dish out to serve immediately or refrigerate for about 2 days wrapped in a plastic sheet for meal prepping.

Nutrition Calories per serving: 197 Fat: 13.8g Carbohydrates: 4.7g Protein: 14.3g Sugar: 1.9g Sodium: 662mg

Tofu with Mushrooms

Serves: 2/Prep Time: 25 mins
Ingredients
- 1 cup fresh mushrooms, chopped finely
- 1 block tofu, pressed and cubed into 1-inch pieces

- 4 tablespoons butter
- Salt and black pepper, to taste
- 4 tablespoons Parmesan cheese, shredded

Directions

1. Season the tofu with salt and black pepper.
2. Put butter and seasoned tofu in a pan and cook for about 5 minutes.
3. Add mushrooms and Parmesan cheese and cook for another 5 minutes, stirring occasionally.
4. Dish out and serve immediately or refrigerate for about 3 days wrapped in a foil for meal prepping and microwave it to serve again.

Nutrition Calories per serving: 423 Fat: 37g Carbohydrates: 4g Protein: 23.1g Sugar: 0.9g Sodium: 691mg

Ham Spinach Ballet

Serves: 2/Prep Time: 40 mins
Ingredients

- 4 teaspoons cream
- ¾ pound fresh baby spinach
- 7-ounce ham, sliced
- Salt and black pepper, to taste
- 1 tablespoon unsalted butter, melted

Directions

1. Preheat the oven to 360 degrees F. and grease 2 ramekins with butter.
2. Put butter and spinach in a skillet and cook for about 3 minutes.
3. Add cooked spinach in the ramekins and top with ham slices, cream, salt and black pepper.
4. Bake for about 25 minutes and dish out to serve hot.
5. For meal prepping, you can refrigerate this ham spinach ballet for about 3 days wrapped in a foil.

Nutrition Calories per serving: 188 Fat: 12.5g Carbohydrates: 4.9g Protein: 14.6g Sugar: 0.3g Sodium: 1098mg

Creamy Parsley Soufflé

Serves: 2/Prep Time: 25 mins
Ingredients

- 2 fresh red chili peppers, chopped
- Salt, to taste
- 4 eggs
- 4 tablespoons light cream
- 2 tablespoons fresh parsley, chopped

Directions

1. Preheat the oven to 375 degrees F and grease 2 soufflé dishes.
2. Combine all the ingredients in a bowl and mix well.
3. Put the mixture into prepared soufflé dishes and transfer in the oven.
4. Cook for about 6 minutes and dish out to serve immediately.
5. For meal prepping, you can refrigerate this creamy parsley soufflé in the ramekins covered in a foil for about 2-3 days.

Nutrition Calories per serving: 108 Fat: 9g Carbohydrates: 1.1g Protein: 6g Sugar: 0.5g Sodium: 146mg

Vegetarian Three Cheese Quiche Stuffed Peppers

Serves: 2/Prep Time: 50 mins

Ingredients

- 2 large eggs
- ¼ cup mozzarella, shredded
- 1 medium bell peppers, sliced in half and seeds removed
- ¼ cup ricotta cheese
- ¼ cup grated Parmesan cheese
- ½ teaspoon garlic powder
- 1/8 cup baby spinach leaves
- ¼ teaspoon dried parsley
- 1 tablespoon Parmesan cheese, to garnish

Directions

8. Preheat oven to 375 degrees F.
9. Blend all the cheeses, eggs, garlic powder and parsley in a food processor and process until smooth.
10. Pour the cheese mixture into each sliced bell pepper and top with spinach leaves.
11. Stir with a fork, pushing them under the cheese mixture and cover with foil.
12. Bake for about 40 minutes and sprinkle with Parmesan cheese.
13. Broil for about 5 minutes and dish out to serve.

Nutrition Calories: 157 Carbs: 7.3g Fats: 9g Proteins: 12.7g Sodium: 166mg Sugar: 3.7g

Spinach Artichoke Egg Casserole

Serves: 2/Prep Time: 45 mins

Ingredients

- 1/8 cup milk
- 2.5-ounce frozen chopped spinach, thawed and drained well
- 1/8 cup parmesan cheese
- 1/8 cup onions, shaved
- ¼ teaspoon salt
- ¼ teaspoon crushed red pepper
- 4 large eggs
- 3.5-ounce artichoke hearts, drained
- ¼ cup white cheddar, shredded
- 1/8 cup ricotta cheese
- ½ garlic clove, minced
- ¼ teaspoon dried thyme

Directions

1. Preheat the oven to 350 degrees F and grease a baking dish with non-stick cooking spray.
2. Whisk eggs and milk together and add artichoke hearts and spinach.
3. Mix well and stir in rest of the ingredients, withholding the ricotta cheese.
4. Pour the mixture into the baking dish and top evenly with ricotta cheese.
5. Transfer in the oven and bake for about 30 minutes.
6. Dish out and serve warm.

Nutrition Calories: 228 Carbs: 10.1g Fats: 13.3g Proteins: 19.1g Sodium: 571mg Sugar: 2.5g

Avocado Baked Eggs

Serves: 2/Prep Time: 25 mins

Ingredients

- 2 eggs
- 1 medium sized avocado, halved and pit removed
- ¼ cup cheddar cheese, shredded
- Kosher salt and black pepper, to taste

Directions

1. Preheat oven to 425 degrees and grease a muffin pan.

3. Crack open an egg into each half of the avocado and season with salt and black pepper.
4. Top with cheddar cheese and transfer the muffin pan in the oven.
5. Bake for about 15 minutes and dish out to serve.

Nutrition Calories: 210 Carbs: 6.4g Fats: 16.6g Proteins: 10.7g Sodium: 151mg Sugar: 2.2g

Cinnamon Faux-St Crunch Cereal

Serves: 2/Prep Time: 35 mins

Ingredients
- ¼ cup hulled hemp seeds
- ½ tablespoon coconut oil
- ¼ cup milled flax seed
- 1 tablespoon ground cinnamon
- ¼ cup apple juice

Directions
1. Preheat the oven to 300 degrees F and line a cookie sheet with parchment paper.
2. Put hemp seeds, flax seed and ground cinnamon in a food processor.
3. Add coconut oil and apple juice and blend until smooth.
4. Pour the mixture on the cookie sheet and transfer in the oven.
5. Bake for about 15 minutes and lower the temperature of the oven to 250 degrees F.
6. Bake for another 10 minutes and dish out from the oven, turning it off.
7. Cut into small squares and place in the turned off oven.
8. Place the cereal in the oven for 1 hour until it is crisp.
9. Dish out and serve with unsweetened almond milk.

Nutrition Calories: 225 Carbs: 9.2g Fats: 18.5g Proteins: 9.8g Sodium: 1mg Sugar: 1.6g

Quick Keto McMuffins

Serves: 2/Prep Time: 15 mins

Ingredients

Muffins:
- ¼ cup flaxmeal
- ¼ cup almond flour
- ¼ teaspoon baking soda
- 1 large egg, free-range or organic
- 2 tablespoons water
- 1 pinch salt
- 2 tablespoons heavy whipping cream
- ¼ cup cheddar cheese, grated

Filling:
- 1 tablespoon ghee
- 2 slices cheddar cheese
- Salt and black pepper, to taste
- 2 large eggs
- 1 tablespoon butter
- 1 teaspoon Dijon mustard

Directions
1. **For Muffins:** Mix together all the dry ingredients for muffins in a small bowl and add egg, cream, cheese and water.
2. Combine well and pour in 2 single-serving ramekins.
3. Microwave on high for about 90 seconds.
4. **For Filling:** Fry the eggs on ghee and season with salt and black pepper.
5. Cut the muffins in half and spread butter on the inside of each half.
6. Top each buttered half with cheese slices, eggs and Dijon mustard.
7. Serve immediately.

Nutrition Calories: 299 Carbs: 8.8g Fats: 24.3g Proteins: 13g Sodium: 376mg Sugar: 0.4g

Keto Egg Fast Snickerdoodle Crepes

Serves: 2/Prep Time: 15 mins
Ingredients
For the crepes:
- 5 oz cream cheese, softened
- 6 eggs
- 1 teaspoon cinnamon
- Butter, for frying
- 1 tablespoon Swerve

For the filling:
- 2 tablespoons granulated Swerve
- 8 tablespoons butter, softened
- 1 tablespoon cinnamon

Directions
1. **For the crepes:** Put all the ingredients together in a blender except the butter and process until smooth.
2. Heat butter on medium heat in a non-stick pan and pour some batter in the pan.
3. Cook for about 2 minutes, then flip and cook for 2 more minutes.
4. Repeat with the remaining mixture.
5. Mix Swerve, butter and cinnamon in a small bowl until combined.
6. Spread this mixture onto the centre of the crepe and serve rolled up.

Nutrition Calories: 543 Carbs: 8g Fats: 51.6g Proteins: 15.7g Sodium: 455mg Sugar: 0.9g

Cauliflower Hash Brown Breakfast Bowl

Serves: 2/Prep Time: 30 mins
Ingredients
- 1 tablespoon lemon juice
- 1 egg
- 1 avocado
- 1 teaspoon garlic powder
- 2 tablespoons extra virgin olive oil
- 2 oz mushrooms, sliced
- ½ green onion, chopped
- ¼ cup salsa
- ¾ cup cauliflower rice
- ½ small handful baby spinach
- Salt and black pepper, to taste

Directions
1. Mash together avocado, lemon juice, garlic powder, salt and black pepper in a small bowl.
2. Whisk eggs, salt and black pepper in a bowl and keep aside.
3. Heat half of olive oil over medium heat in a skillet and add mushrooms.
4. Sauté for about 3 minutes and season with garlic powder, salt, and pepper.
5. Sauté for about 2 minutes and dish out in a bowl.
6. Add rest of the olive oil and add cauliflower, garlic powder, salt and pepper.
7. Sauté for about 5 minutes and dish out.
8.   Return the mushrooms to the skillet and add green onions and baby spinach.
9. Sauté for about 30 seconds and add whisked eggs.
10.   Sauté for about 1 minute and scoop on the sautéed cauliflower hash browns.
11.   Top with salsa and mashed avocado and serve.

Nutrition Calories: 400 Carbs: 15.8g Fats: 36.7g Proteins: 8g Sodium: 288mg Sugar: 4.2g

Cheesy Thyme Waffles

Serves: 2/Prep Time: 15 mins
Ingredients
- ½ cup mozzarella cheese, finely shredded
- ¼ cup Parmesan cheese
- ¼ large head cauliflower
- ½ cup collard greens
- 1 large egg
- 1 stalk green onion
- ½ tablespoon olive oil
- ½ teaspoon garlic powder
- ¼ teaspoon salt
- ½ tablespoon sesame seed
- 1 teaspoon fresh thyme, chopped
- ¼ teaspoon ground black pepper

Directions
1. Put cauliflower, collard greens, spring onion and thyme in a food processor and pulse until smooth.
2. Dish out the mixture in a bowl and stir in rest of the ingredients.
3. Heat a waffle iron and transfer the mixture evenly over the griddle.
4. Cook until a waffle is formed and dish out in a serving platter.
Nutrition Calories: 144 Carbs: 8.5g Fats: 9.4g Proteins: 9.3g Sodium: 435mg Sugar: 3g

Baked Eggs and Asparagus with Parmesan

Serves: 2/Prep Time: 30 mins
Ingredients
- 4 eggs
- 8 thick asparagus spears, cut into bite-sized pieces
- 2 teaspoons olive oil
- 2 tablespoons Parmesan cheese
- Salt and black pepper, to taste

Directions
1. Preheat the oven to 400 degrees F and grease two gratin dishes with olive oil.
2. Put half the asparagus into each gratin dish and place in the oven.
3. Roast for about 10 minutes and dish out the gratin dishes.
4. Crack eggs over the asparagus and transfer into the oven.
5. Bake for about 5 minutes and dish out the gratin dishes.
6. Sprinkle with Parmesan cheese and put the dishes back in the oven.
7. Bake for another 3 minutes and dish out to serve hot.
Nutrition Calories: 336 Carbs: 13.7g Fats: 19.4g Proteins: 28.1g Sodium: 2103mg Sugar: 4.7g

Low Carb Green Smoothie

Serves: 2/Prep Time: 15 mins
Ingredients
- 1/3 cup romaine lettuce
- 1/3 tablespoon fresh ginger, peeled and chopped
- 1½ cups filtered water
- 1/8 cup fresh pineapple, chopped
- ¾ tablespoon fresh parsley
- 1/3 cup raw cucumber, peeled and sliced
- ¼ Hass avocado
- ¼ cup kiwi fruit, peeled and chopped
- 1/3 tablespoon Swerve

Directions
1. Put all the ingredients in a blender and blend until smooth.
2. Pour into 2 serving glasses and serve chilled.

Nutrition Calories: 108 Carbs: 7.8g Fats: 8.9g Proteins: 1.6g Sodium: 4mg Sugar: 2.2g

Hard Boiled Eggs

Serves: 16

Ingredients:

- 1 cup water
- 16 large eggs

Directions:

1. Place the metal rack in the Instant Pot and pour in the water.

2. Place the eggs on the rack and fit in as many as you can. Lock the lid and seal the valve. Press the Manual button and cook on high pressure for 4 minutes.

3. When cooking time is up, press Cancel and open the valve to release pressure. Transfer the eggs to a large bowl and add cold water until all is covered. Let rest for about 5 minutes.

4. While still warm, peel the eggs and rinse off any remaining shell pieces. Serve immediately and store the rest in the fridge.

Crispy Potatoes

Serves: 4

Ingredients:

- ½ cup water
- 1 lb. Yukon Gold potatoes, skinned and cut into 1-inch cubes
- 2 tbsp. ghee
- Kosher salt and ground black pepper
- Juice of 1 small lemon
- ¼ cup fresh chives, minced

Directions:

1. Add water into the pot and fit with a steamer insert. Add the potatoes.

2. Lock the lid and set the valve in sealing position. Hit the Manual button and cook on high pressure for 5 minutes.

3. When the timer goes off, turn off the Instant Pot and release pressure naturally for about 10 minutes. Transfer the potatoes to a bowl.

4. In a large nonstick skillet set over medium-high heat, melt and ghee until it begins to sputter. Add the steamed potatoes and season with generous amount of salt and pepper. Allow to cook by itself for 1 minute.

5. After 1 minutes, flip the potatoes to cook the other side for another minute or until slightly browned.

6. Transfer the crispy potatoes to a serving bowl. Pour the lemon juice over and top with minced chives. Serve warm.

Breakfast Casserole

Serves: 6

Ingredients:

- 2 tbsp. coconut oil
- 2 tsp. minced garlic
- 1 cup chopped kale
- 1 1/3 cups sliced leeks
- 8 eggs
- 1 ½ cups breakfast sausage, cooked
- 2/3 cup sweet potato, skinned and grated
- 1 ½ cups water

Directions:

1. Set the pot to Sauté and add coconut oil. Once melted, sauté garlic, kale, and leeks until softened.

2. Transfer sautéed vegetables to a large mixing bowl and combine with eggs, sausage, and sweet potatoes. Clean the Instant Pot.

3. Grease an oven-proof bowl or pan and pour in the mixture.

4. Add water to the pot and place the wire rack inside. Lower the greased pan or bowl onto the rack. Lock the lid and seal the valve. Set timer to 25 minutes and cook on high pressure.

5. Once done, quick-release pressure. Remove casserole from the pot and slice into equal parts. Serve immediately.

Lunch Recipes

Salmon Stew

Serves: 2/Prep Time: 20 mins

Ingredients

- 1 pound salmon fillet, sliced
- 1 onion, chopped
- Salt, to taste
- 1 tablespoon butter, melted
- 1 cup fish broth
- ½ teaspoon red chili powder

Directions

1. Season the salmon fillets with salt and red chili powder.
2. Put butter and onions in a skillet and sauté for about 3 minutes.
3. Add seasoned salmon and cook for about 2 minutes on each side.
4. Add fish broth and secure the lid.
5. Cook for about 7 minutes on medium heat and open the lid.
6. Dish out and serve immediately.
7. Transfer the stew in a bowl and keep aside to cool for meal prepping. Divide the mixture into 2 containers. Cover the containers and refrigerate for about 2 days. Reheat in the microwave before serving.

Nutrition Calories per serving: 272 Carbohydrates: 4.4g Protein: 32.1g Fat: 14.2g Sugar: 1.9g Sodium: 275mg

Asparagus Salmon Fillets

Serves: 2/Prep Time: 30 mins
Ingredients

- 1 teaspoon olive oil
- 4 asparagus stalks
- 2 salmon fillets
- ¼ cup butter
- ¼ cup champagne
- Salt and freshly ground black pepper, to taste

Directions

1. Preheat the oven to 355 degrees F and grease a baking dish.
2. Put all the ingredients in a bowl and mix well.
3. Put this mixture in the baking dish and transfer it in the oven.
4. Bake for about 20 minutes and dish out.
5. Place the salmon fillets in a dish and keep aside to cool for meal prepping. Divide it into 2 containers and close the lid. Refrigerate for 1 day and reheat in microwave before serving.

Nutrition Calories per serving: 475 Carbohydrates: 1.1g Protein: 35.2g Fat: 36.8g Sugar: 0.5g Sodium: 242mg

Crispy Baked Chicken

Serves: 2/Prep Time: 40 mins
Ingredients

- 2 chicken breasts, skinless and boneless
- 2 tablespoons butter
- ¼ teaspoon turmeric powder
- Salt and black pepper, to taste
- ¼ cup sour cream

Directions

1. Preheat the oven to 360 degrees F and grease a baking dish with butter.
2. Season the chicken with turmeric powder, salt and black pepper in a bowl.
3. Put the chicken on the baking dish and transfer it in the oven.
4. Bake for about 10 minutes and dish out to serve topped with sour cream.
5. Transfer the chicken in a bowl and set aside to cool for meal prepping. Divide it into 2 containers and cover the containers. Refrigerate for up to 2 days and reheat in microwave before serving.

Nutrition Calories per serving: 304 Carbohydrates: 1.4g Protein: 26.1g Fat: 21.6g Sugar: 0.1g Sodium: 137mg

Sour and Sweet Fish

Serves: 2/Prep Time: 25 mins
Ingredients

- 1 tablespoon vinegar
- 2 drops stevia
- 1 pound fish chunks
- ¼ cup butter, melted
- Salt and black pepper, to taste

Directions

6. Put butter and fish chunks in a skillet and cook for about 3 minutes.
7. Add stevia, salt and black pepper and cook for about 10 minutes, stirring continuously.
8. Dish out in a bowl and serve immediately.

10. Place fish in a dish and set aside to cool for meal prepping. Divide it in 2 containers and refrigerate for up to 2 days. Reheat in microwave before serving.

Nutrition Calories per serving: 258 Carbohydrates: 2.8g Protein: 24.5g Fat: 16.7g Sugar: 2.7g Sodium: 649mg

Creamy Chicken

Serves: 2/Prep Time: 25 mins

Ingredients

- ½ small onion, chopped
- ¼ cup sour cream
- Salt and black pepper, to taste
- 1 tablespoon butter
- ¼ cup mushrooms
- ½ pound chicken breasts

Directions

1. Heat butter in a skillet and add onions and mushrooms.
2. Sauté for about 5 minutes and add chicken breasts and salt.
3. Secure the lid and cook for about 5 more minutes.
4. Add sour cream and cook for about 3 minutes.
5. Open the lid and dish out in a bowl to serve immediately.
6. Transfer the creamy chicken breasts in a dish and set aside to cool for meal prepping. Divide them in 2 containers and cover their lid. Refrigerate for 2-3 days and reheat in microwave before serving.

Nutrition Calories per serving: 335 Carbohydrates: 2.9g Protein: 34g Fat: 20.2g Sugar: 0.8g Sodium: 154mg

Paprika Butter Shrimps

Serves: 2/Prep Time: 30 mins

Ingredients

- ¼ tablespoon smoked paprika
- 1/8 cup sour cream
- ½ pound tiger shrimps
- 1/8 cup butter
- Salt and black pepper, to taste

Directions

1. Preheat the oven to 390 degrees F and grease a baking dish.
2. Mix together all the ingredients in a large bowl and transfer into the baking dish.
3. Place in the oven and bake for about 15 minutes.
4. Place paprika shrimp in a dish and set aside to cool for meal prepping. Divide it in 2 containers and cover the lid. Refrigerate for 1-2 days and reheat in microwave before serving.

Nutrition Calories per serving: 330 Carbohydrates: 1.5g Protein: 32.6g Fat: 21.5g Sugar: 0.2g Sodium: 458mg

Bacon Wrapped Asparagus

Serves: 2/Prep Time: 30 mins

Ingredients

- 1/3 cup heavy whipping cream
- 2 bacon slices, precooked
- 4 small spears asparagus
- Salt, to taste
- 1 tablespoon butter

Directions

1. Preheat the oven to 360 degrees F and grease a baking sheet with butter.
2. Meanwhile, mix cream, asparagus and salt in a bowl.
3. Wrap the asparagus in bacon slices and arrange them in the baking dish.
4. Transfer the baking dish in the oven and bake for about 20 minutes.
5. Remove from the oven and serve hot.
6. Place the bacon wrapped asparagus in a dish and set aside to cool for meal prepping. Divide it in 2 containers and cover the lid. Refrigerate for about 2 days and reheat in the microwave before serving.

Nutrition Calories per serving: 204 Carbohydrates: 1.4g Protein: 5.9g Fat: 19.3g Sugar: 0.5g Sodium: 291mg

Spinach Chicken

Serves: 2/Prep Time: 20 mins
Ingredients

- 2 garlic cloves, minced
- 2 tablespoons unsalted butter, divided
- ¼ cup parmesan cheese, shredded
- ¾ pound chicken tenders
- ¼ cup heavy cream
- 10 ounce frozen spinach, chopped
- Salt and black pepper, to taste

Directions

1. Heat 1 tablespoon of butter in a large skillet and add chicken, salt and black pepper.
2. Cook for about 3 minutes on both sides and remove the chicken in a bowl.
3. Melt remaining butter in the skillet and add garlic, cheese, heavy cream and spinach.
4. Cook for about 2 minutes and transfer the chicken in it.
5. Cook for about 5 minutes on low heat and dish out to immediately serve.
6. Place chicken in a dish and set aside to cool for meal prepping. Divide it in 2 containers and cover them. Refrigerate for about 3 days and reheat in microwave before serving.

Nutrition Calories per serving: 288 Carbohydrates: 3.6g Protein: 27.7g Fat: 18.3g Sugar: 0.3g Sodium: 192mg

Chicken with Herbed Butter

Serves: 2/Prep Time: 35 mins
Ingredients

- 1/3 cup baby spinach
- 1 tablespoon lemon juice
- ¾ pound chicken breasts
- 1/3 cup butter
- ¼ cup parsley, chopped
- Salt and black pepper, to taste
- 1/3 teaspoon ginger powder
- 1 garlic clove, minced

Directions

1. Preheat the oven to 450 degrees F and grease a baking dish.
2. Mix together parsley, ginger powder, lemon juice, butter, garlic, salt and black pepper in a bowl.
3. Add chicken breasts in the mixture and marinate well for about 30 minutes.
4. Arrange the marinated chicken in the baking dish and transfer in the oven.
5. Bake for about 25 minutes and dish out to serve immediately.

7. Place chicken in 2 containers and refrigerate for about 3 days for meal prepping. Reheat in microwave before serving.

Nutrition Calories per serving: 568 Carbohydrates: 1.6g Protein: 44.6g Fat: 42.1g Sugar: 0.3g Sodium: 384mg

Lemongrass Prawns

Serves: 2/Prep Time: 25 mins
Ingredients

- ½ red chili pepper, seeded and chopped
- 2 lemongrass stalks
- ½ pound prawns, deveined and peeled
- 6 tablespoons butter
- ¼ teaspoon smoked paprika

Directions

1. Preheat the oven to 390 degrees F and grease a baking dish.
2. Mix together red chili pepper, butter, smoked paprika and prawns in a bowl.
3. Marinate for about 2 hours and then thread the prawns on the lemongrass stalks.
4. Arrange the threaded prawns on the baking dish and transfer it in the oven.
5. Bake for about 15 minutes and dish out to serve immediately.
6. Place the prawns in a dish and set aside to cool for meal prepping. Divide it in 2 containers and close the lid. Refrigerate for about 4 days and reheat in microwave before serving.

Nutrition Calories per serving: 322 Carbohydrates: 3.8g Protein: 34.8g Fat: 18g Sugar: 0.1g Sodium: 478mg

Stuffed Mushrooms

Serves: 2/Prep Time: 45 mins
Ingredients

- 2 ounce bacon, crumbled
- ½ tablespoon butter
- ¼ teaspoon paprika powder
- 2 portobello mushrooms
- 1 ounce cream cheese
- ¾ tablespoon fresh chives, chopped
- Salt and black pepper, to taste

Directions

1. Preheat the oven to 400 degrees F and grease a baking dish.
2. Heat butter in a skillet and add mushrooms.
3. Sauté for about 4 minutes and keep aside.
4. Mix together cream cheese, chives, paprika powder, salt and black pepper in a bowl.
5. Stuff the mushrooms with this mixture and transfer on the baking dish.
6. Place in the oven and bake for about 20 minutes.
7. These mushrooms can be refrigerated for about 3 days for meal prepping and can be served with scrambled eggs.

Nutrition Calories per serving: 570 Carbohydrates: 4.6g Protein: 19.9g Fat: 52.8g Sugar: 0.8g Sodium: 1041mg

Honey Glazed Chicken Drumsticks

Serves: 2/Prep Time: 30 mins
Ingredients

- ½ tablespoon fresh thyme, minced
- 1/8 cup Dijon mustard
- ½ tablespoon fresh rosemary, minced
- ½ tablespoon honey
- 2 chicken drumsticks
- 1 tablespoon olive oil
- Salt and black pepper, to taste

Directions

1. Preheat the oven at 325 degrees F and grease a baking dish.
2. Combine all the ingredients in a bowl except the drumsticks and mix well.
3. Add drumsticks and coat generously with the mixture.
4. Cover and refrigerate to marinate overnight.
5. Place the drumsticks in in the baking dish and transfer it in the oven.
6. Cook for about 20 minutes and dish out to immediately serve.
7. Place chicken drumsticks in a dish and set aside to cool for meal prepping. Divide it in 2 containers and cover them. Refrigerate for about 3 days and reheat in microwave before serving.

Nutrition Calories per serving: 301 Carbs: 6g Fats: 19.7g Proteins: 4.5g Sugar: 4.5g Sodium: 316mg

Keto Zucchini Pizza

Serves: 2/Prep Time: 15 mins
Ingredients

- 1/8 cup spaghetti sauce
- ½ zucchini, cut in circular slices
- ½ cup cream cheese
- Pepperoni slices, for topping
- ½ cup mozzarella cheese, shredded

Directions

1. Preheat the oven to 350 degrees F and grease a baking dish.
2. Arrange the zucchini on the baking dish and layer with spaghetti sauce.
3. Top with pepperoni slices and mozzarella cheese.
4. Transfer the baking dish in the oven and bake for about 15 minutes.
5. Remove from the oven and serve immediately.
6. Meal prep tip: Prevent burning of cheese, otherwise it will taste bitter.

Nutrition Calories per serving: 445 Carbohydrates: 3.6g Protein: 12.8g Fat: 42g Sugar: 0.3g Sodium: 429mg

Omega-3 Salad

Serves: 2/Prep Time: 15 mins
Ingredients

- ½ pound skinless salmon fillet, cut into 4 steaks
- ¼ tablespoon fresh lime juice
- 1 tablespoon olive oil, divided
- 4 tablespoons sour cream
- ¼ zucchini, cut into small cubes
- ¼ teaspoon jalapeño pepper, seeded and chopped finely
- Salt and black pepper, to taste
- ¼ tablespoon fresh dill, chopped

Directions

1. Put olive oil and salmon in a skillet and cook for about 5 minutes on both sides.

3. Season with salt and black pepper, stirring well and dish out.
4. Mix remaining ingredients in a bowl and add cooked salmon to serve.
5. Meal Prep Tip: You can refrigerate it for 1 day and not more than that.

Nutrition Calories per serving: 291 Fat: 21.1g Carbohydrates: 2.5g Protein: 23.1g Sugar: 0.6g Sodium: 112mg

Crab Cakes

Serves: 2/Prep Time: 30 mins
Ingredients
- ½ pound lump crabmeat, drained
- 2 tablespoons coconut flour
- 1 tablespoon mayonnaise
- ¼ teaspoon green Tabasco sauce
- 3 tablespoons butter
- 1 small organic egg, beaten
- ¾ tablespoon fresh parsley, chopped
- ½ teaspoon yellow mustard
- Salt and black pepper, to taste

Directions
1. Mix together all the ingredients in a bowl except butter.
2. Make patties from this mixture and keep aside.
3. Heat butter in a skillet over medium heat and add patties.
4. Cook for about 10 minutes on each side and dish out to serve hot.
5. You can store the raw patties in the freezer for about 3 weeks for meal prepping. Place patties in a container and place parchment paper in between the patties to avoid stickiness.

Nutrition Calories per serving: 153 Fat: 10.8g Carbohydrates: 6.7g Protein: 6.4g Sugar: 2.4g Sodium: 46mg

Salmon Burgers

Serves: 2/Prep Time: 20 mins
Ingredients
- 1 tablespoon sugar-free ranch dressing
- ½-ounce smoked salmon, chopped roughly
- ½ tablespoon fresh parsley, chopped
- ½ tablespoon avocado oil
- 1 small organic egg
- 4-ounce pink salmon, drained and bones removed
- 1/8 cup almond flour
- ¼ teaspoon Cajun seasoning

Directions
1. Mix together all the ingredients in a bowl and stir well.
2. Make patties from this mixture and keep aside.
3. Heat a skillet over medium heat and add patties.
4. Cook for about 3 minutes per side and dish out to serve.
5. You can store the raw patties in the freezer for about 3 weeks for meal prepping. Place patties in a container and place parchment paper in between the patties to avoid stickiness.

Nutrition Calories per serving: 59 Fat: 12.7g Carbohydrates: 2.4g Protein: 6.3g Sugar: 0.7g Sodium: 25mg

Indian Style Butter Chicken

Serves: 2/Prep Time: 25 mins
Ingredients
- ½ medium onion, chopped
- ½ teaspoon fresh ginger, minced
- ½ tablespoon garam masala
- ½ teaspoon fenugreek seeds
- ½ teaspoon ground cumin
- ½ cup heavy cream
- 1 tablespoon unsalted butter
- 1 garlic clove, minced
- 3-ounce sugar-free tomato paste
- ¾ pound grass-fed chicken breasts, cut into ¾-inch chunks
- ½ teaspoon red chili powder
- Salt and black pepper, to taste

Directions
1. Put butter, garlic, ginger and onions in a skillet and sauté for about 4 minutes.
2. Add chicken, tomato paste and spices and cook for about 5 minutes.
3. Stir in heavy cream and allow it to simmer for about 10 minutes.
4. Dish out to serve hot and enjoy.
5. Stir continuously while adding heavy cream in the skillet for meal prepping. You can store in the refrigerator for up to 4 days.

Nutrition Calories per serving: 427 Fat: 24g Carbohydrates: 9g Protein: 42.1g Sugar: 4.4g Sodium: 258mg

Burrito Bowl

Serves: 2/Prep Time: 40 mins
Ingredients
For Chicken:
- 1 tablespoon olive oil
- Salt and black pepper, to taste
- ¼ cup fresh cilantro, chopped
- 1 teaspoon garlic, minced
- ½ pound grass-fed skinless, boneless chicken breasts
- 1/8 cup fresh lime juice

For Cauliflower Rice:
- 1½ cups cauliflower rice
- 1 tablespoon olive oil
- 1 teaspoon garlic powder
- Salt, to taste
- 1/8 cup yellow onion, sliced thinly
- ½ teaspoon ground cumin
- ¼ cup carrot, peeled and shredded

Directions
For Chicken:
1. Put oil, garlic, chicken, salt and black pepper in a large skillet and cook for about 8 minutes each side.
2. Remove it from heat and allow it to cool down, shredding chicken lightly.
3. Mix together rest of the ingredients in a bowl and add chicken, tossing well.

For Cauliflower Rice:
4. Put oil, cumin and onions in a large skillet and sauté for about 3 minutes.
5. Add cauliflower rice, garlic powder and salt and cook for about 5 minutes.
6. Stir in carrots and remove from heat to cool down.
7. Combine chicken and cauliflower rice in a serving bowl and serve.
8. You can store both chicken and cauliflower rice in separate containers up to 5 days for meal prepping. Reheat before serving it.

Nutrition Calories per serving: 303 Fat: 18.3g Carbohydrates: 8.8g Protein: 27.6g
Sugar: 3.4g Sodium: 135mg

Tuna Salad

Serves: 2/Prep Time: 20 mins
Ingredients
- 2/3 cup mayonnaise
- 6 hard-boiled organic eggs, peeled and chopped
- ½ teaspoon seasoned salt
- 1 can water packed tuna, drained
- ½ cup cucumber, chopped

Directions
1. Put all the ingredients in a bowl and mix until well combined.
2. Serve immediately.
3. For meal prepping, place the salad in a container and refrigerate it for 1 day, not more than that.

Nutrition Calories per serving: 615 Fat: 38.9g Carbohydrates: 2.2g Protein: 39.9g
Sugar: 0.4g Sodium: 224mg

Chicken Meal

Serves: 2/Prep Time: 35 mins
Ingredients
- ½ medium zucchini, chopped
- ½ small yellow onion, chopped
- 1 (6-ounce) grass-fed skinless, boneless chicken breasts, cut into ½-inch pieces
- ½ cup fresh broccoli florets
- 1 garlic clove, minced
- ¼ teaspoon paprika
- 1 tablespoon olive oil
- ½ teaspoon Italian seasoning
- Salt and black pepper, to taste

Directions
1. Preheat the oven to 450 degrees F and line a baking dish with foil.
2. Put all the ingredients in a bowl and toss to coat well.
3. Place the chicken mixture in the baking dish and transfer into the oven.
4. Bake for about 20 minutes and dish out to serve hot.
5. For meal prepping, cool the mixture and wrap it with plastic wrap. Refrigerate for about 5 days.

Nutrition Calories per serving: 195 Fat: 10.6g Carbohydrates: 5.6g Protein: 20.5g
Sugar: 2.1g Sodium: 134mg

Tangy Chicken

Serves: 2/Prep Time: 25 mins
Ingredients
- ¾ pound grass-fed skinless, boneless chicken thighs
- 1/8 cup onion, chopped finely
- 1 tablespoon unsalted butter, divided
- Freshly ground black pepper, to taste
- ½ cup chicken broth
- ½ tablespoon fresh lemon juice
- 1 tablespoon maple syrup
- 1 tablespoon fresh ginger, minced
- ½ cup fresh cranberries

Directions

2. Put butter, chicken, salt and black pepper in a large skillet and cook for about 5 minutes per side.
3. Dish out the chicken in a bowl and wrap it with foil to keep it warm.
4. Put onions, ginger and lemon juice in the same skillet and sauté for about 4 minutes.
5. Stir in broth and bring it to boil while continuously stirring.
6. Add cranberries and cook for about 5 minutes.
7. Stir in maple syrup and black pepper and cook for about 2 minutes.
8. Unwrap the chicken and pour this mixture over it.
9. Serve hot.
10. For meal prepping, you can store this cranberry mixture for 2 days and reheat in microwave when you want to use it again.

Nutrition Calories per serving: 199 Fat: 8g Carbohydrates: 4.2g Protein: 25.9g Sugar: 1.4g Sodium: 78mg

Mushroom Risotto with Cauliflower Rice

Serves: 2/Prep Time: 50 mins
Ingredients

- ¾ tablespoon olive oil
- 1/3 small onion, diced
- 3 ounces cremini mushrooms, thinly sliced
- ¾ tablespoon butter
- 2 cloves garlic, minced
- ½ small shallot, minced
- ¾ cup vegetable stock, divided
- 1/3 cup heavy cream
- ¾ tablespoon fresh flat-leaf parsley, chopped
- 1½ cups riced cauliflower
- ¼ cup Parmesan cheese, grated
- Sea salt and black pepper, to taste

Directions
1. Heat butter and olive oil in a large sauté pan over medium heat and add garlic, onion and shallot.
2. Sauté for about 4 minutes and add mushrooms and half of vegetable stock.
3. Sauté for about 5 minutes and add cauliflower and remaining vegetable stock.
4. Sauté for about 10 minutes and reduce the heat to low.
5. Stir in the Parmesan cheese, heavy cream, parsley, salt and black pepper.
6. Allow it to simmer for about 15 minutes and dish out.

Nutrition Calories: 207 Carbs: 9.4g Fats: 17.9g Proteins: 4.7g Sodium: 117mg Sugar: 3.7g

Cheesy Zucchini Gratin

Serves: 2/Prep Time: 55 mins
Ingredients

- ¼ small onion, peeled and sliced thinly
- ½ cup pepper jack cheese, shredded
- ¼ teaspoon garlic powder
- 1 cup raw zucchini, sliced
- Salt and black pepper, to taste
- ¾ tablespoon butter
- ¼ cup heavy whipping cream
- 1/8 teaspoon xanthan gum

Directions
1. Preheat the oven to 375 degrees F and grease an oven proof pan.
2. Mix together zucchini, onions, half of pepper jack cheese, salt and black pepper in a bowl.
3. Put the mixture in the pan and top with rest of the cheese.

5. Combine butter, garlic powder, xanthan gum and heavy cream in a microwave safe dish.
6. Microwave for about 1 minute and whisk until smooth.
7. Pour this mixture over the zucchini layers and transfer the pan in the oven.
8.   Bake for about 45 minutes and dish out to serve warm.

Nutrition Calories: 136 Carbs: 9.7g Fats: 12.2g Proteins: 3.5g Sodium: 296mg Sugar: 1.5g

Eggplant Gratin with Feta Cheese

Serves: 2/Prep Time: 55 mins
Ingredients
- ¼ cup Crème Fraiche
- 1 oz Feta cheese, crumbled
- 2 basil leaves
- ¼ cup tomato sauce
- ¾ eggplant, sliced ½ inch thick
- ¼ cup half and half
- 1/3 teaspoon thyme leaves, chopped
- ½ tablespoon chives, chopped
- ¼ cup Gruyere cheese, grated
- 1 tablespoon olive oil
- Salt and black pepper, to taste

Directions
1. Preheat the oven to 375 degrees F and line a baking pan with parchment paper.
2. Sprinkle both sides of eggplant slices with salt and black pepper and drizzle with olive oil.
3. Transfer the eggplant slices into the baking pan and bake for about 20 minutes until eggplant is tender.
4. Mix together Crème Fraiche, half and half and Feta cheese in a small saucepan.
5. Bring to a boil and add thyme and chives and keep aside.
6. Spread tomato sauce in the bottom of a gratin dish and place eggplant slices.
7. Layer with tomato sauce and sprinkle half of Gruyere cheese.
8.   Top with basil leaves and continue layering with remaining eggplant, sauce and basil.
9. Top with cream, Feta cheese and the remaining Gruyere cheese.
10.   Bake for about 20 minutes until the top is browned and serve warm.

Nutrition Calories: 244 Carbs: 13.8g Fats: 18.3g Proteins: 9.1g Sodium: 380mg Sugar: 7.1g

Garlic and Chive Cauliflower Mash

Serves: 2/Prep Time: 25 mins
Ingredients
- 1/6 cup avocado mayonnaise
- ½ tablespoon water
- 2 pinches black pepper
- 2 cups cauliflower florets
- ½ clove garlic, peeled
- ¼ teaspoon Kosher salt
- 1/8 teaspoon lemon juice
- ½ tablespoon fresh chives, chopped
- ¼ teaspoon lemon zest

Directions
1. Mix together cauliflower, avocado mayonnaise, water, garlic, salt and black pepper in a large microwave safe bowl.

3. Microwave on high for about 15 minutes and transfer the cooked mixture to a food processor.
4. Puree until smooth and add lemon juice, zest and chives.
5. Pulse until combined and dish out in a platter to serve.

Nutrition Calories: 160 Carbs: 5.7g Fats: 16.1g Proteins: 2.1g Sodium: 474mg Sugar: 2.4g

Stuffed Zucchini with Goat Cheese and Marinara

Serves: 2/Prep Time: 25 mins
Ingredients
- 2½-ounces log goat cheese
- 2 medium-sized zucchinis, cut in half lengthwise
- ¾ cup marinara sauce
- Chopped parsley, for garnish

Directions
1. Preheat the oven to 400 degrees F and grease a baking sheet.
2. Season the zucchini with salt and black pepper and transfer on a baking sheet.
3. Layer with half of goat cheese followed by marinara sauce and top with remaining goat cheese.
4. Bake for about 10 minutes and serve immediately.

Nutrition Calories: 145 Carbs: 9.2g Fats: 10.2g Proteins: 8.1g Sodium: 263mg Sugar: 4.2g

Spinach & Artichoke Dip Cauliflower Casserole

Serves: 2/Prep Time: 45 mins
Ingredients
- 4 tablespoons butter
- 2 oz full fat cream cheese
- 2 pinches ground nutmeg
- 1/8 teaspoon smoked paprika
- ¼ cup frozen artichoke hearts, drained and chopped
- 1 cup raw cauliflower florets, roughly chopped
- 1/8 cup Silk Cashew Milk, unsweetened
- Kosher salt and black pepper, to taste
- 1/8 teaspoon garlic powder
- ¼ cup frozen spinach, chopped
- ½ cup whole milk mozzarella cheese, shredded
- 1/8 cup parmesan cheese, grated

Directions
1. Preheat the oven to 400 degrees F and grease a casserole.
2. Mix together the cauliflower, Silk Cashew Milk, butter, cream cheese, nutmeg, garlic powder, salt, black pepper and paprika in a microwave safe dish.
3. Microwave for 10 minutes on high and add spinach, artichoke hearts, half of the mozzarella cheese and parmesan cheese.
4. Stir well and dish out the mixture in an ovenproof casserole dish.
5. Sprinkle the remaining mozzarella cheese over the top and transfer in the oven.
6. Bake for about 20 minutes at 400 degrees F and dish out to serve hot.

Nutrition Calories: 357 Carbs: 6.8g Fats: 34.2g Proteins: 8.9g Sodium: 697mg Sugar: 2.7g

Parmesan Cauliflower Steak

Serves: 2/Prep Time: 35 mins

Ingredients
- 2 tablespoons butter
- ½ large head cauliflower, sliced lengthwise and core into 1-inch steaks
- 1 tablespoon Urban Accents Manchego and Roasted Garlic seasoning blend
- Salt and black pepper, to taste
- 1/8 cup parmesan cheese

Directions
1. Preheat the oven to 400 degrees F and line a baking sheet with parchment paper.
2. Melt butter in microwave and combine with seasoning blend to make paste.
3. Brush this mixture over cauliflower steaks and season with salt and black pepper.
4. Cook cauliflower steaks in a non-stick pan over medium heat for about 3 minutes on each side until browned lightly.
5. Transfer the cauliflower steaks on baking sheet and place in the oven.
6. Bake for about 20 minutes until golden and sprinkle with parmesan cheese to serve.

Nutrition Calories: 160 Carbs: 11.2g Fats: 12.1g Proteins: 4.9g Sodium: 161mg Sugar: 5.1g

Mediterranean Zucchini Noodle Pasta

Serves: 2/Prep Time: 25 mins

Ingredients
- ½ cup spinach, packed
- 1 tablespoon butter
- Sea salt and black pepper, to taste
- 1 tablespoon capers
- 5 kalamata olives, halved
- 1/8 cup feta cheese, crumbled
- 1 large zucchini, spiral sliced
- 1 tablespoon olive oil
- 3 cloves garlic, minced
- 1/8 cup sun-dried tomatoes
- 1 tablespoon Italian flat leaf parsley, chopped
- 1/8 cup Parmesan cheese, shredded

Directions
1. Put zucchini, spinach, olive oil, butter, garlic, sea salt and black pepper over medium heat in a large sauté pan.
2. Sauté for about 5 minutes and drain excess liquid.
3. Add sun-dried tomatoes, capers, parsley, and kalamata olives in the pan and sauté for about 3 minutes.
4. Remove from heat and top with feta and Parmesan cheeses to serve.

Nutrition Calories: 192 Carbs: 9.1g Fats: 16.7g Proteins: 4.8g Sodium: 410mg Sugar: 3.6g

Vegetarian Red Coconut Curry

Serves: 2/Prep Time: 35 mins

Ingredients

- ¾ cup spinach
- ¼ medium onion, chopped
- 1 teaspoon ginger, minced
- 1 cup broccoli florets
- 4 tablespoons coconut oil
- 1 teaspoon garlic, minced
- 2 teaspoons coconut aminos
- 1 tablespoon red curry paste
- 2 teaspoons soy sauce
- ½ cup coconut cream

Directions

1. Heat 2 tablespoons of coconut oil in a pan and add garlic and onions.
2. Sauté for about 3 minutes and add broccoli.
3. Sauté for about 3 minutes and move vegetables to the side of the pan.
4. Add curry paste and cook for about 1 minute.
5. Mix well and add spinach, cooking for about 3 minutes.
6. Add coconut cream, remaining coconut oil, ginger, soy sauce and coconut aminos.
7. Allow it to simmer for about 10 minutes and dish out to serve.

Nutrition Calories: 439 Carbs: 12g Fats: 44g Proteins: 3.6g Sodium: 728mg Sugar: 3.5g

Zucchini Noodles with Avocado Sauce

Serves: 2/Prep Time: 10 mins

Ingredients

- 1¼ cup basil
- 4 tablespoons pine nuts
- 1 zucchini, spiralized
- 1/3 cup water
- 2 tablespoons lemon juice
- 2 cherry tomatoes, sliced
- 1 avocado

Directions

1. Put all the ingredients except the cherry tomatoes and zucchini in a blender and blend until smooth.
2. Mix together the blended sauce and zucchini noodles and cherry tomatoes in a serving bowl and serve.

Nutrition Calories: 366 Carbs: 19.7g Fats: 32g Proteins: 7.1g Sodium: 27mg Sugar: 6.4g

Zucchini and Sweet Potato Latkes

Serves: 4/Prep Time: 5 mins

Ingredients

- 1 cup shredded zucchini
- 1 cup shredded sweet potato
- 1 egg, beaten
- 1 Tbsp coconut flour
- 1/2 tsp garlic powder
- 1/4 tsp ground cumin
- 1/2 tsp dried parsley
- Salt & pepper to taste
- 1 Tbsp ghee or clarified butter
- 1 Tbsp EV olive oil

Directions

1. Combine the zucchini, sweet potato and egg in a medium bowl.
2. In a small bowl, mix the coconut flour and spices together. Add the dry ingredients to the zucchini mixture and stir until fully combined.

4. Heat the ghee and olive oil in a medium nonstick pan. Divide the mixture into four equal portions and drop into the pan, pressing down with a fork until a 1/2 inch thick cake is formed. Cook on medium heat until golden and crisp, then flip carefully and cook the other side. Remove to a plate lined with paper towels to drain.
5. Season with an additional sprinkle of kosher salt. Serve hot.

Nutrition Calories: 109 Carbs: 6.2g Fats: 9.6g Proteins: 0.9g Sodium: 227mg Sugar: 1.8g

Tomato Basil and Mozzarella Galette

Serves: 2/Prep Time: 35 mins
Ingredients
- 1 large egg
- 1 teaspoon garlic powder
- ¾ cup almond flour
- 2 tablespoons mozzarella liquid
- ¼ cup Parmesan cheese, shredded
- 3 leaves fresh basil
- 2 plum tomatoes
- 1½ tablespoons pesto
- 1/3-ounce Mozzarella cheese

Directions
1. Preheat oven to 365 degrees F and line a cookie sheet with parchment paper.
2. Mix together the garlic powder, almond flour and mozzarella liquid in a bowl.
3. Add Parmesan cheese and egg and mix to form a dough.
4. Form balls out of this dough mixture and transfer on the cookie sheet.
5. Press the dough balls with a fork and spread pesto over the centre of the crust evenly.
6. Layer mozzarella, tomatoes and basil leaves, and fold the edges of the crust up and over the filling.
7. Transfer in the oven and bake for about 20 minutes.
8.   Dish out to serve.

Nutrition Calories: 396 Carbs: 17.6g Fats: 29.2g Proteins: 17.5g Sodium: 199mg Sugar: 6.2g

Quick Spiralized Zucchini and Plum Tomatoes

Serves: 2/Prep Time: 30 mins
Ingredients
- 3 garlic cloves, chopped
- 1 pinch red crushed pepper flakes
- 1 large zucchini, spiralized with thicker blade
- 2 tablespoons olive oil
- ½ pound whole plum tomatoes, cut in half
- Kosher salt and black pepper, to taste
- 1 tablespoon fresh basil, chopped

Directions
1. Heat olive oil in a large non-stick pan and add garlic.
2. Sauté for about 30 seconds and add tomatoes, red pepper flakes, salt and black pepper.
3. Reduce the heat to low and simmer for about 15 minutes.
4. Increase heat to medium-high and stir in the basil and zucchini.
5. Season with salt and cook for about 2 minutes and serve.

Nutrition Calories: 174 Carbs: 11.3g Fats: 14.3g Proteins: 3.2g Sodium: 180mg Sugar: 5.5g

Cheesy Spaghetti Squash with Pesto

Serves: 2/Prep Time: 25 mins

Ingredients

- ½ tablespoon olive oil
- ¼ cup whole milk ricotta cheese
- 1/8 cup basil pesto
- 1 cup cooked spaghetti squash, drained
- Salt and black pepper, to taste
- 2 oz fresh mozzarella cheese, cubed

Directions

1. Preheat the oven to 375 degrees F and grease a casserole dish.
2. Mix together squash and olive oil in a medium-sized bowl and season with salt and black pepper.
3. Put the squash in the casserole dish and top with ricotta and mozzarella cheese.
4. Bake for about 10 minutes and remove from the oven.
5. Drizzle the pesto over the top and serve hot.

Nutrition Calories: 169 Carbs: 6.2g Fats: 11.3g Proteins: 11.9g Sodium: 217mg Sugar: 0.1g

Vegan Sesame Tofu and Eggplant

Serves: 2/Prep Time: 30 mins

Ingredients

- ½ cup cilantro, chopped
- 2 tablespoons toasted sesame oil
- ½ teaspoon crushed red pepper flakes
- ½ eggplant, julienned
- ½ pound block firm tofu, pressed
- 1½ tablespoons rice vinegar
- 1 clove garlic, finely minced
- 1 teaspoon Swerve
- ½ tablespoon olive oil
- 1/8 cup sesame seeds
- Salt and black pepper, to taste
- 1/8 cup soy sauce

Directions

1. Preheat the oven to 200 degrees F.
2. Mix together cilantro, eggplant, rice vinegar, half of toasted sesame oil, garlic, red pepper flakes and Swerve in a bowl.
3. Heat olive oil in a skillet and add the marinated eggplant.
4. Sauté for about 4 minutes and transfer the eggplant noodles to an oven safe dish.
5. Cover with a foil and place into the oven to keep warm.
6. Spread the sesame seeds on a plate and press both sides of each piece of tofu into the seeds.
7. Add remaining sesame oil and tofu to the skillet and fry for about 5 minutes.
8. Pour soy sauce into the pan and cook until the tofu slices are browned.
9. Remove the eggplant noodles from the oven and top with tofu to serve.

Nutrition Calories: 333 Carbs: 13.9g Fats: 26.6g Proteins: 13.3g Sodium: 918mg Sugar: 4.5g

Cheesy Spinach Puffs

Serves: 2/Prep Time: 25 mins

Ingredients
- ½ cup almond flour
- 1 large egg
- ¼ cup feta cheese, crumbled
- ½ teaspoon kosher salt
- ½ teaspoon garlic powder
- 1½ tablespoons heavy whipping cream

Directions
1. Preheat the oven to 350 degrees F and grease a cookie sheet.
2. Put all the ingredients in a blender and pulse until smooth.
3. Allow to cool down and form 1-inch balls from this mixture.
4. Arrange on a cookie sheet and transfer into the oven.
5. Bake for about 12 minutes and dish out to serve.

Nutrition Calories: 294 Carbs: 7.8g Fats: 24g Proteins: 12.2g Sodium: 840mg Sugar: 1.1g

Dinner Recipes

Lobster Salad

Serves: 2/Prep Time: 15 mins

Ingredients
- ¼ yellow onion, chopped
- ¼ yellow bell pepper, seeded and chopped
- ¾ pound cooked lobster meat, shredded
- 1 celery stalk, chopped
- Black pepper, to taste
- ¼ cup avocado mayonnaise

Directions
1. Mix together all the ingredients in a bowl and stir until well combined.
2. Refrigerate for about 3 hours and serve chilled.
3. Put the salad into a container for meal prepping and refrigerate for about 2 days.

Nutrition Calories per serving: 336 Carbohydrates: 2g Protein: 27.2g Fat: 25.2g Sugar: 1.2g Sodium: 926mg

Beef Sausage Pancakes

Serves: 2/Prep Time: 30 mins

Ingredients
- 4 gluten-free Italian beef sausages, sliced
- 1 tablespoon olive oil
- 1/3 large red bell peppers, seeded and sliced thinly
- 1/3 cup spinach
- ¾ teaspoon garlic powder
- 1/3 large green bell peppers, seeded and sliced thinly
- ¾ cup heavy whipped cream
- Salt and black pepper, to taste

Directions
1. Mix together all the ingredients in a bowl except whipped cream and keep aside.
2. Put butter and half of the mixture in a skillet and cook for about 6 minutes on both sides.

4. Repeat with the remaining mixture and dish out.
5. Beat whipped cream in another bowl until smooth.
6. Serve the beef sausage pancakes with whipped cream.
7. For meal prepping, it is compulsory to gently slice the sausages before mixing with other ingredients.

Nutrition Calories per serving: 415 Carbohydrates: 7g Protein: 29.5g Fat: 31.6g Sugar: 4.3g Sodium: 1040mg

Holiday Chicken Salad

Serves: 2/Prep Time: 25 mins
Ingredients
- 1 celery stalk, chopped
- 1½ cups cooked grass-fed chicken, chopped
- ¼ cup fresh cranberries
- ¼ cup sour cream
- ½ apple, chopped
- ¼ yellow onion, chopped
- 1/8 cup almonds, toasted and chopped
- 2-ounce feta cheese, crumbled
- ¼ cup avocado mayonnaise
- Salt and black pepper, to taste

Directions
1. Stir together all the ingredients in a bowl except almonds and cheese.
2. Top with almonds and cheese to serve.
3. Meal Prep Tip: Don't add almonds and cheese in the salad if you want to store the salad. Cover with a plastic wrap and refrigerate to serve.

Nutrition Calories per serving: 336 Carbohydrates: 8.8g Protein: 24.5g Fat: 23.2g Sugar: 5.4g Sodium: 383mg

Luncheon Fancy Salad

Serves: 2/Prep Time: 40 mins
Ingredients
- 6-ounce cooked salmon, chopped
- 1 tablespoon fresh dill, chopped
- Salt and black pepper, to taste
- 4 hard-boiled grass-fed eggs, peeled and cubed
- 2 celery stalks, chopped
- ½ yellow onion, chopped
- ¾ cup avocado mayonnaise

Directions
1. Put all the ingredients in a bowl and mix until well combined.
2. Cover with a plastic wrap and refrigerate for about 3 hours to serve.
3. For meal prepping, put the salad in a container and refrigerate for up to 3 days.

Nutrition Calories per serving: 303 Carbohydrates: 1.7g Protein: 10.3g Fat: 30g Sugar: 1g Sodium: 314mg

Italian Platter

Serves: 2/Prep Time: 45 mins
Ingredients
- 1 garlic clove, minced
- 5-ounce fresh button mushrooms, sliced

- 1/8 cup unsalted butter
- ¼ teaspoon dried thyme
- 1/3 cup heavy whipping cream
- Salt and black pepper, to taste
- 2 (6-ounce) grass-fed New York strip steaks

Directions
1. Preheat the grill to medium heat and grease it.
2. Season the steaks with salt and black pepper, and transfer to the grill.
3. Grill steaks for about 10 minutes on each side and dish out in a platter.
4. Put butter, mushrooms, salt and black pepper in a pan and cook for about 10 minutes.
5. Add thyme and garlic and thyme and sauté for about 1 minute.
6. Stir in the cream and let it simmer for about 5 minutes.
7. Top the steaks with mushroom sauce and serve hot immediately.
8. Meal Prep Tip: You can store the mushroom sauce in refrigerator for about 2 days. Season the steaks carefully with salt and black pepper to avoid low or high quantities.

Nutrition Calories per serving: 332 Carbohydrates: 3.2g Protein: 41.8g Fat: 20.5g Sugar: 1.3g Sodium: 181mg

Meat Loaf

Serves: 12/Prep Time: 1 hour 15 mins
Ingredients
- 1 garlic clove, minced
- ½ teaspoon dried thyme, crushed
- ½ pound grass-fed lean ground beef
- 1 organic egg, beaten
- Salt and black pepper, to taste
- ¼ cup onions, chopped
- 1/8 cup sugar-free ketchup
- 2 cups mozzarella cheese, freshly grated
- ¼ cup green bell pepper, seeded and chopped
- ½ cup cheddar cheese, grated
- 1 cup fresh spinach, chopped

Directions
1. Preheat the oven to 350 degrees F and grease a baking dish.
2. Put all the ingredients in a bowl except spinach and cheese and mix well.
3. Arrange the meat over a wax paper and top with spinach and cheese.
4. Roll the paper around the mixture to form a meatloaf.
5. Remove the wax paper and transfer the meat loaf in the baking dish.
6. Put it in the oven and bake for about 1 hour.
7. Dish out and serve hot.
8. Meal Prep Tip: Let the meat loafs cool for about 10 minutes to bring them to room temperature before serving.

Nutrition Calories per serving: 439 Carbohydrates: 8g Protein: 40.8g Fat: 26g Sugar: 1.6g Sodium: 587mg

Grilled Steak

Serves: 2/Prep Time: 15 mins
Ingredients
- ¼ cup unsalted butter
- 2 garlic cloves, minced
- ¾ pound beef top sirloin steaks
- ¾ teaspoon dried rosemary, crushed
- 2 oz. parmesan cheese, shredded
- Salt and black pepper, to taste

Directions

2. Preheat the grill and grease it.
3. Season the sirloin steaks with salt and black pepper.
4. Transfer the steaks on the grill and cook for about 5 minutes on each side.
5. Dish out the steaks in plates and keep aside.
6. Meanwhile, put butter and garlic in a pan and heat until melted.
7. Pour it on the steaks and serve hot.
8. Divide the steaks in 2 containers and refrigerate for about 3 days for meal prepping purpose. Reheat in microwave before serving.

Nutrition Calories per serving: 383 Carbohydrates: 1.5g Protein: 41.4g Fat: 23.6g Sugar: 0g Sodium: 352mg

Cheese Casserole

Serves: 2/Prep Time: 46 mins
Ingredients
- 2½ ounce marinara sauce
- ½ tablespoon olive oil
- 4 ounce parmesan cheese, shredded
- ½ pound sausages, scrambled
- 4 ounce mozzarella cheese, shredded

Directions
1. Preheat the oven to 375 degrees F and grease a baking dish with olive oil.
2. Place half of the sausage scramble in it and top with half of marinara sauce, mozzarella cheese and parmesan cheese.
3. Place the remaining sausage scramble in the baking dish and top again with marinara sauce, mozzarella cheese and parmesan cheese.
4. Transfer in the oven and bake for about 20 minutes.
5. Place the casserole in a dish and set aside to cool for meal prepping. Divide it in 6 containers and refrigerate for 1-2 days. Reheat in microwave before serving.

Nutrition Calories per serving: 353 Carbohydrates: 5.5g Protein: 28.4g Fat: 24.3g Sugar: 5g Sodium: 902mg

Air Fried Simple Steak

Serves: 2/Prep Time: 15 mins
Ingredients
- ½ pound quality cut steaks
- Salt and black pepper, to taste

Directions
1. Preheat the Air fryer to 385 degrees F.
2. Rub the steaks evenly with salt and black pepper.
3. Place the steak in an Air fryer basket and cook for about 15 minutes.
4. Dish out and serve immediately.
5. Divide the steaks in 2 containers and refrigerate for about 3 days for meal prepping purpose. Reheat in microwave before serving.

Nutrition Calories per serving: 301 Carbs: 0g Fats: 25.1g Proteins: 19.1g Sugar: 0g Sodium: 65mg

Almonds Crusted Rack of Lamb

Serves: 2/Prep Time: 50 mins

Ingredients

- ¾ pound rack of lamb
- 2-ounce almonds, finely chopped
- ½ tablespoon fresh rosemary, chopped
- 1 garlic clove, minced
- ½ tablespoon olive oil
- 1 small egg
- 1 tablespoon breadcrumbs
- Salt and black pepper, to taste

Directions

1. Preheat the oven to 350 degrees F and grease a baking tray.
2. Mix together garlic, oil, salt and black pepper in a bowl.
3. Coat the rack of lamb evenly with the garlic rub.
4. Whisk egg in a bowl and keep aside.
5. Mix together breadcrumbs, almonds and rosemary in another dish.
6. Dip the rack of lamb in egg and coat with almond mixture.
7. Place the rack of lamb in the baking tray and transfer in the oven.
8. Bake for about 35 minutes and dish out to serve.
9. Put the rack of lamb in a container and refrigerate for about 3 days for meal prepping purpose. Reheat in microwave before serving.

Nutrition Calories per serving: 471 Carbs: 8.5g Fats: 31.6g Proteins: 39g Sugar: 1.5g Sodium: 145mg

Rib Eye Steak

Serves: 2/Prep Time: 35 mins

Ingredients

- 1 tablespoon steak rub
- ¾ pound rib eye steak
- 1 tablespoon olive oil

Directions

1. Preheat the oven to 400 degrees and grease a baking tray.
2. Drizzle the steak with olive oil and coat with steak rub generously.
3. Place the steak in the baking tray and transfer in the oven.
4. Bake for about 25 minutes and dish out to immediately serve.
5. Put the rib eye steak in a container and refrigerate for about 3 days for meal prepping purpose. Reheat in microwave before serving.

Nutrition Calories per serving: 462 Carbs: 1g Fats: 38.1g Proteins: 26.8g Sugar: 0g Sodium: 307mg

Spicy Skirt Steak

Serves: 2/Prep Time: 40 mins

Ingredients

- 2 tablespoons fresh mint leaves, finely chopped
- 2 tablespoons fresh oregano, finely chopped
- ¾ tablespoon ground cumin
- ¾ cup olive oil
- ¾ teaspoon cayenne pepper
- 2 (8-ounce) skirt steaks
- ¾ cup fresh parsley leaves, finely chopped
- 2 garlic cloves, minced
- 1½ teaspoons smoked paprika
- ¾ teaspoon red pepper flakes, crushed
- 2 tablespoons red wine vinegar
- Salt and black pepper, to taste

Directions

1. Preheat the oven to 390 degrees F and grease a baking tray.
2. Put all the ingredients in a bowl except the steaks and stir well.
3. Add steaks and coat well with the marinade.
4. Put marinated steaks and ¼ cup of the herb mixture in a resealable bag and shake to coat well.
5. Refrigerate for about 1 day and reserve the remaining herb mixture.
6. Remove steaks from the refrigerator and keep at room temperature for about half an hour.
7. Arrange the steaks in the baking tray and transfer in the oven.
8. Bake for about 25 minutes and top with the remaining herb mixture to serve.
9. Put the steaks in a container and refrigerate for about 3 days for meal prepping purpose. Reheat in microwave before serving.

Nutrition Calories per serving: 445 Carbs: 5.8g Fats: 43.1g Proteins: 12.9g Sugar: 0.5g Sodium: 46mg

Leg of Lamb

Serves: 2/Prep Time: 1 hour 30 mins

Ingredients

- ¾ pound leg of lamb
- ¾ tablespoon olive oil
- Salt and black pepper, to taste
- 1 fresh rosemary sprig
- 1 fresh thyme sprig

Directions

1. Preheat the oven to 330 degrees F and grease a baking tray.
2. Season with salt and black pepper and drizzle the leg of lamb with olive oil.
3. Cover the leg of lamb with rosemary and thyme sprigs.
4. Arrange the leg of lamb in the baking tray and transfer in the oven.
5. Bake for about 1 hour 15 minutes and dish out to serve.
6. Put the leg of lamb in a container and refrigerate for about 3 days for meal prepping purpose. Reheat in microwave before serving.

Nutrition Calories per serving: 325 Carbs: 0.7g Fats: 15.9g Proteins: 42.5g Sugar: 0g Sodium: 115mg

Jamaican Jerk Pork

Serves: 2/Prep Time: 35 mins

Ingredients

- ¾ pound pork shoulder
- ¼ cup whipped cream
- ¼ cup butter, melted
- ¼ cup Jamaican jerk spice blend
- ¼ cup beef broth

Directions

1. Marinate the pork with Jamaican jerk spice blend and keep aside.
2. Put butter, cream and marinated pork in an instant pot.
3. Sauté for about 5 minutes and add beef broth.
4. Cover the lid and cook on High Pressure for about 20 minutes.
5. Release the pressure naturally and dish out to serve.

7. Place the pork in a dish and keep aside to cool for meal prepping purpose. Divide it in 2 containers and refrigerate for about 3 days. Reheat in microwave before serving.

Nutrition Calories per serving: 457 Carbohydrates: 0.3g Protein: 27g Fat: 38.2g Sugar: 0.1g Sodium: 209mg

Creamy Turkey Breasts

Serves: 2/Prep Time: 1 hour
Ingredients
- ¼ cup sour cream
- ¼ cup butter
- Salt and black pepper, to taste
- ¾ pound turkey breasts
- ½ cup heavy whipping cream
- 2 garlic cloves, minced

Directions
1. Preheat the oven to 390 degrees F and grease the baking dish with some butter.
2. Marinate the turkey breasts with butter, garlic, salt and black pepper in a bowl.
3. Place the marinated turkey breasts on a baking dish and top with heavy whipping cream and sour cream.
4. Bake for about 45 minutes and dish out in a platter.
5. For meal prepping, place the creamy turkey breasts on a dish and keep aside to cool. Divide it in 2 containers and refrigerate for about 2 days. Reheat in microwave before serving.

Nutrition Calories per serving: 304 Carbohydrates: 4.8g Protein: 20.3g Fat: 23.1g Sugar: 4.1g Sodium: 1246mg

Buttered Scallops

Serves: 2/Prep Time: 15 mins
Ingredients
- ¾ pound sea scallopsSalt and black pepper, to taste
- 1 tablespoon butter, melted
- ½ tablespoon fresh thyme, minced

Directions
1. Preheat the oven to 390 degrees F and grease a baking dish.
2. Put all the ingredients in a large bowl and toss to coat well.
3. Arrange the scallops in the baking dish and transfer in the oven.
4. Bake for about 5 minutes and dish out to serve.
5. You can store the buttered scallops into a container in refrigerator for about 2 days for meal prepping purpose. You can reheat it in the microwave before serving.

Nutrition Calories per serving: 202 Carbs: 4.4g Fats: 7.1g Proteins: 28.7g Sugar: 0g Sodium: 315mg

Ham Wrapped Prawns with Bell Pepper Dip

Serves: 2/Prep Time: 25 mins
Ingredients
- 1 tablespoon olive oil
- 1 garlic clove, minced
- 2 ham slices, halved
- Salt and black pepper, to taste
- ½ tablespoon paprika

- 4 king prawns, peeled, deveined and chopped

Directions
1. Preheat the air fryer to 400 degrees F and place the bell pepper in a fryer basket
2. Cook for about 10 minutes and dish out the bell pepper in a bowl.
3. Cover with a foil paper and keep aside for about 30 minutes.
4. Add the bell pepper along with garlic, paprika and olive oil in a blender.
5. Pulse to form a puree and keep aside.
6. Wrap each prawn with a ham slice and arrange in the fryer basket.
7. Cook for about 4 minutes until golden brown and serve with bell pepper dip.
8. You can store the bell pepper dip into a container in refrigerator for 3 days for meal prepping purpose. Reheat it in the microwave before serving with the ha, wrapped prawns.

Nutrition Calories per serving: 553 Carbs: 2.5g Fats: 33.6g Proteins: 5g Sugar: 7.2g Sodium: 366mg

Chicken Wraps

Serves: 2/Prep Time: 45 mins
Ingredients
- ¼ pound lean ground chicken
- ¼ green bell pepper, seeded and chopped
- 1/8 cup yellow squash, chopped
- ½ tablespoon low-sodium soy sauce
- Freshly ground black pepper, to taste
- ½ cup Parmesan cheese, shredded
- ½ tablespoon unsalted butter
- ¼ onion, chopped
- 1 garlic clove, minced
- ¼ cup carrot, peeled and chopped
- 1/8 cup zucchini, chopped
- ¼ teaspoon curry powder
- 2 large lettuce leaves

Directions
1. Put butter and chicken in a skillet and cook for about 5 minutes.
2. Break the lumps and stir in the vegetables.
3. Cook for about 5 minutes and add curry powder, soy sauce and black pepper.
4. Cook for 5 more minutes and keep aside.
5. Arrange the lettuce leaves in serving plates and place chicken mixture over them.
6. Sprinkle with cheese and serve.
7. You have to place the mixture on the leaves evenly for meal prepping purpose. You can refrigerate it in a container for about 2 days.

Nutrition Calories per serving: 71 Fat: 6.7g Carbohydrates: 4.2g Protein: 4.8g Sugar: 30.5g Sodium: 142mg

Indian Beef

Serves: 2/Prep Time: 35 mins
Ingredients
- ½ tablespoon olive oil
- ¼ yellow onion, chopped
- 1 garlic clove, minced
- ½ jalapeño pepper, chopped
- ½ pound grass-fed ground beef
- ½ cup cherry tomatoes, quartered
- ½ pound fresh collard greens, trimmed and chopped
- ½ teaspoon fresh lemon juice

Spices

- ½ teaspoon ground coriander
- ½ teaspoon ground cumin
- ¼ teaspoon ground fennel seeds
- ¼ teaspoon ground ginger
- ¼ teaspoon ground cinnamon
- ¼ teaspoon ground turmeric
- Salt and black pepper, to taste

Directions

1. Put olive oil and onions in a skillet and sauté for about 5 minutes.
2. Add garlic and jalapeno and sauté for about 1 minute.
3. Add beef and spices and cook for about 10 minutes, continuously stirring.
4. Stir in tomatoes and collard greens and cook for about 4 minutes.
5. Add lemon juice, salt and black pepper and dish out to serve.
6. You can refrigerate it by placing it in containers for meal prepping purpose and refrigerate it up to 4 days. Reheat in microwave when you want to use it again.

Nutrition Calories per serving: 294 Fat: 13.1g Carbohydrates: 10g Protein: 37.7 Sugar: 5.1g Sodium: 463mg

Hearty Meatballs

Serves: 2/Prep Time: 35 mins
Ingredients
For Meatballs:

- ½ tablespoon sugar-free tomato paste
- 1 garlic clove, minced
- Freshly ground black pepper, to taste
- ½ pound grass-fed lean ground lamb
- 1/8 cup fresh coriander leaves, chopped
- ½ small yellow onion, finely chopped
- ¼ teaspoon ground cumin

For Tomato Gravy:

- ½ large yellow onions, finely chopped
- ½ tablespoon fresh ginger, minced
- ½ teaspoon ground cumin
- 1 large tomato, finely chopped
- ¾ cup chicken broth
- 1 tablespoon olive oil, divided
- 1 garlic clove, minced
- ½ teaspoon dried thyme, crushed
- ½ teaspoon cayenne pepper
- Salt and black pepper, to taste

Directions

For Meatballs:

1. Put all the ingredients in a bowl and mix well.
2. Make small balls of equal sizes out of this mixture and keep aside.

For Gravy:

3. Put ½ tablespoon olive oil and meatballs in a pan and cook for about 5 minutes.
4. Dish out the meatballs in a plate and keep aside.
5. Put remaining olive oil and onions in the same pan and sauté for about 3 minutes.
6. Add garlic, ginger, thyme and spices and sauté for about 1 minute.
7. Stir in the tomatoes and cook for about 4 minutes, crushing them with the back of the spoon.
8. Add beef broth and bring it to boil.
9. Stir in the meatballs in it and cook for about 5 minutes without stirring.
10. Reduce the heat to low and allow it to simmer for about 15 minutes.

12. Dish out to serve hot and enjoy.
13. You can freeze the raw meatballs for over a month covered in a plastic wrap in the freezer for meal prepping purpose.

Nutrition Calories per serving: 250 Fat: 13.3g Carbohydrates: 9.1g Protein: 24g Sugar: 6.3g Sodium: 414mg

Creamy Steak

Serves: 2/Prep Time: 20 mins
Ingredients

- 1½ tablespoons Parmesan cheese, shredded
- 1/8 teaspoon ground nutmeg
- 1/8 teaspoon garlic powder
- 2 (8-ounce) beef tenderloin steaks
- 2 cups heavy cream
- 1½-ounce gorgonzola cheese, crumbled
- Salt and black pepper, to taste
- 1/8 teaspoon onion powder
- 1/8 teaspoon lemon pepper

Directions
1. Preheat the outdoor grill of the oven to medium high and grease it.
2. Boil the heavy cream in a pan and allow to simmer on low heat for about 30 minutes, stirring continuously.
3. Remove from heat and add gorgonzola cheese, Parmesan cheese, nutmeg, salt, pepper, both cheeses and mix well.
4. Meanwhile, mix together garlic powder, onion powder, lemon pepper, salt and black pepper in a bowl.
5. Sprinkle the steaks with the seasoning mixture and transfer to the grill.
6. Grill for about 5 minutes on each side and dish out on the serving plates.
7. Top with creamy sauce and serve immediately.
8. While sprinkling the seasoning on the steaks, sprinkle it evenly for meal prepping purpose. You can refrigerate it in the refrigerator for about 2 days.

Nutrition Calories per serving: 915 Fat: 64.9g Carbohydrates: 4.9g Protein: 76.4g Sugar: 1.2g Sodium: 680mg

Tofu in Purgatory

Serves: 2/Prep Time: 25 mins
Ingredients

- 4 large garlic cloves
- Salt and black pepper, to taste
- 1 tablespoon olive oil
- 1 can diced tomatoes
- 2 teaspoons dried herbs
- 1 block medium tofu, not pressed and cut into rounds
- ½ teaspoon dried chili flakes

Directions
1. Heat olive oil in a skillet over medium heat and add garlic.
2. Sauté for about 1 minute and add tomatoes, chili flakes, herbs, salt and black pepper.
3. Simmer for about 5 minutes over a medium heat and add the tofu.
4. Reduce the heat to medium-low and simmer for about 15 minutes.
5. Dish out and serve with a baguette.

Nutrition Calories: 123 Carbs: 8.3g Fats: 8.9g Proteins: 4.8g Sodium: 10mg Sugar: 1.3g

Caprese Style Portobellos

Serves: 2/Prep Time: 25 mins
Ingredients
- 4 plum tomatoes, halved
- 2 large portobello mushroom caps, gills removed
- ¼ cup Mozzarella cheese, shredded
- 4 tablespoons olive oil
- ¼ cup fresh basil

Directions
1. Preheat the oven to 400 degrees F and line a baking sheet with foil.
2. Brush the mushrooms with olive oil.
3. Place cherry tomatoes in a bowl and add remaining olive oil, basil, salt and black pepper.
4. Put Mozzarella cheese on the bottom of the mushroom cap and add tomato basil mixture.
5. Bake for about 15 minutes and dish out to serve.

Nutrition Calories: 315 Carbs: 14.2g Fats: 29.2g Proteins: 4.7g Sodium: 55mg Sugar: 10.4g

Four Cheese Pesto Zoodles

Serves: 2/Prep Time: 20 mins
Ingredients
- 1/8 cup parmesan cheese, grated
- ¼ teaspoon kosher salt
- 2 pinches ground nutmeg
- ½ cup mozzarella cheese, grated
- 4 ounces Mascarpone cheese
- 1/8 cup Romano cheese, grated
- ½ teaspoon ground black pepper
- 1/8 cup basil pesto
- 4 cups raw zucchini noodles

Directions
1. Preheat the oven to 400 degrees F and grease a casserole dish.
2. Microwave the zucchini noodles for 3 minutes on high and keep aside.
3. Mix together the parmesan cheese, mascarpone cheese, Romano cheese, nutmeg, salt and black pepper in a large microwave safe bowl.
4. Microwave for 1 minute on high and whisk together until smooth.
5. Fold in the basil pesto, mozzarella cheese and cooked zoodles.
6. Transfer to a casserole dish and place in the oven.
7. Bake for about 10 minutes and serve immediately.

Nutrition Calories: 139 Carbs: 3.3g Fats: 9.7g Proteins: 10.2g Sodium: 419mg Sugar: 0.2g

Roasted Baby Eggplant with Ricotta

Serves: 2/Prep Time: 45 mins
Ingredients
- ¼ tablespoon olive oil
- 1 eggplant, halved
- ¼ teaspoon Wild Fennel Pollen
- ¼ teaspoon black pepper
- ¼ teaspoon sea salt

To serve:

- 1/8 cup ricotta cheese
- Sea salt and black pepper, to taste
- ¼ tablespoon extra-virgin olive oil

Directions

1. Preheat the oven to 350 degrees F and grease a cookie sheet.
2. Place the eggplant halves on a cookie sheet, cut side up and top with olive oil, fennel pollen, salt and black pepper.
3. Transfer in the oven and bake for about 45 minutes, until lightly browned.
4. Remove from the oven and allow to cool slightly.
5. Serve warm topped with ricotta cheese, olive oil, salt and black pepper.

Nutrition Calories: 69 Carbs: 3.4g Fats: 5.5g Proteins: 2.4g Sodium: 247mg Sugar: 1.6g

Moroccan Roasted Green Beans

Serves: 2/Prep Time: 45 mins

Ingredients

- 1/3 teaspoon kosher salt
- 2 cups raw green beans, trimmed
- ¼ teaspoon ground black pepper
- 2 tablespoons olive oil
- 1/3 tablespoon Ras el Hanout seasoning

Directions

1. Preheat the oven to 400 degrees F and grease a roasting pan.
2. Mix together green beans, olive oil and seasonings in a bowl and transfer into the roasting pan.
3. Roast for about 20 minutes and remove from the oven.
4. Return to the oven and roast for another 10 minutes.
5. Dish out and serve warm.

Nutrition Calories: 160 Carbs: 8.5g Fats: 14.1g Proteins: 2g Sodium: 437mg Sugar: 1.5g

Spinach Artichoke Stuffed Portobello

Serves: 8/Prep Time: 30 mins

Ingredients

- 1 medium portobello mushrooms, stems and gills removed
- ¼ can artichoke hearts drained and chopped, 14 ounce can
- ½ tablespoon sour cream
- 1 clove garlic, chopped
- ½ tablespoon olive oil
- ¼ package (10 ounces) frozen spinach, chopped, cooked and drained
- 1-ounce cream cheese
- ¼ cup Parmesan cheese, grated
- Salt and black pepper, to taste
- ¾-ounce mozzarella cheese, shredded

Directions

1. Preheat the oven to 375 degrees F and line a baking pan with foil.
2. Brush the mushrooms with olive oil and transfer on baking pan.
3. Broil for about 5 minutes each side and dish out.

5. Mix together the spinach, cream cheese, artichoke, sour cream, garlic, Parmesan cheese, salt and black pepper until well combined.
6. Stuff each mushroom cap with the spinach mixture and sprinkle with mozzarella cheese.
7. Transfer into the oven and bake for about 12 minutes.
8. Dish out and serve warm.

Nutrition Calories: 143 Carbs: 4g Fats: 11.9g Proteins: 6.8g Sodium: 218mg Sugar: 0.5g

Grilled Halloumi Bruschetta

Serves: 2/Prep Time: 20 mins
Ingredients
- 2 tablespoons fresh basil, chopped
- ½ tablespoon olive oil
- 1/3 medium tomatoes, chopped
- ½ clove garlic, minced
- Salt and black pepper, to taste
- 1½-ounce package Halloumi cheese, sliced

Directions
1. Mix together tomatoes, basil, garlic, olive oil, salt and black pepper in a bowl.
2. Refrigerate for about 1 hour.
3. Grill the Halloumi cheese for about 2 minutes on each side and transfer to a serving platter.
4. Top with tomato basil mixture and serve chilled.

Nutrition Calories: 84 Carbs: 1.6g Fats: 7.2g Proteins: 3.8g Sodium: 1mg Sugar: 1g

Roasted Mushroom and Walnut Cauliflower Grits

Serves: 2/Prep Time: 25 mins
Ingredients
- 1½ cloves garlic, minced
- ¼ cup walnuts, chopped
- 1 tablespoon olive oil
- ¼ cup water
- ½ cup cheddar cheese, shredded
- Salt, to taste
- 3 ounces portobello mushrooms, sliced
- ½ tablespoon rosemary
- ½ tablespoon smoked paprika
- ½ medium cauliflower
- ½ cup half and half
- 1 tablespoon butter

Directions
1. Preheat oven to 400 degrees F and line a cookie sheet with foil.
2. Mix together mushrooms, garlic, rosemary, walnuts, olive oil, smoked paprika and salt in a small dish.
3. Arrange the mixture evenly on the cookie sheet and transfer in the oven.
4. Roast for about 15 minutes and dish out to keep aside.
5. Pulse cauliflower florets in a food processor and steam for 5 minutes with water.
6. Stir in half and half into the cauliflower and simmer for about 3 minutes on medium-low heat.
7. Add sharp cheddar and butter and reduce heat to low.
8. Season with salt and top with the mushroom mixture to serve.

Nutrition Calories: 456 Carbs: 15.8g Fats: 38.9g Proteins: 17.3g Sodium: 367mg Sugar: 4.8g

Cheesy Ranch Roasted Broccoli

Serves: 2/Prep Time: 45 mins
Ingredients
- 1/8 cup ranch dressing
- 1½ cups broccoli florets
- ¼ cup sharp cheddar cheese, shredded
- Kosher salt and black pepper, to taste
- 1/8 cup heavy whipping cream

Directions
1. Preheat the oven to 375 degrees F and grease oven proof casserole dish.
2. Mix together all the ingredients in a medium-sized bowl and transfer to the casserole dish.
3. Place in the oven and bake for about 30 minutes.
4. Dish out in a platter and serve hot.

Nutrition Calories: 111 Carbs: 5.7g Fats: 7.7g Proteins: 5.8g Sodium: 198mg Sugar: 1.6g

Easy Low-Carb Cauliflower Fried Rice

Serves: 2/Prep Time: 15 mins
Ingredients
- 6 ounces cauliflower fresh or frozen, riced
- 1 large green onion, sliced with white and green parts separated
- 1 tablespoon butter
- 1/8 cup carrots, finely diced
- 1 clove garlic, crushed
- 1 tablespoon gluten-free soy sauce
- 1 small egg, beaten
- ½ teaspoon toasted sesame oil

Directions
1. Melt butter in a large heavy skillet over medium-high heat and add carrots and riced cauliflower.
2. Cook for about 5 minutes and stir in garlic and white part of the green onions.
3. Cook for about 3 minutes and whisk in the egg.
4. Cook for about 2 minutes and stir in the soy sauce, green part of green onions, and the sesame oil.
5. Dish out and serve hot.

Nutrition Calories: 123 Carbs: 7.3g Fats: 8.9g Proteins: 5g Sodium: 484mg Sugar: 2.8g

Creamy Avocado Pasta with Shirataki

Serves: 2/Prep Time: 5 mins
Ingredients
- ½ avocado
- ½ teaspoon dried basil
- ½ packet shirataki noodles
- 1/8 cup heavy cream
- ½ teaspoon black pepper
- ½ teaspoon salt

Directions
1. Boil some water and cook the shirataki for about 2 minutes.

3. Mash avocado in a bowl and add cream, basil, salt and black pepper.
4. Transfer into a blender and blend until smooth.
5. Put shirataki noodles in the frying pan and add blended mixture.
6. Cook for about 2 minutes and dish out to serve hot.

Nutrition Calories: 131 Carbs: 4.9g Fats: 12.6g Proteins: 1.2g Sodium: 588mg Sugar: 0.3g

Spicy Crockpot Cauliflower Mac & Cheese

Serves: 2/Prep Time: 2 hours 15 mins
Ingredients
- ¼ stick butter
- 4 ounces sharp cheddar cheese shredded
- ¼ teaspoon garlic powder
- ½ large head cauliflower, boiled
- 2 ounces cream cheese
- 1/8 cup pickled jalapenos, diced
- ¼ teaspoon onion powder
- 1/3 cup half and half cream
- ¼ teaspoon dry mustard
- 1/8 teaspoon paprika

Directions
1. Put all the ingredients in a crockpot and stir well.
2. Cover the lid and cook for about 2 hours on high heat.
3. Dish out in large serving bowl and let it cool for about 10 minutes before serving

Nutrition Calories: 540 Carbs: 15.4g Fats: 45.2g Proteins: 22g Sodium: 597mg Sugar: 5.9g

Cheesy Broccoli & Cauliflower Rice

Serves: 2/Prep Time: 15 mins
Ingredients
- ½ cup broccoli, riced
- ¼ teaspoon kosher salt
- 1½ cups cauliflower, riced
- ½ tablespoon butter
- ¼ teaspoon ground black pepper
- Pinch of ground nutmeg
- 1/8 cup mascarpone cheese
- ¼ teaspoon garlic powder
- ¼ cup sharp cheddar cheese, shredded

Directions
1. Mix together cauliflower, butter, broccoli, garlic powder, nutmeg, salt and black pepper in a medium sized microwave safe bowl.
2. Microwave for about 5 minutes on high and add the cheddar cheese.
3. Microwave for 2 more minutes and stir in the mascarpone cheese until creamy.
4. Dish out and serve hot.

Nutrition Calories: 138 Carbs: 6.6g Fats: 9.8g Proteins: 7.5g Sodium: 442mg Sugar: 2.4g

Zucchini Noodle Alfredo

Serves: 2/Prep Time: 25 mins
Ingredients

- ½ tablespoon olive oil
- ½ pound zucchini, spiralized into noodles
- ¾ ounces cream cheese
- ¼ cup Parmesan cheese, grated
- ½ tablespoon sour cream

Directions

1. Heat olive oil in a large pan over medium heat and add zucchini noodles.
2. Sauté for about 5 minutes and add cream cheese, sour cream and Parmesan cheese.
3. Stir well and pour this mixture over noodles.
4. Dish out and serve hot.

Nutrition Calories: 103 Carbs: 4.3g Fats: 8.8g Proteins: 3.4g Sodium: 77mg Sugar: 2g

Creamy Mushroom and Cauliflower Risotto

Serves: 2/Prep Time: 5 mins

Ingredients

- 1 garlic clove, sliced
- ½ cup cream
- ½ cup cauliflower, riced
- ½ cup mushrooms, sliced
- Coconut oil, for frying
- Parmesan cheese, for topping

Directions

1. Heat coconut oil over medium-high heat in a frying pan and add garlic and mushrooms.
2. Sauté for about 4 minutes and add cauliflower and cream.
3. Simmer for about 12 minutes and dish out in a bowl.
4. Top with Parmesan cheese and serve.

Nutrition Calories: 179 Carbs: 4.4g Fats: 17.8g Proteins: 2.8g Sodium: 61mg Sugar: 2.1g

Appetizer Recipes

Cheesy Cauliflower Breadsticks

Serves: 2/Prep Time: 40 mins

Ingredients

- ½ cup Monterey jack cheese, freshly grated
- 1/8 teaspoon ground sage
- 1/8 teaspoon ground mustard
- ½ cup cauliflower, riced
- 1 small egg, beaten
- 1/8 teaspoon ground oregano
- 1/8 teaspoon dried thyme
- Salt and black pepper, to taste
- Fresh parsley, minced

Directions

1. Put the cauliflower in a toaster oven and cook for about 8 minutes.
2. Dish out the cauliflower in a mixing bowl and season with sage, oregano, thyme and mustard.
3. Add egg and ½ of cheese to the seasoned cauliflower and sprinkle with salt and black pepper.
4. Preheat the oven to 450 degrees F and grease a baking sheet.
5. Place cauliflower in the baking sheet and transfer into the oven.
6. Bake for about 8 minutes and top with rest of the cheese.
7. Bake for 5 more minutes and dish out to serve with garnished parsley.

Nutrition Calories: 142 Carbs: 2.2g Fats: 10.5g Proteins: 10g Sodium: 188mg Sugar: 0.9g

Low Carb Broccoli and Cheese Fritters

Serves: 2/Prep Time: 15 mins
Ingredients
The Fritters
- 2 tablespoons + 1 tablespoon flaxseed meal
- 4 tablespoons almond flour
- 1-ounce fresh broccoli
- 1 small egg
- Salt and black pepper, to taste
- 1-ounce mozzarella cheese
- ¼ teaspoon baking powder

The Sauce
- 4 tablespoons fresh chopped dill
- 4 tablespoons mayonnaise
- ½ teaspoon lemon juice
- Salt and black pepper, to taste

Directions
1. Put broccoli into a food processor and process until completely chopped.
2. Place the broccoli in a bowl and add mozzarella cheese, egg, 2 tablespoons flaxseed meal, baking powder, almond flour, salt and black pepper.
3. Mix well and roll the batter into balls.
4. Coat the balls in 1 tablespoon flaxseed meal and keep aside.
5. Heat a deep fat fryer to 375 degrees F and drop the balls in the basket.
6. Fry the fritters for about 5 minutes until golden brown and dish out in a platter.
7. Mix together all the ingredients for the sauce and make a dip to serve with fritters.

Nutrition Calories: 428 Carbs: 11.4g Fats: 38.6g Proteins: 12.9g Sodium: 367mg Sugar: 0.6g

Sun Dried Tomato Pesto Mug Cake

Serves: 2/Prep Time: 15 mins
Ingredients
Base
- 4 tablespoons butter
- 2 large eggs
- 4 tablespoons almond flour
- 1 teaspoon baking powder

Flavor
- 10 teaspoons sun dried tomato pesto
- 2 pinches salt
- 2 tablespoons almond flour

Directions
1. Mix together all the ingredients in a mug and transfer into a microwave oven.
2. Microwave on high for 70 seconds.
3. Take the mug cake out and top with extra tomato pesto to serve.

Nutrition Calories: 404 Carbs: 6.1g Fats: 38g Proteins: 11.1g Sodium: 400mg Sugar: 0.4g

Fried Goat Cheese

Serves: 2/Prep Time: 15 mins
Ingredients
- 2 ounces (package) goat cheese log, cold and chopped
- 1/8 tsp dried parsley
- ¼ oz almond crumbs
- 1 small egg
- 1/8 teaspoon pink salt
- 1/8 cup coconut flour
- 1/3 cup coconut oil, for cooking

Directions
1. Whisk egg in a small bowl, put coconut flour in another bowl and place almond crumbs in a third bowl.
2. Coat the goat cheese in coconut flour, egg wash and then almond crumbs.
3. Heat coconut oil in a small saucepan on medium-high and add coated goat cheese.
4. Cook for about 30 seconds and flip gently.
5. Cook for another 30 seconds and repeat with the remaining goat cheese.
6. Dish out and serve with your favourite dip.

Nutrition Calories: 456 Carbs: 8.1g Fats: 45.8g Proteins: 7.5g Sodium: 540mg Sugar: 1.3g

Low Carb Cauliflower Hummus

Serves: 2/Prep Time: 15 mins
Ingredients
- ¾ tablespoon water
- ¼ teaspoon salt
- ½ tablespoon Tahini paste
- ¾ tablespoon extra-virgin olive oil
- 1 cup raw cauliflower florets
- ¾ tablespoon avocado oil
- 2 whole garlic cloves
- ¾ tablespoon lemon juice
- 1/3 tsp kosher salt
- ¼ teaspoon smoked paprika

Directions
1. Mix together cauliflower, water, 1 garlic clove and half of salt, avocado oil and olive oil in a microwave safe dish.
2. Microwave for about 15 minutes and transfer the mixture into a food processor.
3. Add tahini paste, lemon juice and rest of the garlic clove, avocado oil, olive oil and kosher salt to the blender and blend until smooth.
4. Dish out the hummus in a bowl and sprinkle with paprika to serve.

Nutrition Calories: 93 Carbs: 5g Fats: 8.1g Proteins: 2g Sodium: 312mg Sugar: 1.4g

Eggplant Fries

Serves: 2/Prep Time: 15 mins
Ingredients
- 1 egg, beaten
- 1/8 cup parmesan cheese, grated
- 1/8 teaspoon parsley flakes
- ½ large eggplant, peeled and cut into 4 inches strips
- 1/8 cup coconut flour
- 1/8 teaspoon garlic powder
- Salt and black pepper, to taste
- 1/8 cup olive oil, for frying

Directions

1. Beat egg in a small bowl and keep aside.
2. Mix together coconut flour, parmesan cheese, garlic powder, parsley flakes, salt and black pepper in another bowl.
3. Dip the eggplant in the egg mixture for 1 minute and then dredge in a coconut flour mixture.
4. Heat olive oil in a pan and drop some eggplant fries.
5. Cook until brown on both sides and dish out in a serving platter to serve.

Nutrition Calories: 204 Carbs: 12.1g Fats: 16.1g Proteins: 5.5g Sodium: 49mg Sugar: 3.7g

Cheesy Herb Muffins

Serves: 2/Prep Time: 28 mins

Ingredients

- ¼ teaspoon granulated erythritol
- ¾ tablespoon coconut flour
- ½ teaspoon baking powder
- 1 egg
- 1½ tablespoons butter
- ¼ cup blanched almond flour
- ¼ teaspoon kosher salt
- 1/8 teaspoon garlic powder
- 1/8 teaspoon xanthan gum
- 1/8 teaspoon fresh thyme leaves
- 1/8 cup almond milk, unsweetened
- 1/8 cup sharp cheddar cheese, shredded

Directions

1. Preheat the oven to 375 degrees F and grease 2 muffin cups.
2. Put the butter in a microwave safe bowl and microwave uncovered, for 30 seconds on high.
3. Combine the butter, erythritol, coconut flour, almond flour, baking powder, xanthan gum, garlic powder, almond milk, fresh thyme, cheddar cheese and salt in a bowl.
4. Transfer the mixture into the muffin cups and place in the oven.
5. Bake for about 20 minutes and remove from the oven to serve.

Nutrition Calories: 272 Carbs: 13.7g Fats: 23.7g Proteins: 8.9g Sodium: 646mg Sugar: 1.4g

Spicy Keto Roasted Nuts

Serves: 2/Prep Time: 13 mins

Ingredients

- 1/3 teaspoon salt
- 2 oz. pecans, almonds and walnuts
- 1/3 tablespoon olive oil
- 1/3 teaspoon paprika powder or chili powder
- 1/3 teaspoon ground cumin

Directions

1. Mix together all the ingredients and transfer in a medium frying pan.
2. Cook for about 5 minutes on medium heat until the nuts are completely warmed.
3. Allow to cool and serve immediately.

Nutrition Calories: 220 Carbs: 4.4g Fats: 22.7g Proteins: 3.2g Sodium: 393mg Sugar: 1.1g

Roasted Caprese Tomatoes with Basil dressing

Serves: 2/Prep Time: 35 mins
Ingredients
- 1 tablespoon olive oil
- 4 large ripe tomatoes, halved
- 2 tablespoons Balsamic vinegar

For the dressing
- 1 garlic clove
- Small handful fresh basil
- ½ teaspoon lemon

- Salt and black pepper, to taste
- 4 basil leaves
- 4 thin Mozzarella slices

- Salt, to taste
- 2 tablespoons olive oil

Directions
1. Preheat the oven to 360 degrees F and grease a baking sheet.
2. Place the tomatoes on the baking sheet, cut side up.
3. Drizzle the olive oil and Balsamic vinegar and season with salt and black pepper.
4. Roast for about 20 minutes and top the tomatoes with the mozzarella cheese.
5. Roast for another 5 minutes and remove from the oven.
6. Place a basil leaf on each bottom half and close with the top half.
7. **For the dressing:** Put all the ingredients in a small food processor until finely chopped.
8.   Serve the tomatoes with the dressing.

Nutrition Calories: 412 Carbs: 17g Fats: 31.8g Proteins: 19.4g Sodium: 359mg Sugar: 9.7g

Caprese Grilled Eggplant Roll Ups

Serves: 2/Prep Time: 15 mins
Ingredients
- 2 oz mozzarella cheese, thinly sliced
- ½ eggplant, thinly sliced
- ½ large tomato, thinly sliced

- 3 tablespoons olive oil
- 1 basil leaf, thinly shredded
- ¼ teaspoon black pepper

Directions
1. Brush the eggplant slices with olive oil and keep aside.
2. Heat a griddle pan and transfer the eggplant slices in a pan.
3. Grill for about 3 minutes on each side and top with mozzarella slice, tomato slice, basil leaf and black pepper.
4. Grill for another 1 minute and roll the eggplant holding it with a cocktail stick.
5. Dish out and serve warm.

Nutrition Calories: 298 Carbs: 9.7g Fats: 26.3g Proteins: 9.6g Sodium: 175mg Sugar: 4.6g

Salads Recipes

Snap Pea Salad

Serves: 2/Prep Time: 15 mins

Ingredients

- 1/8 cup lemon juice
- ½ clove garlic, crushed
- 4 ounces cauliflower riced
- 1/8 cup olive oil
- ¼ teaspoon coarse grain Dijon mustard
- ½ teaspoon granulated stevia
- ¼ cup sugar snap peas, ends removed and each pod cut into three pieces
- 1/8 cup chives
- 1/8 cup red onions, minced
- Sea salt and black pepper, to taste
- ¼ cup almonds, sliced

Directions

1. Pour water in a pot fitted with a steamer basket and bring water to a boil.
2. Place riced cauliflower in the steamer basket and season with sea salt.
3. Cover the pot and steam for about 10 minutes until tender.
4. Drain the cauliflower and dish out in a bowl to refrigerate for about 1 hour.
5. Meanwhile, make a dressing by mixing olive oil, lemon juice, garlic, mustard, stevia, salt and black pepper in a bowl.
6. Mix together chilled cauliflower, peas, chives, almonds and red onions in another bowl.
7. Pour the dressing over this mixture and serve.

Nutrition Calories: 203 Carbs: 7.6g Fats: 18.8g Proteins: 4.2g Sodium: 28mg Sugar: 2.9g

Creamy Cilantro Lime Coleslaw

Serves: 2/Prep Time: 10 mins

Ingredients

- ¾ avocado
- 1 lime, juiced
- 1/8 cup water
- Cilantro, to garnish
- 6 oz coleslaw, bagged
- 1/8 cup cilantro leaves
- 1 garlic clove
- ¼ teaspoon salt

Directions

1. Put garlic and cilantro in a food processor and process until chopped.
2. Add lime juice, avocado and water and pulse until creamy.
3. Put coleslaw in a large bowl and stir in the avocado mixture.
4. Refrigerate for a few hours before serving.

Nutrition Calories: 240 Carbs: 17.4g Fats: 19.6g Proteins: 2.8g Sodium: 530mg Sugar: 0.5g

Simple Greek Salad

Serves: 2/Prep Time: 15 mins

Ingredients

- ½ pint grape tomatoes, halved
- 1 cucumber, peeled and chopped
- 2 oz feta cheese, cubed
- 1 tablespoon extra-virgin olive oil
- 1 tablespoon fresh dill

Directions

1. Mix together all the ingredients in a bowl except olive oil.
2. Drizzle with the olive oil and mix well to serve.

Nutrition Calories: 178 Carbs: 11g Fats: 13.5g Proteins: 6.1g Sodium: 327mg Sugar: 6g

Crispy Tofu and Bok Choy Salad

Serves: 2/Prep Time: 15 mins
Ingredients
- 7 ounces extra firm tofu, pressed and chopped

For Marinade
- ½ tablespoon soy sauce
- ½ tablespoon sesame oil
- 1 teaspoon garlic, minced

- ½ teaspoon lemon juice
- ½ tablespoon water
- ½ tablespoon rice wine vinegar

For Salad
- ½ stalk green onion
- 1½ tablespoons coconut oil
- 4 ounces bok choy, sliced
- 1 tablespoon cilantro, chopped
- 1 tablespoon soy sauce

- ½ tablespoon peanut butter
- 3 drops liquid stevia
- ½ tablespoon sambal olek
- ½ teaspoon lemon juice

Directions
1. Preheat the oven to 350 degrees F and line a baking sheet with parchment paper.
2. Mix together all the ingredients for the marinade in a bowl.
3. Place the tofu in a plastic bag along with marinade, allowing it to marinate overnight.
4. Transfer the marinated tofu on the baking sheet and place in the oven.
5. Bake for about 30 minutes and dish out.
6. Mix together all the salad ingredients except bok choy in a bowl.
7. Top the salad with baked tofu and bok choy to serve.

Nutrition Calories: 230 Carbs: 5.2g Fats: 19.9g Proteins: 10.9g Sodium: 745mg Sugar: 1.9g

Keto Asian Noodle Salad with Peanut Sauce

Serves: 2/Prep Time: 10 mins
Ingredients
For the salad:
- ½ cup green cabbage, shredded
- 1/8 cup cilantro, chopped
- 1/8 cup peanuts, chopped
- 2 cups shirataki noodles, drained and rinsed

- ½ cup red cabbage, shredded
- 1/8 cup scallions, chopped

For the dressing:
- ½ teaspoon garlic, minced
- ½ tablespoon lime juice
- 1 tablespoon ginger, minced
- ¼ cup filtered water
- ½ tablespoon toasted sesame oil
- ½ tablespoon coconut aminos

- ¼ teaspoon cayenne pepper
- ½ tablespoon granulated erythritol sweetener
- ½ tablespoon wheat-free soy sauce
- 1/8 cup sugar free peanut butter
- ¼ teaspoon kosher salt

Directions
1. Mix together all of the salad ingredients in a large bowl.
2. Put all the dressing ingredients in a blender and blend until smooth.
3. Pour the dressing over the salad and mix well to coat.
4. Serve immediately in a serving bowl.

Nutrition Calories: 118 Carbs: 8.2g Fats: 12.9g Proteins: 3.8g Sodium: 250mg Sugar: 5.7g

Zucchini Noodles Salad with Parmesan & Walnuts

Serves: 2/Prep Time: 15 mins
Ingredients
For the salad:
- ½ cup fresh radicchio, shredded
- 2 cups zucchini noodles, spiralized
- 1/8 cup fresh parsley, roughly chopped
- 1/8 cup walnuts, roughly chopped
- ½ oz parmesan cheese, shaved

For the vinaigrette:
- 1/8 cup fresh lemon juice
- ½ cup avocado oil
- ½ teaspoon fresh garlic, minced
- Kosher salt and black pepper, to taste
- ¼ teaspoon granulated Swerve

Directions
1. Mix together all the salad ingredients in a bowl.
2. Whisk together the vinaigrette ingredients in a small bowl.
3. Drizzle the vinaigrette over the salad and toss to coat well.
4. Serve immediately in a serving bowl.

Nutrition Calories: 173 Carbs: 9.4g Fats: 13.6g Proteins: 6.6g Sodium: 87mg Sugar: 2.6g

Zoodles Greek Salad

Serves: 2/Prep Time: 10 mins
Ingredients
- 1/3 tablespoon balsamic vinegar
- 1/3 teaspoon fresh oregano, minced
- 1 medium zucchini, peeled and spiralized
- 1 oz. feta cheese, crumbled
- 4 tablespoons lemon juice
- 1/3 tablespoon olive oil
- Kosher salt and black pepper, to taste
- ½ cup cherry tomatoes, halved
- ¼ cup pitted kalamata olives, halved

Directions
1. Whisk together the balsamic vinegar, lemon juice, olive oil, oregano, salt and black pepper in a small bowl to make a dressing.
2. Mix together the dressing, zucchini noodles, tomatoes, olives and feta cheese in a large bowl until coated evenly.

Nutrition Calories: 109 Carbs: 7.5g Fats: 7.7g Proteins: 4g Sodium: 323mg Sugar: 4.1g

Charred Veggie and Fried Goat Cheese Salad

Serves: 2/Prep Time: 15 mins
Ingredients
- 1 teaspoon garlic flakes
- 1 tablespoon avocado oil
- 4 ounces goat cheese, cut into 4½" in thick medallions

- 4 cups arugula, divided between two bowls
- 2 tablespoons sesame seeds
- 1 medium red bell pepper, seeds removed and cut into 8 pieces
- 2 tablespoons poppy seeds
- 1 teaspoon onion flakes
- ½ cup baby portobello mushrooms, sliced

Directions

1. Mix together poppy seeds, sesame seeds, garlic flakes and onion in a bowl.
2. Coat goat cheese pieces with this mixture on both sides.
3. Transfer in the refrigerator for about 1 hour.
4. Put a skillet on medium heat and add bell pepper and portobello mushrooms.
5. Cook for about 5 minutes and dish out in a bowl with arugula.
6. Add cold goat cheese in the skillet and fry for about 30 seconds on each side.
7. Add the cheese to the salad and pour avocado oil.
8.   Dish out and serve warm.

Nutrition Calories: 406 Carbs: 14.2g Fats: 29.9g Proteins: 23.3g Sodium: 213mg Sugar: 7g

Crunchy and Nutty Cauliflower Salad

Serves: 2/Prep Time: 15 mins
Ingredients
- ½ cup leek (the green part), finely chopped
- 1½ cups cauliflower, very finely chopped
- ¼ cup organic walnuts, chopped
- Sea salt, to taste
- ½ cup full-fat sour cream

Directions

1. Mix together all the ingredients in a large bowl until well combined.
2. Refrigerate for at least 3 hours and serve chilled.

Nutrition Calories: 252 Carbs: 11.1g Fats: 21.4g Proteins: 7.4g Sodium: 175mg Sugar: 2.9g

"Anti" Pasta Cauliflower Salad

Serves: 2/Prep Time: 15 mins
Ingredients
- 1/8 cup radicchio, chopped
- 1/8 cup fresh basil, chopped
- ½ cup raw cauliflower, chopped
- 1/8 cup artichoke hearts, chopped
- 1/8 cup parmesan cheese, freshly grated
- ¾ tablespoon kalamata olives, chopped
- ¾ tablespoon balsamic vinegar
- Salt and black pepper, to taste
- ¾ tablespoon sundried tomatoes, chopped
- ½ clove garlic, minced
- ¾ tablespoon extra-virgin olive oil

Directions

1. Cook chopped cauliflower in the microwave for about 5 minutes.
2. Mix together the radicchio, basil, artichoke hearts, parmesan, olives, sundried tomatoes and garlic in a bowl.
3. Whisk together the olive oil and vinegar in another bowl and drizzle it over the salad.

5. Season with salt and pepper and toss well to serve.

Nutrition Calories: 71 Carbs: 3.6g Fats: 6.1g Proteins: 1.7g Sodium: 86mg Sugar: 1.2g

Clear Soups Recipes

Clear Chicken Soup

Serves: 4/Prep Time: 25 mins
Ingredients
- ¼ cup onions,chopped
- ¾ pound chicken with bones
- 4 garlic cloves, smashed
- 2bay leaves
- 4cupswater
- ¼ teaspoon black pepper, freshly cracked
- ¼ cup carrots,chopped
- 3sprigsthyme
- Salt, to taste

Directions
1. Put the chicken, garlic, onions, carrot, thyme, bay leaves and water in a pressure cooker.
2. Season with salt and black pepper and pressure cook on high heat until one whistle.
3. Cook on low heat for about 12 minutes and release the pressure naturally.
4. Strain the soup using a soup strainer and shred the chicken pieces.
5. Place the shredded chicken pieces in each serving bowl and pour clear soup on top.
6. Dish out and serve hot.

Nutrition: Calories: 194 Carbs: 3.1g Fats: 12.9g Proteins: 15.5g Sodium: 77mg Sugar: 0.7g

Chinese Clear Vegetable Soup

Serves: 6/Prep Time: 15 mins
Ingredients
- ¾ cup cabbage
- 3stickscelery
- 1carrot, thinly sliced
- 3lettuce leaves
- 5 cups boiling water
- 3spring onions with greens, chopped
- 50 g cauliflower, sliced
- Pinch of baking powder
- 2 teaspoons soy sauce
- 4 tablespoons olive oil
- Pinch of citric acid
- Salt,to taste

Directions
1. Heat oil in a pot and add baking powder, citric acid and vegetables.
2. Cook for about 4 minutes on high flame and add boiling water, salt and soy sauce.
3. Boil for about 4 minutes and dish out to serve hot.

Nutrition Calories: 109 Carbs: 6.2g Fats: 9.6g Proteins: 0.9g Sodium: 227mg Sugar: 1.8g

Miso Soup

Serves: 5/Prep Time: 25 mins
Ingredients
- 2spring onions, chopped
- 8mushrooms, cut into quarters
- 1 cup cottage cheese cubes
- ½ cup red pumpkin cubes
- ½ carrot, cubed
- 5 cups water

- ½ cup spinach,chopped
- ½ tablespoon ginger, grated
- 1largegarlic clove, finely chopped
- Salt,to taste
- 4 tablespoons butter

Directions
1. Boil water in a pan and add ginger and garlic.
2. Add the spring onions, pumpkin and carrot and let it simmer for about 15 minutes.
3. Add the spinach, mushrooms, cottage cheese, butter and salt.
4. Simmer for about 5 minutes and serve hot.

Nutrition Calories: 169 Carbs: 26.5g Fats: 4.7g Proteins: 5.3g Sodium: 262mg Sugar: 2.7g

Hot Mushroom Clear Soup

Serves: 2/Prep Time: 15 mins
Ingredients
- ½ cup mushrooms, finely chopped
- 2 cups water
- 2 teaspoons butter
- Salt and black pepper, to taste

Directions
1. Put butter and mushrooms in a deep non-stick pan and cook for about 5 minutes on a low flame.
2. Stir in water, salt and black pepper and cook for another 5 minutes, stirring occasionally.
3. Dish out and serve hot.

Nutrition Calories: 37 Carbs: 0.6g Fats: 3.9g Proteins: 0.6g Sodium: 35mg Sugar: 0.3g

Spinach and Mushrooms Clear Soup

Serves: 3/Prep Time: 10 mins
Ingredients
- 1 cup spinach, torn into small pieces
- 3 cups clear vegetable stock
- ½ cup mushrooms, chopped
- 1 tablespoon olive oil
- ½ teaspoon soy sauce
- 1 teaspoon sesame seeds, roasted
- 1 teaspoon garlic, finely chopped
- Salt and black pepper, to taste

Directions
1. Heat olive oil in a deep non-stick pan and add garlic.
2. Sauté for 30 seconds on a high flame and add the mushrooms and spinach.
3. Sauté for about 1 minute and stir in clear vegetable stock, soya sauce, salt and black pepper.
4. Cook for about 3 minutes on a medium flame, stirring occasionally and serve topped with sesame seeds.

Nutrition Calories: 62 Carbs: 3.4g Fats: 7.2g Proteins: 1g Sodium: 778mg Sugar: 2.3g

Cream Soups Recipes

Creamy Roasted Butternut Squash Soup

Serves: 4/Prep Time: 55 mins
Ingredients
- 1potato, peeled and chopped
- 1onion, chopped

- 1large butternut squash, peeled and cubed
- 3 tablespoons extra-virgin olive oil
- 2 tablespoons butter
- 1 cup heavy cream
- 1stalk celery, thinly sliced
- 1 tablespoon fresh thyme leaves
- 1 quartlow-sodium chicken broth
- Salt and black pepper, to taste

Directions

1. Preheat oven to 400 degrees and grease a large baking sheet.
2. Toss potatoes and butternut squash with olive oil and season generously with salt and black pepper.
3. Transfer on the baking sheet and roast for about 25 minutes.
4. Meanwhile, melt butter over medium heat in a large pot and add onion, carrots and celery.
5. Cook for about 10 minutes until softened and season generously with salt, black pepper and thyme.
6. Add potatoes, chicken broth and roasted squash and allow it to simmer for about 10 minutes.
7. Transfer the mixture into an immersion blender and blend soup until creamy.
8. Dish out and serve garnished with thyme.

Nutrition Calories: 214 Carbs: 11g Fats: 18.3g Proteins: 2.8g Sodium: 87mg Sugar: 1.6g

Creamy Garlic Chicken Soup

Serves: 4/Prep Time: 20 mins

Ingredients

- 1 large chicken breast
- 2tablespoonsbutter
- 40uncescream cheese,cubed
- 14.50zchicken broth
- ½ cup heavy cream
- 2tablespoonsStacey Hawkins Garlic Gusto Seasoning
- Salt,to taste

Directions

1. Melt butter over medium heat in a saucepan and add shredded chicken.
2. Sauté for about 2 minutes and add Stacey Hawkins Garlic Gusto seasoning and cream cheese.
3. Cook for about 3 minutes and add chicken broth and heavy cream.
4. Bring to a boil and reduce heat to low.
5. Simmer for about 4 minutes and season with salt to serve.

Nutrition Calories: 247 Carbs: 7g Fats: 22.4g Proteins: 9.9g Sodium: 470mg Sugar: 0.4g

Creamy Curried Cauliflower Soup

Serves: 4/Prep Time: 35 mins

Ingredients

- 2 tablespoons avocado oil
- 1-inch ginger, chopped
- 2 teaspoons curry powder
- 1 large cauliflower, cut into florets
- 1 white onion, chopped
- 4 garlic cloves, chopped
- ½ Serrano pepper, seeds removed and chopped
- 1teaspoonsalt
- ¼teaspoon turmeric powder
- 1 cup chicken broth
- ½ teaspoon black pepper
- 1 cup water

- 1 can full fat coconut milk
- Cilantro, for garnishing

Directions
1. Put oil and onions over medium heat in a heavy bottomed pot and sauté for about 3 minutes.
2. Add Serrano pepper, garlic and ginger and stir-fry for about 2 minutes.
3. Add curry powder, turmeric, salt and black pepper and stir fry for 1 minute.
4. Add cauliflower florets and water and cover with a lid.
5. Cook for about 10 minutes, stirring occasionally.
6. Turn off heat and allow it to cool.
7. Transfer into the blender and blend until smooth.
8. Pour blended cauliflower back into pot and add coconut milk and broth.
9. Cook for another about 10 minutes then garnish with cilantro and serve.

Nutrition Calories: 263 Carbs: 8.9g Fats: 23.9g Proteins: 3.3g Sodium: 838mg Sugar: 4.1g

Cream of Zucchini Soup

Serves: 4/Prep Time: 25 mins
Ingredients
- 2 garlic cloves
- ½ small onion, quartered
- 2 medium zucchini, cut in large chunks
- 4 tablespoons sour cream
- 1 cup Parmesan cheese, freshly grated
- 2 tablespoons butter
- 32 oz chicken broth
- Salt and black pepper, to taste

Directions
1. Mix together chicken broth, onion, garlic and zucchini over medium heat in a pot and bring to a boil.
2. Lower the heat and simmer for about 20 minutes until tender.
3. Remove from heat and transfer into an immersion blender.
4. Add the sour cream and purée until smooth.
5. Season with salt and black pepper and serve hot.

Nutrition Calories: 179 Carbs: 6.5g Fats: 7.6g Proteins: 10.9g Sodium: 909mg Sugar: 2.8g

Cream of Asparagus Soup

Serves: 6/Prep Time: 30 mins
Ingredients
- 4 tablespoons unsalted butter
- 6 cups reduced sodium chicken broth
- 2 pounds asparagus, cut in half
- 1 small onion, chopped
- ½ cup sour cream
- Salt and black pepper, to taste

Directions
1. Heat butter in a large pot over low heat and add onions.
2. Sauté for about 2 minutes until soft and add asparagus, chicken broth and black pepper.
3. Bring to a boil, cover and cook for about 20 minutes on low heat.
4. Remove from heat and transfer into blender along with sour cream.
5. Pulse until smooth and dish out to serve.

Nutrition Calories: 161 Carbs: 8.7g Fats: 11.9g Proteins: 7.4g Sodium: 623mg Sugar: 3.9g

Creamy Broccoli Cheddar Soup

Serves: 6/Prep Time: 40 mins

Ingredients
- 1small white onion, diced
- 4 cups vegetable broth
- 3 tablespoons unsalted butter
- 2 garlic cloves, minced
- 3 tablespoons almond flour
- 2 cups half-and-half
- 1½ cups cheddar cheese, grated
- Pinch of nutmeg
- 2small heads broccoli, cut into florets
- Salt and black pepper, to taste
- 4 tablespoons sour cream, for garnishing

Directions
1. Melt butter in a large pot over medium-high heat and add onions.
2. Cook for about 5 minutes until soft and add garlic.
3. Sauté for about 1 minute and add almond flour.
4. Cook for about 3 minutes, stirring constantly and add half-and-half and broth.
5. Bring to a boil and reduce heat to medium.
6. Add broccoli and simmer for about 20 minutes.
7. Transfer into an immersion blender and blend until smooth.
8. Pulse until smooth and dish out in a bowl.
9. Whisk in cheddar cheese and season with nutmeg, salt and pepper.
10. Garnish with sour cream and serve.

Nutrition Calories: 345 Carbs: 8g Fats: 28.8g Proteins: 14.3g Sodium: 769mg Sugar: 1.5g

Cream of Brown Butter Mushroom Soup

Serves: 6/Prep Time: 25 mins

Ingredients
- 2tablespoons fresh sage,chopped
- 4cups chicken stock
- ½ cup heavy cream
- 6tablespoonsbutter
- 1poundmushrooms,sliced
- Salt and black pepper, to taste

Directions
1. Heat butter in a large pot over medium heat and add sage.
2. Cook for about 2 minutes and add mushrooms.
3. Sauté for about 4 minutes and stir in stock.
4. Allow it to simmer and cook for about 5 more minutes.
5. Transfer to food processor and blend until smooth.
6. Return to pot and stir in heavy cream to serve.

Nutrition Calories: 161 Carbs: 3.7g Fats: 15.9g Proteins: 3.2g Sodium: 599mg Sugar: 1.8g

Creamy Low-Carb Red Gazpacho

Serves: 10/Prep Time: 30 mins

Ingredients
- 1 large red pepper, halved
- 2 medium avocados
- 2 tablespoons fresh lemon juice
- 2 tablespoons basil, freshly chopped
- 2 medium spring onions, diced
- 1 cup extra virgin olive oil
- 1 large green pepper, halved
- 1 small red onion
- 4 medium tomatoes
- 2 garlic cloves
- 2 tablespoons apple cider vinegar
- 1 large cucumber, diced

- Salt and black pepper, to taste
- 200 g feta cheese

Directions

1. Preheat the oven to 400 degrees F and line a baking sheet with parchment paper.
2. Transfer in the oven and roast for about 20 minutes.
3. Peel the skin of roasted bell peppers and transfer into a blender along with red onions, tomatoes, fresh herbs, cucumber, spring onions, lemon juice, vinegar, garlic, olive oil, salt and black pepper.
4. Pulse until smooth and season with more salt and black pepper.
5. Top with feta cheese and serve.

Nutrition: Calories: 293 Carbs: 8.4g Fats: 28.6g Proteins: 4.3g Sodium: 230mg Sugar: 4.2g

Creamy Keto Taco Soup with Ground Beef

Serves: 8/Prep Time: 30 mins

Ingredients

- ½ cup onions, chopped
- 1 tablespoon ground cumin
- 1 pound ground beef
- 2 garlic cloves, minced
- 1 teaspoon chili powder
- 2 (14.5 ounce) cans beef broth
- ½ cup heavy cream
- 1 (8 ounce) package cream cheese, softened
- 2 (10 ounce) cans diced tomatoes and green chiles
- 2 teaspoons salt

Directions

1. Mix together ground beef, onions and garlic over medium-high heat in a large soup pot.
2. Cook for about 7 minutes until beef is browned and add cumin and chili powder.
3. Cook for about 2 more minutes and add cream cheese into the pot.
4. Mash it into the beef with a big spoon for about 5 minutes until no white spots remain.
5. Stir in broth, diced tomatoes, heavy cream and salt and cook for about 10 more minutes.
6. Dish out and serve.

Nutrition Calories: 262 Carbs: 4.3g Fats: 17g Proteins: 22.4g Sodium: 1175mg Sugar: 0.7g

Creamy Tomato Basil Soup

Serves: 4/Prep Time: 45mins

Ingredients

- 4 cups tomato juice
- 14 leaves fresh basil
- 1 cup butter
- 3 tomatoes, peeled, seeded and diced
- 2 cups water
- 1 cup heavy whipping cream
- Salt and black pepper, to taste

Directions

1. Place tomatoes, water and tomato juice over medium heat in a pot.
2. Simmer for about 30 minutes and transfer into blender along with basil leaves.
3. Blend until smooth and return to the pot.
4. Place the pot over medium heat and stir in heavy cream and butter.
5. Season with salt and black pepper and stir until the butter is melted.

Nutrition Calories: 284 Carbs: 7.4g Fats: 28.7g Proteins: 1.9g Sodium: 500mg Sugar: 5.6g

Vegetable Soups Recipes

Tomato Basil Soup

Serves: 2/Prep Time: 20 mins
Ingredients

- ¾ cup filtered water
- ¼ teaspoon onion powder
- 3 ounces mascarpone cheese
- 1/3 teaspoon apple cider vinegar
- 1/8 cup prepared basil pesto
- 12 ounces whole plum tomatoes
- ½ teaspoon kosher salt
- 1/8 teaspoon garlic powder
- 1½ tablespoons butter
- ¾ tablespoon granulated erythritol
- 1/8 teaspoon dried basil leaves

Directions

1. Mix together the canned tomatoes, salt, water, garlic powder and onion powder in a medium saucepan.
2. Bring to a boil over medium-high heat and allow to simmer for about 2 minutes.
3. Transfer into an immersion blender and blend until smooth.
4. Return to the saucepan and add butter and mascarpone cheese.
5. Stir well over low heat for about 2 minutes until creamy.
6. Remove from the heat and stir in the erythritol, dried basil, pesto and apple cider vinegar.
7. Ladle into serving bowls and serve warm.

Nutrition Calories: 228 Carbs: 16.3g Fats: 18.2g Proteins: 8.3g Sodium: 967mg Sugar: 9.8g

Cream of Broccoli and Cheddar Soup

Serves: 2/Prep Time: 15 mins
Ingredients

- ¾ cup vegetable stock
- ¼ teaspoon garlic powder
- ¼ teaspoon mustard powder
- Salt and black pepper, to taste
- 1/8 cup butter
- 1 cup broccoli florets
- 1/3 cup sharp cheddar cheese, shredded
- ¼ teaspoon onion powder
- 1 pinch nutmeg
- ¼ cup heavy whipping cream

Directions

1. Place the broccoli florets in the microwave for about 4 minutes on high.
2. Transfer the broccoli in a blender along with other ingredients and blend until smooth.
3. Place this mixture in the microwave for about 2 minutes on high.
4. Stir well and cook for another 4 minutes to serve hot.

Nutrition Calories: 264 Carbs: 4.8g Fats: 24.1g Proteins: 8.4g Sodium: 506mg Sugar: 1.4g

Anti-Inflammatory Egg Drop Soup

Serves: 2/Prep Time: 15 mins

Ingredients

- 1/3 teaspoon ground turmeric
- 1 clove garlic, minced
- ¾ quart vegetable stock
- 1/3 teaspoon ground ginger
- 1/3 small chile pepper, sliced
- ¾ cup brown mushrooms, sliced
- 1 cup Swiss chard, chopped
- 1 small spring onion, sliced
- 1/3 teaspoon salt
- 2 tablespoons extra-virgin olive oil
- ¾ tablespoon coconut aminos
- 1 large egg
- ¾ tablespoon cilantro, freshly chopped
- Black pepper, to taste

Directions

1. Heat vegetable stock in a large pot and simmer for about 3 minutes.
2. Place the ginger, garlic, turmeric, chile pepper, chard stalks, coconut aminos and mushrooms into the pot and let it simmer for about 5 minutes.
3. Add chard leaves and cook for about 1 minute.
4. Whisk the eggs and pour them slowly into the simmering soup.
5. Cook for about 3 minutes and add cilantro and spring onions.
6. Season with salt and pepper and dish out in a bowl.
7. Drizzle with olive oil and serve immediately.

Nutrition Calories: 184 Carbs: 5.4g Fats: 16.9g Proteins: 4.7g Sodium: 489mg Sugar: 1.7g

Ginger Zucchini Noodle Egg Drop Soup

Serves: 2/Prep Time: 25 mins

Ingredients

- 1 tablespoon extra-virgin olive oil
- 1¼ cups portobello mushrooms, sliced
- ½ cup plus ½ tablespoon water, divided
- 1¼ tablespoons low-sodium soy sauce
- 1 medium zucchini, spiralized
- ½ tablespoon ginger, minced
- 2 cups vegetable broth, divided
- ¼ teaspoon red pepper flakes
- ½ cup scallions, thinly sliced and divided
- 1 large egg, beaten
- Salt and black pepper, to taste
- ¾ tablespoon corn starch

Directions

1. Heat olive oil in a large pot over medium-high heat and add ginger.
2. Sauté for about 2 minutes and add shiitake mushrooms and ½ tablespoon of water.
3. Cook for about 4 minutes and add 1½ cup vegetable broth, ½ cup water, ½ cup scallions, red pepper flakes and tamari sauce.
4. Bring to a boil, stirring occasionally and pour in the beaten eggs slowly.
5. Meanwhile, mix ½ cup of vegetable broth with the corn starch.
6. Add this mixture to the soup while continuously stirring and cook for about 5 minutes.
7. Season with salt and black pepper and add zucchini noodles.
8. Cook for about 2 minutes until the noodles are soft and top with the remaining scallions to serve.

Nutrition Calories: 193 Carbs: 11g Fats: 11.3g Proteins: 11.8g Sodium: 1366mg Sugar: 4.8g

Creamiest Low-Carb Vegetable Soup

Serves: 2/Prep Time: 45 mins
Ingredients
- ½ small brown onion, finely chopped
- ½ cup water
- ½ garlic clove, finely chopped
- ½ cup vegetable stock
- ¼ teaspoon onion powder
- 1 tablespoon extra-virgin olive oil
- ½ pound zucchini
- ½ tablespoon butter
- Sea salt and black pepper, to taste
- ½ pound cauliflower, green parts removed
- 1 celery stalk
- ½ teaspoon fresh thyme, plus extra for garnish
- ½ cup cream

Directions
1. Heat butter in a large saucepan over medium-high heat and add onion and garlic.
2. Sauté for about 3 minutes and add cauliflower, zucchini, celery and seasonings.
3. Add water and vegetable stock and bring to the boil.
4. Allow to simmer for about 15 minutes and transfer into an immersion blender.
5. Blend until smooth and add cream.
6. Return to the saucepan and cook for about 3 minutes.
7. Ladle the soup into 2 bowls and drizzle ½ tablespoon of olive oil and a thyme sprig in each bowl to serve.

Nutrition Calories: 183 Carbs: 13.6g Fats: 14.4g Proteins: 4.6g Sodium: 106mg Sugar: 7g

Hearty Veggies Low-Carb Miso Soup

Serves: 2/Prep Time: 25 mins
Ingredients
- 1 clove garlic, chopped
- 1 small rainbow carrot, peeled and diced
- ¼ head Romanesco, florets chopped
- ¾ small zucchini, sliced and halved
- 1¼ oz baby spinach
- 2 tablespoons coconut oil
- ¼ medium purple onion, peeled and diced
- 3 cups water
- ¼ head purple cauliflower, florets chopped
- ¾ tablespoon Bouillon
- 1/8 cup mellow white miso
- Fresh dill
- Salt and black pepper, to taste
- Fresh parsley

Directions
1. Put coconut oil in a large pot over medium-high heat and add garlic and onions.
2. Cook for about 3 minutes and add carrots and water.
3. Bring to a boil and cook for about 14 minutes.
4. Add cauliflower and Romanesco and cook for about 5 minutes.
5. Stir in spinach, miso and bouillon and mix until miso is dissolved.
6. Stir in dill and parsley and season with salt and black pepper to serve.

Nutrition Calories: 173 Carbs: 11.7g Fats: 14.1g Proteins: 4.4g Sodium: 102mg Sugar: 3.4g

Cauliflower Parmesan Soup

Serves: 2/Prep Time: 35 mins
Ingredients
- Salt and black pepper, to taste
- 2¾ tablespoons butter
- ½ onion, sliced
- 1/3 head cauliflower, chopped
- ½ cup water
- 1/3 cup Parmesan cheese
- ½ leek, sliced
- ¾ cup vegetable broth
- ¾ tablespoon thyme, chopped

Directions
1. Melt ¾ tablespoon butter in large pot and add onion, leek and salt.
2. Cook for about 3 minutes and add remaining butter, cauliflower, broth and water.
3. Allow it to simmer for about 15 minutes and add thyme.
4. Simmer for about 10 minutes until cauliflower is tender and transfer to a blender along with cheese.
5. Blend until smooth and dish out in a bowl to serve.

Nutrition Calories: 208 Carbs: 9.2g Fats: 17.6g Proteins: 5.1g Sodium: 463mg Sugar: 3.4g

Cheesy Keto Zucchini Soup

Serves: 2/Prep Time: 20 mins
Ingredients
- ½ medium onion, peeled and chopped
- 1 cup bone broth
- 1 tablespoon coconut oil
- 1½ zucchinis, cut into chunks
- ½ tablespoon nutritional yeast
- Dash of black pepper
- ½ tablespoon parsley, chopped, for garnish
- ½ tablespoon coconut cream, for garnish

Directions
1. Melt the coconut oil in a large pan over medium heat and add onions.
2. Sauté for about 3 minutes and add zucchinis and bone broth.
3. Reduce the heat to simmer for about 15 minutes and cover the pan.
4. Add nutritional yeast and transfer to an immersion blender.
5. Blend until smooth and season with black pepper.
6. Top with coconut cream and parsley to serve.

Nutrition Calories: 154 Carbs: 8.9g Fats: 8.1g Proteins: 13.4g Sodium: 93mg Sugar: 3.9g

Spring Soup with Poached Egg

Serves: 2/Prep Time: 20 mins
Ingredients
- 32 oz vegetable broth
- 2 eggs
- 1 head romaine lettuce, chopped
- Salt, to taste

Directions
1. Bring the vegetable broth to a boil and reduce the heat.
2. Poach the eggs for 5 minutes in the broth and remove them into 2 bowls.

4. Stir in romaine lettuce into the broth and cook for 4 minutes.
5. Dish out in a bowl and serve hot.

Nutrition Calories: 158 Carbs: 6.9g Fats: 7.3g Proteins: 15.4g Sodium: 1513mg Sugar: 3.3g

Mint Avocado Chilled Soup

Serves: 2/Prep Time: 15 mins
Ingredients
- 2 romaine lettuce leaves
- 1 Tablespoon lime juice
- 1 medium ripe avocado
- 1 cup coconut milk, chilled
- 20 fresh mint leaves
- Salt to taste

Directions
1. Put all the ingredients in a blender and blend until smooth.
2. Refrigerate for about 10 minutes and serve chilled.

Nutrition Calories: 432 Carbs: 16.1g Fats: 42.2g Proteins: 5.2g Sodium: 33mg Sugar: 4.5g

Easy Butternut Squash Soup

Serves: 4/Prep Time: 1 hour 45 mins
Ingredients
- 1 small onion, chopped
- 4 cups chicken broth
- 1 butternut squash
- 3 tablespoons coconut oil
- Salt, to taste
- Nutmeg and pepper, to taste

Directions
1. Put oil and onions in a large pot and add onions.
2. Sauté for about 3 minutes and add chicken broth and butternut squash.
3. Simmer for about 1 hour on medium heat and transfer into an immersion blender.
4. Pulse until smooth and season with salt, pepper and nutmeg.
5. Return to the pot and cook for about 30 minutes.
6. Dish out and serve hot.

Nutrition Calories: 149 Carbs: 6.6g Fats: 11.6g Proteins: 5.4g Sodium: 765mg Sugar: 2.2g

Spring Soup Recipe with Poached Egg

Serves: 2/Prep Time: 20 mins
Ingredients
- 2 eggs
- 2 tablespoons butter
- 4 cups chicken broth
- 1 head of romaine lettuce, chopped
- Salt, to taste

Directions
1. Boil the chicken broth and lower heat.
2. Poach the eggs in the broth for about 5 minutes and remove the eggs.

4. Place each egg into a bowl and add chopped romaine lettuce into the broth.
5. Cook for about 10 minutes and ladle the broth with the lettuce into the bowls.

Nutrition Calories: 264 Carbs: 7g Fats: 18.9g Proteins: 16.1g Sodium: 1679mg Sugar: 3.4g

Cauliflower, leek & bacon soup

Serves: 4/Prep Time: 10 mins

Ingredients
- 4 cups chicken broth
- ½ cauliflower head, chopped
- 1 leek, chopped
- Salt and black pepper, to taste
- 5 bacon strips

Directions
1. Put the cauliflower, leek and chicken broth into the pot and cook for about 1 hour on medium heat.
2. Transfer into an immersion blender and pulse until smooth.
3. Return the soup into the pot and microwave the bacon strips for 1 minute.
4. Cut the bacon into small pieces and put into the soup.
5. Cook on for about 30 minutes on low heat.
6. Season with salt and pepper and serve.

Nutrition Calories: 185 Carbs: 5.8g Fats: 12.7g Proteins: 10.8g Sodium: 1153mg Sugar: 2.4g

Swiss Chard Egg Drop Soup

Serves: 4/Prep Time: 20 mins

Ingredients
- 3 cups bone broth
- 2 eggs, whisked
- 1 teaspoon ground oregano
- 3 tablespoons butter
- 2 cups Swiss chard, chopped
- 2 tablespoons coconut aminos
- 1 teaspoon ginger, grated
- Salt and black pepper, to taste

Directions
1. Heat the bone broth in a saucepan and add whisked eggs while stirring slowly.
2. Add the swiss chard, butter, coconut aminos, ginger, oregano and salt and black pepper.
3. Cook for about 10 minutes and serve hot.

Nutrition Calories: 185 Carbs: 2.9g Fats: 11g Proteins: 18.3g Sodium: 252mg Sugar: 0.4g

Mushroom Spinach Soup

Serves: 4/Prep Time: 25 mins

Ingredients
- 1cupspinach,cleaned and chopped
- 100gmushrooms,chopped
- 1onion
- 6 garlic cloves
- ½ teaspoon red chili powder
- Salt and black pepper, to taste
- 3 tablespoons buttermilk
- 1 teaspoon almond flour
- 2 cups chicken broth
- 3 tablespoons butter
- ¼ cup fresh cream,for garnish

Directions

1. Heat butter in a pan and add onions and garlic.
2. Sauté for about 3 minutes and add spinach, salt and red chili powder.
3. Sauté for about 4 minutes and add mushrooms.
4. Transfer into a blender and blend to make a puree.
5. Return to the pan and add buttermilk and almond flour for creamy texture.
6. Mix well and simmer for about 2 minutes.
7. Garnish with fresh cream and serve hot.

Nutrition Calories: 160 Carbs: 7g Fats: 13.3g Proteins: 4.7g Sodium: 462mg Sugar: 2.7g

Delicata Squash Soup

Serves: 5/Prep Time: 45mins
Ingredients
- 1½ cups beef bone broth
- 1small onion, peeled and grated.
- ½ teaspoon sea salt
- ¼ teaspoon poultry seasoning
- 2small Delicata Squash, chopped
- 2 garlic cloves, minced
- 2tablespoons olive oil
- ¼ teaspoon black pepper
- 1 small lemon, juiced
- 5 tablespoons sour cream

Directions
1. Put Delicata Squash and water in a medium pan and bring to a boil.
2. Reduce the heat and cook for about 20 minutes.
3. Drain and set aside.
4. Put olive oil, onions, garlic and poultry seasoning in a small sauce pan.
5. Cook for about 2 minutes and add broth.
6. Allow it to simmer for 5 minutes and remove from heat.
7. Whisk in the lemon juice and transfer the mixture in a blender.
8. Pulse until smooth and top with sour cream.

Nutrition Calories: 109 Carbs: 4.9g Fats: 8.5g Proteins: 3g Sodium: 279mg Sugar: 2.4g

Broccoli Soup

Serves: 6/Prep Time: 10 mins
Ingredients
- 3 tablespoons ghee
- 5 garlic cloves
- 1 teaspoon sage
- ¼ teaspoon ginger
- 2 cups broccoli
- 1 small onion
- 1 teaspoon oregano
- ½ teaspoon parsley
- Salt and black pepper, to taste
- 6 cups vegetable broth
- 4 tablespoons butter

Directions
1. Put ghee, onions, spices and garlic in a pot and cook for 3 minutes.
2. Add broccoli and cook for about 4 minutes.
3. Add vegetable broth, cover and allow it to simmer for about 30 minutes.
4. Transfer into a blender and blend until smooth.
5. Add the butter to give it a creamy delicious texture and flavor

Nutrition Calories: 183 Carbs: 5.2g Fats: 15.6g Proteins: 6.1g Sodium: 829mg Sugar: 1.8g

Apple Pumpkin Soup

Serves: 8/Prep Time: 10 mins
Ingredients

- 1 apple, chopped
- 1 whole kabocha pumpkin, peeled, seeded and cubed
- 1 cup almond flour
- ¼ cup ghee
- 1 pinch cardamom powder
- 2 quarts water
- ¼ cup coconut cream
- 1 pinch ground black pepper

Directions

1. Heat ghee in the bottom of a heavy pot and add apples.
2. Cook for about 5 minutes on a medium flame and add pumpkin.
3. Sauté for about 3 minutes and add almond flour.
4. Sauté for about 1 minute and add water.
5. Lower the flame and cook for about 30 minutes.
6. Transfer the soup into an immersion blender and blend until smooth.
7. Top with coconut cream and serve.

Nutrition Calories: 186 Carbs: 10.4g Fats: 14.9g Proteins: 3.7g Sodium: 7mg Sugar: 5.4g

Keto French Onion Soup

Serves: 6/Prep Time: 40 mins
Ingredients

- 5 tablespoons butter
- 500 g brown onion medium
- 4 drops liquid stevia
- 4 tablespoons olive oil
- 3 cups beef stock

Directions

1. Put the butter and olive oil in a large pot over medium low heat and add onions and salt.
2. Cook for about 5 minutes and stir in stevia.
3. Cook for another 5 minutes and add beef stock.
4. Reduce the heat to low and simmer for about 25 minutes.
5. Dish out into soup bowls and serve hot.

Nutrition Calories: 198 Carbs: 6g Fats: 20.6g Proteins: 2.9g Sodium: 883mg Sugar: 1.7g

Cauliflower and Thyme Soup

Serves: 6/Prep Time: 30 mins
Ingredients

- 2teaspoonsthyme powder
- 1head cauliflower
- 3cupsvegetable stock
- ½ teaspoon matcha green tea powder
- 3tablespoonsolive oil
- Salt and black pepper, to taste
- 5garlic cloves,chopped

Directions

1. Put the vegetable stock, thyme and matcha powder to a large pot over medium-high heat and bring to a boil.
2. Add cauliflower and cook for about 10 minutes.
3. Meanwhile, put the olive oil and garlic in a small sauce pan and cook for about 1 minute.
4. Add the garlic, salt and black pepper and cook for about 2 minutes.
5. Transfer into an immersion blender and blend until smooth.

7. Dish out and serve immediately.

Nutrition Calories: 79 Carbs: 3.8g Fats: 7.1g Proteins: 1.3g Sodium: 39mg Sugar: 1.5g

Chicken Soups Recipes

Homemade Thai Chicken Soup

Serves: 12/Prep Time: 8 hours 25 mins

Ingredients

- 1 lemongrass stalk, cut into large chunks
- 5 thick slices of fresh ginger
- 1 whole chicken
- 20 fresh basil leaves
- 1 lime, juiced
- 1 tablespoon salt

Directions

1. Place the chicken, 10 basil leaves, lemongrass, ginger, salt and water into the slow cooker.
2. Cook for about 8 hours on low and dish out into a bowl.
3. Stir in fresh lime juice and basil leaves to serve.

Nutrition Calories: 255 Carbs: 1.2g Fats: 17.6g Proteins: 25.2g Sodium: 582mg Sugar: 0.1g

Chicken Kale Soup

Serves: 6/Prep Time: 6 hours 10 mins

Ingredients

- 2poundschicken breast, skinless
- 1/3cuponion
- 1tablespoonolive oil
- 14ounceschicken bone broth
- ½ cup olive oil
- 4 cups chicken stock
- ¼ cup lemon juice
- 5ouncesbaby kale leaves
- Salt, to taste

Directions

1. Season chicken with salt and black pepper.
2. Heat olive oil over medium heat in a large skillet and add seasoned chicken.
3. Reduce the temperature and cook for about 15 minutes.
4. Shred the chicken and place in the crock pot.
5. Process the chicken broth and onions in a blender and blend until smooth.
6. Pour into crock pot and stir in the remaining ingredients.
7. Cook on low for about 6 hours, stirring once while cooking.

Nutrition Calories: 261 Carbs: 2g Fats: 21g Proteins: 14.1g Sodium: 264mg Sugar: 0.3g

Chicken Veggie Soup

Serves: 6/Prep Time: 20 mins

Ingredients

- 5 chicken thighs
- 12 cups water
- 1 tablespoon adobo seasoning
- 4 celery ribs
- 1 yellow onion
- 1½ teaspoons whole black peppercorns
- 6 sprigs fresh parsley
- 2 teaspoons coarse sea salt
- 2 carrots
- 6 mushrooms, sliced

- 2 garlic cloves
- 1 bay leaf
- 3 sprigs fresh thyme

Directions
1. Put water, chicken thighs, carrots, celery ribs, onion, garlic cloves and herbs in a large pot.
2. Bring to a boil and reduce the heat to low.
3. Cover the pot and simmer for about 30 minutes.
4. Dish out the chicken and shred it, removing the bones.
5. Put the bones back into the pot and simmer for about 20 minutes.
6. Strain the broth, discarding the chunks and put the liquid back into the pot.
7. Bring it to a boil and simmer for about 30 minutes.
8. Put the mushrooms in the broth and simmer for about 10 minutes.
9. Dish out to serve hot.

Nutrition: Calories: 250 Carbs: 6.4g Fats: 8.9g Proteins: 35.1g Sodium: 852mg Sugar: 2.5g

Chicken Mulligatawny Soup

Serves: 10/Prep Time: 30 mins

Ingredients
- 1½ tablespoons curry powder
- 3 cups celery root, diced
- 2 tablespoons Swerve
- 10 cups chicken broth
- 5 cups chicken, chopped and cooked
- ¼ cup apple cider
- ½ cup sour cream
- ¼ cup fresh parsley, chopped
- 2 tablespoons butter
- Salt and black pepper, to taste

Directions
1. Combine the broth, butter, chicken, curry powder, celery root and apple cider in a large soup pot.
2. Bring to a boil and simmer for about 30 minutes.
3. Stir in Swerve, sour cream, fresh parsley, salt and black pepper.
4. Dish out and serve hot.

Nutrition Calories: 215 Carbs: 7.1g Fats: 8.5g Proteins: 26.4g Sodium: 878mg Sugar: 2.2g

Buffalo Ranch Chicken Soup

Serves: 4/Prep Time: 40 mins

Ingredients
- 2 tablespoons parsley
- 2 celery stalks, chopped
- 6 tablespoons butter
- 1 cup heavy whipping cream
- 4 cups chicken, cooked and shredded
- 4 tablespoons ranch dressing
- ¼ cup yellow onions, chopped
- 8 oz cream cheese
- 8 cups chicken broth
- 7 hearty bacon slices, crumbled

Directions
1. Heat butter in a pan and add chicken.
2. Cook for about 5 minutes and add 1½ cups water.
3. Cover and cook for about 10 minutes.

5. Put the chicken and rest of the ingredients into the saucepan except parsley and cook for about 10 minutes.
6. Top with parsley and serve hot.

Nutrition Calories: 444 Carbs: 4g Fats: 34g Proteins: 28g Sodium: 1572mg Sugar: 2g

Traditional Chicken Soup

Serves: 6/Prep Time: 1 hour 45 mins

Ingredients

- 3 pounds chicken
- 4 quarts water
- 4 stalks celery
- 1/3 large red onion
- 1 large carrot
- 3 garlic cloves
- 2 thyme sprigs
- 2 rosemary sprigs
- Salt and black pepper, to taste

Directions

1. Put water and chicken in the stock pot on medium high heat.
2. Bring to a boil and allow it to simmer for about 10 minutes.
3. Add onion, garlic, celery, salt and pepper and simmer on medium low heat for 30 minutes.
4. Add thyme and carrots and simmer on low for another 30 minutes.
5. Dish out the chicken and shred the pieces, removing the bones.
6. Return the chicken pieces to the pot and add rosemary sprigs.
7. Simmer for about 20 minutes at low heat and dish out to serve.

Nutrition Calories: 357 Carbs: 3.3g Fats: 7g Proteins: 66.2g Sodium: 175mg Sugar: 1.1g

Chicken Noodle Soup

Serves: 6/Prep Time: 30 mins

Ingredients

- 1 onion, minced
- 1 rib celery, sliced
- 3 cups chicken, shredded
- 3 eggs, lightly beaten
- 1 green onion, for garnish
- 2 tablespoons coconut oil
- 1 carrot, peeled and thinly sliced
- 2 teaspoons dried thyme
- 2½ quarts homemade bone broth
- ¼ cup fresh parsley, minced
- Salt and black pepper, to taste

Directions

1. Heat coconut oil over medium-high heat in a large pot and add onions, carrots, and celery.
2. Cook for about 4 minutes and stir in the bone broth, thyme and chicken.
3. Simmer for about 15 minutes and stir in parsley.
4. Pour beaten eggs into the soup in a slow steady stream.
5. Remove soup from heat and let it stand for about 2 minutes.
6. Season with salt and black pepper and dish out to serve.

Nutrition Calories: 226 Carbs: 3.5g Fats: 8.9g Proteins: 31.8g Sodium: 152mg Sugar: 1.6g

Chicken Cabbage Soup

Serves: 8/Prep Time: 35 mins

Ingredients

- 2 celery stalks
- 2 garlic cloves, minced
- 4 oz. butter
- 6 oz. mushrooms, sliced
- 2 tablespoons onions, dried and minced
- 1 teaspoon salt
- 8 cups chicken broth
- 1 medium carrot
- 2 cups green cabbage, sliced into strips
- 2 teaspoons dried parsley
- ¼ teaspoon black pepper
- 1½ rotisserie chickens, shredded

Directions

1. Melt butter in a large pot and add celery, mushrooms, onions and garlic into the pot.
2. Cook for about 4 minutes and add broth, parsley, carrot, salt and black pepper.
3. Simmer for about 10 minutes and add cooked chicken and cabbage.
4. Simmer for an additional 12 minutes until the cabbage is tender.
5. Dish out and serve hot.

Nutrition Calories: 184 Carbs: 4.2g Fats: 13.1g Proteins: 12.6g Sodium: 1244mg Sugar: 2.1g

Green Chicken Enchilada Soup

Serves: 5/Prep Time: 20 mins
Ingredients

- 4 oz. cream cheese, softened
- ½ cup salsa verde
- 1 cup cheddar cheese, shredded
- 2 cups cooked chicken, shredded
- 2 cups chicken stock

Directions

1. Put salsa verde, cheddar cheese, cream cheese and chicken stock in an immersion blender and blend until smooth.
2. Pour this mixture into a medium saucepan and cook for about 5 minutes on medium heat.
3. Add the shredded chicken and cook for about 5 minutes.
4. Garnish with additional shredded cheddar and serve hot.

Nutrition Calories: 265 Carbs: 2.2g Fats: 17.4g Proteins: 24.2g Sodium: 686mg Sugar: 0.8g

Keto BBQ Chicken Pizza Soup

Serves: 6/Prep Time: 1 hour 30 mins
Ingredients

- 6 chicken legs
- 1 medium red onion, diced
- 4 garlic cloves
- 1 large tomato, unsweetened
- 4 cups green beans
- ¾ cup BBQ Sauce
- 1½ cups mozzarella cheese, shredded
- ¼ cup ghee
- 2 quarts water
- 2 quarts chicken stock
- Salt and black pepper, to taste
- Fresh cilantro, for garnishing

Directions

1. Put chicken, water and salt in a large pot and bring to a boil.
2. Reduce the heat to medium-low and cook for about 75 minutes.
3. Shred the meat off the bones using a fork and keep aside.

5. Put ghee, red onions and garlic in a large soup and cook over a medium heat.
6. Add chicken stock and bring to a boil over a high heat.
7. Add green beans and tomato to the pot and cook for about 15 minutes.
8. AddBBQ Sauce, shredded chicken, salt and black pepper to the pot.
9. Ladle the soup into serving bowls and top with shredded mozzarella cheese and cilantro to serve.

Nutrition: Calories: 449 Carbs: 7.1g Fats: 32.5g Proteins: 30.8g Sodium: 252mg Sugar: 4.7g

Seafood Soups Recipes

Salmon Stew Soup

Serves: 5/Prep Time: 25 mins
Ingredients
- 4 cups chicken broth
- 3 salmon fillets, chunked
- 2 tablespoons butter
- 1 cup parsley, chopped
- 3 cups Swiss chard, roughly chopped
- 2 Italian squash, chopped
- 1 garlic clove, crushed
- ½ lemon, juiced
- Salt and black pepper, to taste
- 2 eggs

Directions
1. Put the chicken broth and garlic into a pot and bring to a boil.
2. Add salmon, lemon juice and butter in the pot and cook for about 10 minutes on medium heat.
3. Add Swiss chard, Italian squash, salt and pepper and cook for about 10 minutes.
4. Whisk eggs and add to the pot, stirring continuously.
5. Garnish with parsley and serve.

Nutrition Calories: 262 Carbs: 7.8g Fats: 14g Proteins: 27.5g Sodium: 1021mg Sugar: 1.2g

Spicy Halibut Tomato Soup

Serves: 8/Prep Time: 1 hour 5mins
Ingredients
- 2garliccloves, minced
- 1tablespoonolive oil
- ¼ cup fresh parsley, chopped
- 10anchoviescanned in oil, minced
- 6cupsvegetable broth
- 1teaspoonblack pepper
- 1poundhalibut fillets, chopped
- 3tomatoes, peeled and diced
- 1teaspoonsalt
- 1teaspoonred chili flakes

Directions
1. Heat olive oil in a large stockpot over medium heat and add garlic and half of the parsley.
2. Add anchovies, tomatoes, vegetable broth, red chili flakes, salt and black pepper and bring to a boil.
3. Reduce the heat to medium-low and simmer for about 20 minutes.
4. Add halibut fillets and cook for about 10 minutes.
5. Dish out the halibut and shred into small pieces.
6. Mix back with the soup and garnish with the remaining fresh parsley to serve.

Nutrition Calories: 170 Carbs: 3g Fats: 6.7g Proteins: 23.4g Sodium: 2103mg Sugar: 1.8g

Spicy Shrimp and Chorizo Soup

Serves: 8/Prep Time: 55mins

Ingredients

- 2 tablespoons butter
- 1medium onion, diced
- 3celery ribs, diced
- 4 garlic cloves, sliced
- 12ounces chorizo, diced
- 2tomatoes, diced
- 1½teaspoons smoked paprika
- 1teaspoonground coriander
- 1teaspoonsea salt
- 1quart chicken broth
- 1poundshrimp,peeled, deveined and chopped
- 2tablespoons fresh cilantro, minced
- 1avocado,diced
- Chopped fresh cilantro,for garnish

Directions

1. Heat half of butter over medium-high heat in a large pot and add celery, bell pepper and onions.
2. Cook for about 8 minutes, stirring occasionally and add tomato paste, half of chorizo, garlic, coriander, smoked paprika and salt.
3. Cook for about 1 minute, stirring continuously and add the tomatoes and broth.
4. Cook for about 20 minutes and heat remaining butter in a small pan.
5. Add remaining chorizo and cook for about 5 minutes until crispy.
6. Add smoked paprika, shrimp, coriander and simmer for about 4 minutes.
7. Remove from the heat and stir in minced cilantro.
8. Top with the crispy chorizo and chopped cilantro and serve.

Nutrition Calories: 374 Carbs: 7.9g Fats: 25.9g Proteins: 26.8g Sodium: 1315mg Sugar: 2.1g

Creamy Leek & Salmon Soup

Serves: 4/Prep Time: 30 mins

Ingredients

- 2 tablespoons butter
- 2 leeks, washed, trimmed and sliced
- 3 garlic cloves, minced
- 6 cups seafood broth
- 2 teaspoons dried thyme leaves
- 1 pound salmon, in bite size pieces
- 1½ cups coconut milk
- Salt and black pepper, to taste

Directions

1. Heat butter at a low-medium heat in a large saucepan and add garlic and leeks.
2. Cook for about 3 minutes and add stock and thyme.
3. Simmer for about 15 minutes and season with salt and black pepper.
4. Add salmon and coconut milk to the pan and simmer for about 5 minutes.
5. Dish out and serve immediately.

Nutrition Calories: 332 Carbs: 9.1g Fats: 24.3g Proteins: 21.5g Sodium: 839mg Sugar: 3.9g

Thai Coconut Shrimp Soup

Serves: 5/Prep Time: 40 mins

Ingredients

BROTH
- 4 cups chicken broth
- 1½ cups full fat coconut milk
- 1 organic lime zest
- 1 teaspoondried lemongrass
- 1 cup fresh cilantro
- 1 jalapeno pepper, sliced
- 1 inch piece fresh ginger root
- 1 teaspoon sea salt

SOUP
- 100 grams raw shrimp
- 1 tablespoon coconut oil
- 30 grams mushrooms, sliced
- 1 red onion, thinly sliced
- 1 anchovy, finely smashed
- 1 lime, juiced
- 1 tablespoon cilantro, chopped

Directions
1. Broth: Mix together all the ingredients in a sauce pan and simmer for about 20 minutes.
2. Strain the mixture through a fine mesh colander and pour back into the pan.
3. Soup: Simmer the broth again and add shrimp, onions, mushrooms and anchovy.
4. Allow it to simmer for about 10 minutes and add lime juice.
5. Garnish with cilantro and serve hot.

Nutrition Calories: 247 Carbs: 7.7g Fats: 19g Proteins: 11.5g Sodium: 1061mg Sugar: 3.2g

Salmon Head Soup

Serves: 6/Prep Time: 2 hours 45 mins

Ingredients
- 2 salmon heads
- 1 small onion, sliced
- 1 bulb green garlic, minced
- ½ cup wakame
- 2 tablespoons ginger, peeled and minced
- ¼ cup mirin
- ¼ cup coconut aminos
- 2 zucchinis, spiraled into noodles
- Chives and chilies, for garnish

Directions
1. Put salmon heads, ginger and water in a slow cooker and cook on high for about 2 hours.
2. Strain broth and shredded shrimp meat and transfer into a stock pot along with green garlic, ginger, onions, mirin, wakame and coconut aminos.
3. Cook for about 20 minutes and add zucchinis.
4. Cook for about 15 minutes and garnish with chives and chillies.

Nutrition Calories: 123 Carbs: 7g Fats: 5.8g Proteins: 9.6g Sodium: 163mg Sugar: 3.3g

Carrot Ginger Halibut Soup

Serves: 6/Prep Time: 45 mins

Ingredients
- 1 large onion, chopped
- 2 tablespoons fresh ginger, peeled and minced
- 1 tablespoon coconut oil
- 4 carrots, peeled and sliced
- 2 cups chicken broth
- 1 cup water
- ½ teaspoon black pepper
- 1 pound halibut, cut into 1" chunks
- Sea salt, to taste

Directions
1. Heat coconut oil over medium heat in a large pot and add onions.

3. Sauté for about 8 minutes and add ginger, carrots, broth and water.
4. Bring to a boil, reduce heat and simmer for about 20 minutes.
5. Transfer into an immersion blender and blend until smooth.
6. Return the soup to the pot and add halibut, sea salt and black pepper.
7. Allow to simmer for 5 more minutes and serve.

Nutrition Calories: 246 Carbs: 8g Fats: 16.3g Proteins: 16.3g Sodium: 363mg Sugar: 3.4g

Coconut Seafood Soup

Serves: 5/Prep Time: 30 mins
Ingredients
- 10 button mushrooms, sliced
- 1 cup romaine lettuce, chopped
- 4 cups chicken stock
- ½ cup kale, chopped
- 4 tilapia filets, chopped into large chunks
- 10 prawns
- 1 cup coconut cream
- Salt, to taste
- 10 mussels
- 1 teaspoon Red Boat fish sauce

Directions
1. Put the chicken stock into a large pot and bring to the boil.
2. Add kale, romaine lettuce and mushrooms and boil again.
3. Add tilapia pieces and prawns and bring to the boil again.
4. Boil for around 5 minutes and add coconut cream, fish sauce and salt.
5. Stir gently and dish out to serve immediately.

Nutrition Calories: 300 Carbs: 7.3g Fats: 15.5g Proteins: 34.7g Sodium: 1217mg Sugar: 2.9g

Cheesy Shrimp Soup

Serves: 8/Prep Time: 30 mins
Ingredients
- 8 oz cheddar cheese, shredded
- 24 oz extra small shrimp
- 2 cups mushrooms, sliced
- 32 oz chicken broth
- ½ cup butter
- 1 cup heavy whipping cream

Directions
1. Put chicken broth and mushrooms to a large soup pot and bring to a boil.
2. Reduce heat and stir in butter, heavy whipping cream and cheese.
3. Add shrimp and allow it to simmer for about 15 minutes.
4. Dish out and serve hot.

Nutrition Calories: 395 Carbs: 3.3g Fats: 28.7g Proteins: 29.8g Sodium: 1428mg Sugar: 0.8g

Thai Hot and Sour Shrimp Soup

Serves: 6/Prep Time: 55 mins

Ingredients

- 3 tablespoons butter
- 1 inch piece ginger root, peeled
- 1/2 teaspoon fresh lime zest
- 5 cups chicken broth
- 1 small green zucchini
- 1 pound shrimps, peeled and deveined
- 1 medium onion, diced
- 4 garlic cloves
- 1 lemongrass stalk
- 1 red Thai chili, roughly chopped
- 1/2 pound cremini mushrooms, sliced into wedges
- 2 tablespoons fresh lime juice
- 2 tablespoons fish sauce
- 1/4 bunch fresh Thai basil, coarsely chopped
- 1/4 bunch fresh cilantro, coarsely chopped
- Salt and black pepper, to taste

Directions

1. Heat butter in a large pot over medium heat and add shrimps.
2. Stir well and add garlic, onions, ginger, lemongrass, lime zest, Thai chillies, salt and black pepper.
3. Cook for about 3 minutes and add chicken broth to the pot.
4. Simmer for about 30 minutes and strain it.
5. Heat a large sauté pan over high heat and add coconut oil, mushrooms, zucchini, salt and black pepper.
6. Sauté for about 3 minutes and add to the shrimp mixture.
7. Simmer for about 2 minutes and add fish sauce, lime juice, salt and black pepper.
8. Cook for about 1 minute and add fresh cilantro and basil.
9. Dish out and serve hot.

Nutrition Calories: 223 Carbs: 8.7g Fats: 10.2g Proteins: 23g Sodium: 1128mg Sugar: 3.6g

Beef and Pork Soups Recipes

Creamy Pulled Pork Soup

Serves: 6/Prep Time: 55 mins

Ingredients

- 1 medium onion
- 1 pound cauliflower
- ½ cup butter
- 8 garlic cloves
- 1 teaspoon sea salt
- 7 cups chicken broth
- 1½ cups pulled pork
- 2 teaspoons dried oregano
- 3 tablespoons sour cream

Directions

1. Heat butter in a saucepan and add onions and garlic.
2. Sauté for about 3 minutes and add cauliflower, chicken broth and sea salt.
3. Cook for about 20 minutes and transfer it to an immersion blender.
4. Blend until smooth and add dried oregano.
5. Return to the saucepan and simmer for about 5 minutes.
6. Add sour cream and pulled pork and cook for about 15 minutes.
7. Dish out and serve hot.

Nutrition Calories: 257 Carbs: 8.7g Fats: 19.1g Proteins: 13.6g Sodium: 1351mg Sugar: 3.5g

Thai Beef and Broccoli Soup

Serves: 8/Prep Time: 50 mins
Ingredients
- 1 onion, chopped
- 2 garlic cloves, minced
- 2 tablespoons avocado oil
- 2 tablespoons Thai green curry paste
- 2-inch ginger, minced
- 1 Serrano pepper, minced
- 3 tablespoons coconut aminos
- ½ teaspoon salt
- 4 cups beef bone broth
- 1 cup full-fatcoconut milk
- 1 pound ground beef
- 2 teaspoons fish sauce
- ½ teaspoon black pepper
- 2 large broccoli stalks, cut into florets
- Cilantro, garnish

Directions
1. Put avocado oil and onions into a large pot and sauté for about 4 minutes.
2. Add ginger, garlic, Serrano pepper and curry paste and cook for about 1 minute.
3. Add coconut aminos, fish sauce, ground beef, salt and black pepper.
4. Cook for about 6 minutes and add bone broth.
5. Reduce the heat to low and cook, covered for about 20 minutes.
6. Add coconut milk and broccoli florets to the pot and cover.
7. Cook for another 10 minutes and increase heat to high.
8. Simmer for about 5 minutes and garnish with cilantro to serve.

Nutrition Calories: 240 Carbs: 8.5g Fats: 13.5g Proteins: 22g Sodium: 547mg Sugar: 2.2g

Good Ole'   Southern Potlikker Soup

Serves: 6/Prep Time: 10 mins
Ingredients
- 1 large onion, diced
- 2 garlic cloves, minced
- 6 cups chicken broth
- 4 tablespoons butter
- 1 pound ham steaks, cubed
- 2 celery stalks, chopped
- 1 cup kale, chopped
- 1 tablespoon apple cider vinegar
- 6 cups collards, chopped
- 1 tablespoon Sriracha
- Salt and black pepper, to taste

Directions
1. Put butter, ham, garlic, onions, carrots and celery in a heavy-bottomed pot.
2. Cook for about 3 minutes over medium heat and add rest of the ingredients.
3. Bring to a boil and reduce the heat.
4. Simmer for about 90 minutes and dish out to serve.

Nutrition Calories: 160 Carbs: 7.6g Fats: 10.3g Proteins: 9.4g Sodium: 1055mg Sugar: 2g

Potsticker Meatball Asian Noodle Soup

Serves: 6/Prep Time: 35 mins
Ingredients

For the meatballs:
- 1 egg
- 1 pound ground pork
- 1/3 cup almond flour
- ½ teaspoon garlic powder

- 1 teaspoon ginger, minced
- 1 tablespoon gluten free soy sauce
- ½ teaspoon kosher salt

For the broth:
- 2 tablespoons ginger, minced
- 1 teaspoon sesame oil
- 1 teaspoon garlic, minced
- 2 cups water
- 1 tablespoon fish sauce

- ½ teaspoon kosher salt
- 4 cups chicken broth
- 1 tablespoon gluten free soy sauce
- ½ teaspoon red pepper flakes

To assemble the soup:
- 2 cups Napa cabbage, shredded
- 3 cups shiratake noodles, drained and rinsed

- ¼ cup radish sticks
- 6 lime wedges
- ½ cup cilantro, chopped

Directions
1. *For the meatballs:* Mix together all the ingredients for meatballs in a medium bowl.
2. Make meatballs out of this mixture and transfer on to a baking sheet.
3. Bake for about 12 minutes at 375 degrees F and dish out.
4. *For the broth:* Heat sesame oil and add ginger and garlic
5. Cook for about 1 minute and add water, soy sauce, chicken broth, red pepper flakes, fish sauce and salt.
6. Bring to a boil and simmer for about 10 minutes.
7. Strain the broth and return to the pan.
8. Bring to a boil right before serving.
9. *To assemble the soup:* Place about ½ cup shiratake noodles in a soup bowl and top with a handful of cabbage, four meatballs, a pinch of radish and cilantro.
10. Ladle about 1 cup of hot broth into each bowl and squeeze a lime wedge over it.

Nutrition Calories: 226 Carbs: 7.9g Fats: 8.7g Proteins: 27.4g Sodium: 1476mg Sugar: 1.3g

Beef Noodle Soup with Shitake Mushrooms and Baby Bok Choy

Serves: 1/Prep Time: 25 mins
Ingredients
- 2 teaspoons garlic, minced
- ¼ teaspoon crushed red pepper flakes
- ½ large zucchini, peeled and spiralized
- 3 oz beef steaks, cut into 1" cubes
- 2 tablespoons olive oil
- 1 cup chicken broth, homemade

- 1 head of baby bokchoy, roughly chopped
- ¼ cup green onions, chopped
- ¼ cup water
- 1 tablespoon coconut aminos
- ½ cup mushrooms
- Salt and black pepper, to taste

Directions
1. Season the beef cubes with 1 teaspoon olive oil, salt and black pepper.
2. Heat 1 tablespoon of olive oil over medium heat in a large saucepan and add garlic.
3. Sauté for about 1 minute and add beef.
4. Cook for about 2 minutes on each side and dish out.

6. Add remaining oil in the same saucepan and add mushrooms, bokchoy and red pepper flakes.
7. Stir to combine and cook for about 2 minutes.
8. Add chicken broth and water and bring to a boil.
9. Add coconut aminos and reduce heat to low.
10. Simmer for about 5 minutes and add zucchini noodles, beef and half of the green onions.
11. Cook for about 2 minutes and dish out into a bowl.
12. Top with remaining green onions and serve.

Nutrition Calories: 252 Carbs: 7.2g Fats: 17.6g Proteins: 17.7g Sodium: 262mg Sugar: 2.6g

Thai Tom Saap Pork Ribs Soup

Serves: 6/Prep Time: 2 hours
Ingredients
- 1 red shallot, chopped
- 1 pound pork spare ribs
- 4 small lemongrass stalks, chopped
- 8 cups water
- 1 lime, juiced
- 2 tablespoons fish sauce
- 3 tablespoons ginger
- 10 kaffir lime leaves
- Salt,to taste

Directions
1. Put the pork spare ribs into a large pot of water and bring to a boil.
2. Cook for about 10 minutes and pour out the liquid with the froth.
3. Pour water, lemongrass, shallots, ginger and salt to the pot and simmer for about 1 hour on low heat.
4. Add kaffir lime leaves, fish sauce, lime juice and salt and dish out to serve.

Nutrition Calories: 232 Carbs: 8.9g Fats: 16.4g Proteins: 12.2g Sodium: 424mg Sugar: 0.3g

Creamy Cauliflower & Ham Soup

Serves: 10/Prep Time: 10 mins
Ingredients
- 6 cups chicken broth
- ½ teaspoon onion powder
- 2 tablespoons apple cider vinegar
- 24 oz cauliflower florets
- 2 cups water
- ½ teaspoon garlic powder
- 3 cups ham, chopped
- 1 tablespoon fresh thyme leaves
- 3 tablespoons butter
- Salt and black pepper, to taste

Directions
1. Mix together garlic powder, chicken broth, cauliflower, water and onion powder in a large soup pot.
2. Bring to a boil and simmer for about 30 minutes.
3. Transfer into an immersion blender and blend until smooth.
4. Return to the pot and stir in ham and thyme leaves.
5. Simmer for about 10 minutes and add butter and apple cider vinegar.
6. Remove from the heat and season with salt and black pepper.
7. Dish out and serve hot.

Nutrition Calories: 139 Carbs: 6.1g Fats: 7.9g Proteins: 11.1g Sodium: 1033mg Sugar: 2.1g

Bacon and Pumpkin Soup

Serves: 6/Prep Time: 4 hours 15 mins
Ingredients
- 400gpumpkin,diced
- 3 cups bacon hock, diced
- Boiling water

Directions
1. Place pumpkin, boiling water and bacon hock in the slow cooker.
2. Cook on HIGH for about 4 hours and pull the meat away from the bones.
3. Return the meat to the slow cooker and allow it to simmer for 5 minutes before serving.

Nutrition Calories: 116 Carbs: 3.2g Fats: 5.9g Proteins: 12.1g Sodium: 27mg Sugar: 1.3g

Quick Italian Sausage and Pepper Soup

Serves: 10/Prep Time: 6 hours 20 mins
Ingredients
- 2pounds hot Italian sausage,cut into bite size pieces
- 2sweet bell peppers, chopped
- 2cupschicken broth low sodium
- 2tablespoonsextra virgin olive oil
- 4 garliccloves, minced
- 1onion, chopped
- 2tablespoonsred wine vinegar
- 2cupswater
- 1teaspoondried parsley
- 4ouncesfresh spinach leaves
- 1(28 ounce) can diced tomatoes with juice
- 1teaspoondried basil
- ½ cup Parmesan cheese, grated

Directions
1. Heat olive oil in a large skillet and add sausages.
2. Cook for about 5 minutes until browned and transfer into a slow cooker.
3. Add the remaining ingredients except spinach and fresh herbs.
4. Cook on LOW for about 6 hours.
5. Add fresh herbs and spinach and serve.

Nutrition Calories: 373 Carbs: 6.9g Fats: 29.4g Proteins: 20.4g Sodium: 845mg Sugar: 3.8g

Pork and Tomato Soup

Serves: 8/Prep Time: 45 mins
Ingredients
- 2 tablespoons olive oil
- ½ cup onions, chopped
- 2 pounds boneless pork ribs, cut into 1 inch pieces
- 1 tablespoon garlic, chopped
- ½ cup dry white wine
- 1 cup chicken stock
- 1 cup water
- 2 cups cauliflower, finely chopped
- 2 cups fresh tomatoes, chopped
- 2 tablespoons fresh oregano, chopped
- Salt and black pepper, to taste

Directions
1. Season the pork generously with salt and black pepper.

3. Heat olive oil in a heavy saucepan and add seasoned pork.
4. Cook for about 3 minutes per side until browned and add garlic and onions.
5. Cook for about 2 minutes and add the chicken stock, white wine, fresh tomatoes and water.
6. Bring to a boil and pour into a slow cooker.
7. Cook on HIGH for about 4 hours until the meat is tender.
8. Stir in the cauliflower and fresh oregano and cook for another 20 minutes.
9. Dish out and serve hot.

Nutrition Calories: 228 Carbs: 5.3g Fats: 7.8g Proteins: 31g Sodium: 172mg Sugar: 2.4g

Cold Soups Recipes

Mint Avocado Chilled Soup

Serves: 2/Prep Time: 10 mins
Ingredients
- 2 romaine lettuce leaves
- 1 medium ripe avocado
- 1 cup coconut milk, chilled
- 20 fresh mint leaves
- 1 tablespoon lime juice
- Salt, to taste

Directions
1. Put all the ingredients into a blender and blend until smooth.
2. Refrigerate for about 10 minutes and serve chilled.

Nutrition Calories: 245 Carbs: 8.4g Fats: 24.2g Proteins: 2.6g Sodium: 15mg Sugar: 2.3g

Chilled Zucchini Soup

Serves: 5/Prep Time: 10 mins
Ingredients
- 1 medium zucchini, cut into ½ inch pieces
- 4cupschicken broth
- 8ozcream cheese,cut into cubes
- ½ teaspoon ground cumin
- Salt and black pepper, to taste

Directions
1. Mix chicken broth and zucchini in a large stockpot.
2. Bring to a boil and reduce heat to low.
3. Simmer for about 10 minutes and add cream cheese.
4. Stir well and transfer to an immersion blender.
5. Blend until smooth and season with cumin, salt and black pepper.
6. Refrigerate to chill for about 2 hours and serve.

Nutrition Calories: 196 Carbs: 3.4g Fats: 17g Proteins: 7.8g Sodium: 749mg Sugar: 1.3g

Super Food Keto Soup

Serves: 7/Prep Time: 30 mins
Ingredients
- 1 medium white onion, diced
- 1 bay leaf, crumbled
- 200 g fresh spinach
- 1 medium head cauliflower
- 2 garlic cloves
- 150 g watercress
- 4 cups vegetable stock
- 1/4cupghee

- 1 cup coconut cream
- Salt and black pepper, to taste

Directions
1. Put ghee, onions and garlic in a soup pot over medium-high heat.
2. Cook until golden brown and add cauliflower and bay leaf.
3. Cook for about 5 minutes and add the spinach and watercress.
4. Cook for about 3 minutes and pour in the vegetable stock.
5. Bring to a boil and add coconut cream.
6. Season with salt and black pepper and transfer to an immersion blender.
7. Pulse until smooth and refrigerate for about an hour before serving.

Nutrition Calories: 187 Carbs: 9.4g Fats: 15.8g Proteins: 4.3g Sodium: 115mg Sugar: 4.4g

Chilled Cucumber Soup

Serves: 8/Prep Time: 15mins

Ingredients
- 3 large cucumbers, chopped
- 2 medium avocados, halved
- 2 cloves garlic, minced
- 2 large spring onions, roughly chopped
- 1 bunch fresh basil
- 3 tablespoons fresh lime juiceorlemon juice
- 2 cups water, vegetable stockor chicken stock
- ¾ teaspoon sea salt
- ¼ teaspoon black pepper, or to taste
- ½ cup extra virgin olive oil, divided
- 1 medium cucumber, thinly sliced

Directions
1. Put the cucumbers, avocados, onions, water, garlic, olive oil, basil, lime juice, salt and black pepper in an immersion blender.
2. Pulse until smooth and pour into a container.
3. Refrigerate for about 2 hours before serving.
4. Pour into serving bowls and top with the sliced cucumber.

Nutrition Calories: 203 Carbs: 8.7g Fats: 19.6g Proteins: 1.9g Sodium: 374mg Sugar: 2.4g

Chilled Guacamole Soup

Serves: 6/Prep Time: 10 mins

Ingredients
- 2 avocados, peeled and pitted
- ¼ cup red onion, chopped
- 1 tablespoon fresh cilantro, chopped
- ¼ teaspoon black pepper
- ¼ cup whipping cream
- 2½ cups low-sodium chicken broth, divided
- 6 tablespoons cheddar cheese, shredded
- 2 garlic cloves, coarsely chopped
- 1 jalapeno, seeded and coarsely chopped
- 1 tablespoon lime juice
- ½ teaspoon salt
- ¼ teaspoon cayenne
- 2 tablespoons sour cream

Directions
1. Put 1 cup of chicken broth, garlic, jalapeño, avocados, lime juice, cilantro and onions in a food processor.

3. Pulse until smooth and add remaining broth, cayenne salt and black pepper.
4. Puree until smooth and transfer to a large bowl.
5. Stir in whipping cream and chill for at least 1 hour before serving.
6. Ladle into bowls and top with sour cream and shredded cheese.

Nutrition Calories: 188 Carbs: 7.7g Fats: 15.3g Proteins: 6g Sodium: 317mg Sugar: 0.6g

Spinach Mint Soup with Sumac

Serves: 3/Prep Time: 10 mins

Ingredients

- 350gspinach leaves
- 400mlchicken stock
- ½ cup mint leaves
- 4spring onions,chopped
- 4 tablespoons heavy cream
- Pinch of sumac
- 1 tablespoon olive oil
- 2garlic cloves
- Salt and black pepper, to taste

Directions

1. Heat oil in a pot and add spring onions and garlic.
2. Sauté for about 3 minutes and add spinach leaves.
3. Cook for about 4 minutes and add chicken stock and mint leaves.
4. Transfer into a blender and blend until smooth.
5. Stir in heavy cream, salt, black pepper and a pinch of sumac.
6. Refrigerate and serve chilled.

Nutrition Calories: 157 Carbs: 8.6g Fats: 13g Proteins: 5.1g Sodium: 538mg Sugar: 1.4g

Vegan Gazpacho

Serves: 6/Prep Time: 10 mins

Ingredients

- ½ red onion, finely chopped
- 2 tomatoes, finely chopped
- ½ medium cucumber, finely chopped
- ½ green pepper, seeded and finely chopped
- 6 celery stalks, finely chopped
- 1 garlic clove, crushed
- 2 cups tomato juice
- 1/3 cup extra virgin olive oil
- ¼ cup white wine vinegar
- ¼ cup fresh parsley, finely chopped
- 1 scoop stevia
- Salt and black pepper, to taste

Directions

1. Put all the ingredients into a blender and blend until smooth.
2. Refrigerate for about 3 hours and serve chilled.

Nutrition Calories: 133 Carbs: 8.2g Fats: 11.4g Proteins: 1.6g Sodium: 237mg Sugar: 5.3g

Chilled Avocado Arugula Soup

Serves: 6/Prep Time: 10 mins

Ingredients

- 2 medium ripe hass avocados, diced
- 65 grams arugula
- 1/3 cup mint leaves, roughly chopped
- 1 teaspoon sea salt
- 1 lemon, juiced
- 1 scoop stevia
- 1/3 cup heavy cream
- 3 cups spring water, ice cold

- 1 tablespoon olive oil
- 3 tablespoons goat cheese, for topping

Directions
1. Put all the ingredients into a blender and blend until smooth.
2. Dish out into bowls and top with goat cheese.

Nutrition Calories: 167 Carbs: 6.2g Fats: 15.5g Proteins: 3.2g Sodium: 341mg Sugar: 0.6g

Chilled Cantaloupe Soup

Serves: 4/Prep Time: 10 mins

Ingredients
- 1 cantaloupe, cut into chunks
- 3 tablespoons butter
- 1/3 cup plain, non fat Greek yogurt
- 1 tablespoon ginger, freshly grated
- 1 scoop stevia
- ¼ teaspoon nutmeg
- Pinch of kosher salt
- 3 tablespoons fresh basil leaves, for garnish

Directions
1. Put all the ingredients into food processor except basil and pulse until smooth.
2. Refrigerate at least 2 hours before serving.
3. Garnish with fresh basil leaves and serve.

Nutrition Calories: 87 Carbs: 4.7g Fats: 6.9g Proteins: 2.1g Sodium: 92mg Sugar: 3.2g

Chilled Peach Soup with Fresh Goat Cheese

Serves: 4/Prep Time: 1 hour 20 mins

Ingredients
- 2 peaches, sliced and peeled
- ¼ cup seedless cucumber, finely diced and peeled
- ¼ cup yellow bell pepper, finely diced
- ¼ cup dried apricots, diced
- 2 scoops stevia
- 3 tablespoons fresh goat cheese, crumbled
- ¼ cup white balsamic vinegar
- 1/3 cup extra-virgin olive oil
- 1 large garlic clove
- Basil leaves, for garnish
- Salt and black pepper, to taste

Directions
1. In a bowl, toss the peaches, diced cucumber, yellow pepper and apricots. Add the honey, 3 tablespoons of goat cheese, 1/4 cup of balsamic vinegar and 2 tablespoons of the olive oil. Stir in 1 1/2 teaspoons of salt. Add the garlic. Cover and refrigerate overnight.
2. Discard the garlic. Transfer the contents of the bowl to a blender and puree. Add 1/4 cup of water and puree until very smooth and creamy; add more water if the soup seems too thick. Season with salt and vinegar. Refrigerate the soup until very cold, about 1 hour.
3. Meanwhile, in a medium skillet, heat the remaining 1/4 cup of olive oil. Add the diced bread and cook over moderate heat, stirring, until golden and crisp, about 2 minutes. Using a slotted spoon, transfer the croutons to paper towels and season with salt.
4. Pour the peach soup into shallow bowls and garnish with the sliced cucumber, sliced bell pepper, goat cheese, croutons and basil. Drizzle lightly with olive oil, season with black pepper and serve.

Nutrition Calories: 169 Carbs: 26.5g Fats: 4.7g Proteins: 5.3g Sodium: 262mg Sugar: 2.7g

Chowders Recipes

Manhattan Clam Chowder

Serves: 9/Prep Time: 30 mins

Ingredients

- 1/3 pound bacon, diced
- 4 oz onions, diced
- 2 large garlic cloves, rough chopped
- 10 oz celery root, peeled and diced
- ½ cup dry white wine
- 2 tablespoons tomato paste
- ½ teaspoon dried thyme
- 2 bay leaves
- 4 cups unsalted chicken broth
- 14 oz can whole plum tomatoes and juice
- 20 oz whole baby clams
- 8 oz bottle clam juice
- 6 tablespoons butter
- ¼ cup fresh parsley, chopped
- Salt and black pepper, to taste

Directions

1. Heat butter in a pot and add bacon.
2. Cook for about 6 minutes until crispy, stirring occasionally.
3. Reduce the heat to low and add the garlic, onions and celery root.
4. Sauté for about 3 minutes and pour in the wine, thyme, bay leaves, plum tomatoes, chicken broth, clam juice and tomato paste.
5. Bring to a boil and reduce the heat to simmer for about 15 minutes.
6. Add the clams, parsley, salt and pepper to serve.

Nutrition Calories: 249 Carbs: 8.9g Fats: 16.1g Proteins: 15.6g Sodium: 1071mg Sugar: 2.6g

Chipotle Chicken Chowder

Serves: 8/Prep Time: 35 mins

Ingredients

- 1 medium onion, chopped
- 2 garlic cloves, minced
- 6 bacon slices, chopped
- 4 cups jicama, cubed
- 3 cups chicken stock
- 1 teaspoon salt
- 2 cups heavy cream
- 1 tablespoon olive oil
- 2 tablespoons fresh cilantro, chopped
- 1¼ pounds chicken thighs, boneless, skinless, cut into 1 inch chunks
- ½ teaspoon black pepper
- 1 chipotle pepper in adobo, minced

Directions

1. Heat olive oil over medium heat in a large saucepan and add bacon.
2. Cook until crispy and add onions, garlic and jicama.
3. Cook for about 7 minutes and add chicken stock and chicken.
4. Bring to a boil and reduce temperature to low.
5. Simmer for about 10 minutes and season with salt and black pepper.
6. Add heavy cream and chipotle and simmer for about 5 minutes.
7. Sprinkle with chopped cilantro and dish out into serving bowls.

Nutrition Calories: 350 Carbs: 8.4g Fats: 22.7g Proteins: 27.4g Sodium: 1023mg Sugar: 2g

Smoky Bacon & Turkey Chowder

Serves: 8/Prep Time: 40 mins
Ingredients
- 1 large shallot, peeled and chopped
- 8 cups turkey (or chicken) stock
- ½ cup extra sharp cheddar cheese, shredded
- 8 oz bacon, crumbled
- ½ cup celery, chopped
- ½ cup heavy whipping cream
- 1 cup potatoes, peeled and chopped
- 1 teaspoon dried parsley
- ½ teaspoon liquid smoke
- 1 tablespoon fresh thyme leaves
- 4 cups cooked turkey meat, shredded or chopped
- 1 teaspoon xanthan gum
- 1 tablespoon olive oil
- Salt and black pepper, to taste

Directions
1. Put olive oil, bacon, shallots and celery in a pot and cook for about 5 minutes.
2. Add the turkey stock, cheddar cheese and whipping cream and cook for about 3 minutes.
3. Add the sweet potato, parsley, turkey and liquid smoke and simmer for about 20 minutes.
4. Whisk in the xanthan gum and cook for 5 more minutes.
5. Add fresh thyme, salt and black pepper.
6. Garnish with fresh thyme leaves and serve hot.

Nutrition: Calories: 295 Carbs: 7.4g Fats: 17.3g Proteins: 26.8g Sodium: 1106mg Sugar: 1.1g

Thai Seafood Chowder

Serves: 8/Prep Time: 35 mins
Ingredients
- ¼ cup onions, diced
- 2 celery stalks, chopped
- 3 cups chicken broth
- ½ head cabbage, roughly chopped
- ½ pound raw shrimps, peeled and deveined
- 2 tablespoons avocado oil
- Salt and black pepper, to taste
- 1 jalapeño, seeded and diced
- 2 tablespoons green Thai curry paste
- 1 (15-ounce) can full fat coconut milk
- 1 pound wild pacific cod, cut into 1 inch chunks
- 2 tablespoons fish sauce
- ¼ cup fresh cilantro, chopped
- 2 tablespoons fresh lime juice

Directions
1. Heat oil over medium heat in a large stock pot and add onions, salt and black pepper.
2. Sauté for about 4 minutes and add celery and jalapeño.
3. Cook for about 3 minutes and stir in curry paste for about 30 seconds.
4. Add coconut milk, chicken broth and cabbage and simmer for about 10 minutes.
5. Add shrimp, cod chunks and continue to simmer for 10 more minutes.
6. Remove from heat and stir in lime juice and fish sauce.
7. Top with fresh cilantro and serve.

Nutrition Calories: 206 Carbs: 5.8g Fats: 11.6g Proteins: 18.3g Sodium: 938mg Sugar: 3.1g

Hearty Fish Chowder

Serves: 6/Prep Time: 35 mins

Ingredients

- 4baconslices, chopped
- 1medium onion,chopped
- 3cupsdaikon radish, chopped
- 2½ cups chicken stock
- ½ teaspoon dried thyme
- Salt and black pepper, to taste
- 2cupsheavy cream
- 1pound tilapia, chopped
- 2tablespoonsbutter

Directions

1. Heat butter over medium heat in a large saucepan and add bacon.
2. Cook until crisp and add onions and daikon radish.
3. Cook for about 5 minutes and add chicken stock.
4. Simmer for about 10 minutes and season with thyme, salt and pepper.
5. Add cream and tilapia and simmer for about 4 minutes.
6. Dish out and serve immediately.

Nutrition Calories: 319 Carbs: 4.4g Fats: 24.9g Proteins: 20.6g Sodium: 686mg Sugar: 1.6g

Smoked Salmon Chowder

Serves: 6/Prep Time: 1 hour

Ingredients

- 1 small onion, diced
- 4 garlic cloves, minced
- 4 slicesraw bacon, crumbled
- 1 teaspoon smoked paprika
- 2 cups chicken broth
- 2 celery stalks, diced
- 1bay leaf
- 1 cup squash, cut into ½ inch cubes
- 2½ cups cream, heavy whipping
- 8 ozsmoked salmon, cut into cubes
- Salt and black pepper, to taste

Directions

1. Put chicken stock, celery, onions, bay leaf and garlic in a soup pot and bring to a simmer.
2. Add squash, bell peppers, paprika, salt and black pepper and cook for about 5 minutes.
3. Reduce temperature to low and add cream, salmon and bacon to the chowder.
4. Simmer on low for about 45 minutes and dish out to serve.

Nutrition Calories: 203 Carbs: 6.4g Fats: 13.1g Proteins: 14.6g Sodium: 1343mg Sugar: 3.2g

Lobster Chowder

Serves: 6/Prep Time: 10 mins

Ingredients

- ½ cup onions, chopped
- 2 cups lobster broth
- 3 cups unsweetened almond milk
- 4 strips raw bacon, chopped
- ¼ cup salted butter
- 2 cups raw cauliflower florets
- 2 cups cooked lobster, cut into chunks
- ¼ teaspoon ground black pepper
- ¼ teaspoon garlic powder
- 2 tablespoons apple cider vinegar
- 2 tablespoons fresh parsley, chopped
- 1½ teaspoons kosher salt
- ¼ teaspoon xanthan gum
- 3 tablespoons Cointreau
- 1 tablespoon butter, to finish

Directions

1. Put butter, bacon and onion over low heat in a large pan and cook for about 4 minutes.

3. Add lobster broth and cauliflower, cover and simmer for about 8 minutes.
4. Add almond milk and lobster and cook for about 5 minutes.
5. Remove ½ cup of broth to a small bowl and stir in the xanthan gum.
6. Return it to the chowder and stir in the Cointreau, apple cider vinegar, parsley and 1 tablespoon butter.
7. Dish out and serve hot.

Nutrition Calories: 264 Carbs: 7.5g Fats: 16.1g Proteins: 20.7g Sodium: 1725mg Sugar: 1.6g

Turkey Chowder

Serves: 12/Prep Time: 1 hour 30mins
Ingredients

- ½ cup green onions, sliced into small rounds
- 1 cup celery, diced
- 1 cup cauliflower, broken into small pieces
- ½ cup oat bran
- ½ cup butter
- ½ cup carrots, diced
- 1 cup broccoli, diced
- 2 cups turkey, diced, cooked and smoked
- 1 teaspoon salt
- ½ teaspoon pepper
- 1 tablespoon parsley
- 2 cups heavy cream
- ½ cup frozen corn
- ½ teaspoon thyme
- 4 cups chicken stock
- 1 cup cheddar cheese, shredded

Directions
1. Put butter and vegetables in a pot over medium heat and cook for about 5 minutes.
2. Add the turkey, oat bran and seasonings and cook for about 4 minutes.
3. Add chicken stock and cream and simmer for about 15 minutes.
4. Add the corn and cheese and cook for at least 10 minutes.
5. Dish out and serve hot.

Nutrition: Calories: 236 Carbs: 4.7g Fats: 19.8g Proteins: 10.8g Sodium: 607mg Sugar: 1.4g

Creamy Chicken Bacon Chowder

Serves: 12/Prep Time: 40 mins
Ingredients

- 8ouncefull fat cream cheese
- ½ cup frozen onions
- 6boneless chicken thighs, cubed
- 4teaspoonsgarlic, minced
- 6ounce mushrooms, sliced
- 1teaspoonthyme
- 3cupschicken broth
- 1poundcooked bacon,chopped
- 4tablespoonsbutter
- Salt and black pepper, to taste
- 1cupheavy cream
- 2cupsfresh spinach

Directions
1. Put all the ingredients in a zipper bag except chicken broth, spinach, cream and bacon and zip to seal.
2. Refrigerate for about 2 hours and then, pour into Instant Pot with chicken broth.
3. Cook for about 30 minutes and add spinach and cream.
4. Cover and allow it to sit for 10 minutes.

6. Top with bacon and serve hot.

Nutrition Calories: 330 Carbs: 3.6g Fats: 24.5g Proteins: 23.6g Sodium: 1113mg Sugar: 1.3g

Bay Scallop Chowder

Serves: 6/Prep Time: 35mins

Ingredients
- 1medium onion,chopped
- 2½ cups chicken stock
- 4slicesbacon,chopped
- 3cupschopped daikon radish
- ½ teaspoon dried thyme
- 2cupsheavy cream
- 1tablespoonbutter
- Salt and black pepper, to taste
- 1pound bay scallops

Directions
1. Heat butter over medium heat in a large saucepan and add bacon.
2. Cook until crisp and add onions and daikon radish.
3. Cook for about 5 minutes and add chicken stock.
4. Simmer for about 8 minutes and season with thyme, salt and pepper.
5. Add heavy cream and bay scallops and simmer for about 4 minutes.
6. Dish out and serve immediately.

Nutrition Calories: 307 Carbs: 6.2g Fats: 22.8g Proteins: 19.2g Sodium: 767mg Sugar: 1.6g

Stew Recipes

Brazilian Shrimp Stew

Serves: 6/Prep Time: 25 mins

Ingredients
- 1 garlic clove, minced
- ¼ cup onions, diced
- ¼ cup olive oil
- 1½ pounds raw shrimp, peeled & deveined
- ¼ cup red pepper, roasted and diced
- 1 (14 oz) can diced tomatoes with chilies
- 2 tablespoons lemon juice
- 2 tablespoons Sriracha hot sauce
- 1 cup coconut milk
- ¼ cup fresh cilantro, chopped
- Salt and black pepper, to taste

Directions
1. Heat olive oil in a medium saucepan and add garlic and onions.
2. Sauté for about 3 minutes and add peppers, tomatoes, shrimp and cilantro.
3. Simmer for about 5 minutes and add coconut milk and Sriracha sauce.
4. Cook for about 5 minutes and stir in lime juice, salt and black pepper.
5. Garnish with fresh cilantro and serve hot.

Nutrition Calories: 316 Carbs: 7.4g Fats: 19.9g Proteins: 26.9g Sodium: 593mg Sugar: 3.7g

Southwestern Pork Stew

Serves: 8/Prep Time: 8 hours 10 mins

Ingredients

- 2½ pounds boneless pork chops
- 1 (14-ounce) can diced tomatoes
- 4 cups chicken broth
- 2 garlic cloves
- 1½ teaspoons dried oregano
- ½ teaspoon cumin
- 2 tablespoons butter
- 1½ cups rutabaga, peeled and cubed
- ½ cup onions, chopped
- 1 tablespoon chili powder
- 1 teaspoon kosher salt
- ½ teaspoon black pepper
- 3 tablespoons lemon juice

Directions

1. Mix together all the ingredients in a large slow cooker and stir well.
2. Cook on LOW for about 8 hours and dish out the pork.
3. Shred with fork and return to the pot.
4. Squeeze lime and serve hot.

Nutrition Calories: 276 Carbs: 6.4g Fats: 9g Proteins: 40.7g Sodium: 793mg Sugar: 3.6g

Thai Pumpkin Seafood Stew

Serves: 12/Prep Time: 45 mins

Ingredients

- 1½ tablespoons fresh galangal, roughly chopped
- 1 teaspoon lime zest
- 1 small kabocha squash
- 32 medium-sized mussels, fresh and alive
- 1 pound shrimp
- 16 leaves Thai basil
- 1 (13.5-ounce) can coconut milk
- 1 tablespoon lemongrass, minced
- 4 garlic cloves, roughly chopped
- 32 medium-sized clams, fresh and alive
- 1½ pounds fresh salmon
- 2 tablespoons coconut oil
- Salt and black pepper, to taste

Directions

1. Add coconut milk, lemongrass, galangal, garlic and lime leaves in a small saucepan, and bring to a boil.
2. Allow to simmer for about 25 minutes, stirring occasionally.
3. Strain this mixture through a fine sieve into a large soup pot and bring to a simmer.
4. Meanwhile, heat oil in a pan and add kabocha squash.
5. Season with a bit of salt and pepper and sauté for about 5 minutes.
6. Add this mixture to the coconut milk mixture.
7. Heat oil again in a pan and add fish and shrimp.
8. Season with salt and pepper and sauté for about 4 minutes.
9. Throw this mixture into the coconut milk mixture along with clams and mussels.
10. Simmer for about 8 minutes and garnish with Thai basil to serve.

Nutrition Calories: 389 Carbs: 9.7g Fats: 16.8g Proteins: 48.8g Sodium: 346mg Sugar: 1.4g

Bacon Cabbage Chuck Beef Stew

Serves: 6/Prep Time: 7 hours 10 mins

Ingredients

- ½ pound bacon strips
- 2 pounds grass-fed chuck roast, cut in 2" pieces

- 2 small red onions, peeled and sliced
- 1 garlic clove, minced
- 1 small Napa cabbage
- Salt and black pepper, to taste
- 1 sprig fresh thyme
- 1 cup homemade beef bone broth

Directions
1. Put bacon slices, onion slices and garlic at the bottom of the slow cooker.
2. Layer with the chuck roast, followed by the cabbage slices, thyme and broth.
3. Season with salt and black pepper, and cook on LOW for 7 hours.
4. Dish out and serve hot.

Nutrition Calories: 170 Carbs: 3.7g Fats: 9g Proteins: 19.6g Sodium: 164mg Sugar: 1.2g

Italian Beef Stew with Zucchini, Mushrooms, And Basil

Serves: 8/Prep Time: 1 hour 40 mins
Ingredients
- 5 teaspoons olive oil
- 2 cans (14 oz.) beef broth
- 2 pounds chuck roast, cut into cubes larger than 1 inch
- Salt and black pepper, to taste
- 2 cans (14.5 oz.) diced tomatoes with juice
- 1 tablespoon Italian Herb Blend
- 1 large onion, chopped into ½ inch dice
- ½ pound mushrooms, cut into thick slices
- 1 teaspoon ground fennel seed
- 2 small zucchini, cut into thick slices
- 4 tablespoons fresh basil, chopped

Directions
1. Heat olive oil in a large non-stick pan over medium-high heat and add onions, green peppers and beef cubes.
2. Brown beef on all sides for about 10 minutes and season with salt and black pepper.
3. Add the browned meat mixture to the stew pot along with beef broth, Italian Herb Blend, diced tomatoes with juice and ground fennel.
4. Heat oil again in a non-stick pan and add zucchini and mushroom slices.
5. Cook for about 5 minutes and add to the stew pot.
6. Simmer for about 1 hour and add the chopped basil.
7. Simmer for about 15 more minutes and dish out to serve.

Nutrition Calories: 318 Carbs: 5g Fats: 13.5g Proteins: 42.3g Sodium: 589mg Sugar: 2.4g

Mexico Green Chile Pork Stew

Serves: 8/Prep Time: 1 hour 45 mins
Ingredients
- 2teaspoonsground cumin
- 1teaspoonchili powder
- 2poundspork loin, cubed
- 2teaspoons garlic powder
- ½ cup onions, chopped
- 1can(27 ounce) whole Hatch green chilies and liquid
- 2cupswater
- 2garlic cloves
- 3tablespoons olive oil

Directions
1. Put onions, garlic and green chilies in a blender and blend to make a paste.
2. Heat oil in a pan and add cubed pork loin and onion paste.
3. Sauté for about 8 minutes and add cumin, chili powder and garlic powder.
4. Sauté for about 1 minute and add water.

6. Reduce heat to low and simmer for about 1 hour 30 minutes.
7. Dish out in a bowl and serve hot.

Nutrition Calories: 329 Carbs: 1.9g Fats: 21.3g Proteins: 31.3g Sodium: 176mg Sugar: 0.6g

Mediterranean Beef Stew with Rosemary and Balsamic Vinegar

Serves: 8/Prep Time: 8 hours 20 mins

Ingredients

- 8 oz. mushrooms, sliced
- 2 pounds chuck steak, cut in bite-sized pieces
- 1 can (14.5 oz.) diced tomatoes with juice
- 2 tablespoons olive oil
- 1 onion, diced in ½ inch pieces
- 1 cup beef stock
- ½ cup tomato sauce
- 1 can black olives, cut in half
- 2 tablespoons fresh rosemary, finely chopped
- 1 tablespoon capers
- ¼ cup balsamic vinegar
- ½ cup garlic cloves, thinly sliced
- 2 tablespoons fresh parsley, finely chopped
- Salt and black pepper, to taste

Directions

1. Heat olive oil in a frying pan over medium-high heat and add onions and mushrooms.
2. Cook for about 5 minutes and transfer into a slow cooker.
3. Add a little more oil and add beef.
4. Cook for about 10 minutes until brown and transfer into a slow cooker along with diced tomatoes and juice, beef stock, tomato sauce, olives, garlic, balsamic vinegar, rosemary, capers, parsley, salt and black pepper.
5. Stir well and cook, covered for about 8 hours on LOW.
6. Dish out and serve hot.

Nutrition Calories: 357 Carbs: 7g Fats: 19.4g Proteins: 37.5g Sodium: 350mg Sugar: 1.9g

Belizean Stewed Chicken

Serves: 6/Prep Time: 40 mins

Ingredients

- 2 tablespoons white vinegar
- 2 tablespoons recadorojo seasoning
- 1 tablespoon coconut oil
- 4 whole chicken legs
- 3 tablespoons Worcestershire sauce
- 1 teaspoon dried oregano
- 1 tablespoon erythritol
- 1 teaspoon ground cumin
- ½ cup cilantro
- 2 cups chicken stock
- 3 garlic cloves
- 1 cup yellow onions, sliced
- ½ teaspoon black pepper

Directions

1. Mix together the vinegar, recadorojo paste, Worcestershire sauce, oregano, cumin, erythritol and pepper in a large bowl.
2. Add chicken pieces and rub the marinade into it.
3. Marinate overnight and transfer into an Instant Pot.
4. Select "Sauté" and add coconut oil and chicken.
5. Sauté for about 2 minutes per side and dish out.
6. Add garlic and onions and sauté for about 3 minutes.

8. Return chicken pieces to the Instant Pot and stir in broth.
9. Lock the lid and set to "Manual" at high pressure for about 20 minutes.
10. Release the pressure naturally and garnish with cilantro to serve.

Nutrition Calories: 184 Carbs: 7g Fats: 11.9g Proteins: 14.7g Sodium: 526mg Sugar: 5.1g

Garlic Beef Stew with Olives, Capers and Tomatoes

Serves: 10/Prep Time: 4 hours 30 mins
Ingredients
- 1 cup garlic cloves, peeled
- 1 can (14.5 oz.) diced tomatoes with juice
- 2 tablespoons olive oil
- 3 bay leaves
- 2 tablespoons tomato paste
- 2 pounds beef chuck roast, cut into 1 inch pieces
- 1 cup Kalamata olives, cut in half lengthwise
- 1 teaspoon dried Greek oregano
- 3 tablespoons red wine vinegar
- 1 cup low-sodium beef broth
- 2 tablespoons capers, rinsed
- 1 small can (8 oz.) tomato sauce
- Black pepper, to taste

Directions
1. Heat 1 tablespoon olive oil in a heavy frying pan over medium-high heat and add beef cubes.
2. Cook for about 6 minutes and transfer into crockpot.
3. Heat more oil and add garlic and Kalamata olives.
4. Sauté for about 2 minutes and transfer into crockpot.
5. Add beef broth, bay leaves, oregano, capers, canned tomatoes and juice, red wine vinegar, tomato sauce, tomato paste and black pepper to the crockpot.
6. Cook for about 4 hours on HIGH and dish out to serve hot.

Nutrition Calories: 398 Carbs: 6.8g Fats: 29.6g Proteins: 25.3g Sodium: 311mg Sugar: 0.8g

Kimchi Beef Stew

Serves: 6/Prep Time: 40 mins
Ingredients
- 1poundbeef cubes, cut into 2 inch pieces
- 1cup mushrooms
- 2cupsKimchi
- 1cup onions, chopped
- 1tablespoon garlic, minced
- 1tablespoon sesame oil
- 1tablespoon dark soy sauce
- 1tablespoongochujang
- 2cupswater
- ½ cup green onions, diced
- 1tablespoon ginger, minced
- ½ teaspoon cayenne pepper
- ¼ teaspoon Splenda
- Salt, to taste

Directions
1. Put all the ingredients in an Instant Pot and lock the lid.
2. Set to "Manual" at high pressure for about 15 minutes.
3. Release the pressure naturally and dish out to serve hot.

Nutrition Calories: 157 Carbs: 6.1g Fats: 6.4g Proteins: 17.8g Sodium: 327mg Sugar: 2.4g

Southwestern Beef Stew with Tomatoes, Olives and Chiles

Serves: 6/Prep Time: 8 hours 30 mins

Ingredients

- 2 teaspoons olive oil
- 1 cup beef broth
- 2 teaspoons ground cumin
- 2 pounds lean beef cubes, cut into inch square
- 1 large onion, chopped
- 1 cup salsa
- 1 teaspoon Mexican oregano
- 1 can olives, drained and cut in half
- 1 tomato, crushed
- Sour cream, for serving limes
- 1 tablespoon garlic, crushed
- 1 can (4 oz.) diced green chiles
- Fresh lime slices, to squeeze

Directions

1. Heat the olive oil in a large heavy frying pan and add beef.
2. Sauté for about 10 minutes and add beef broth.
3. Cook for about 5 minutes and transfer to the slow cooker along with onions, cumin, salsa, garlic and Mexican oregano.
4. Cook on LOW for about 7 hours and add olives, crushed tomatoes and green chiles.
5. Cook for about 1 more hour and top with fresh lime slices.
6. Dish out to serve hot.

Nutrition: Calories: 320 Carbs: 8.2g Fats: 10.3g Proteins: 46.6g Sodium: 588mg Sugar: 3.3g

Herb Chicken and Mushroom Stew

Serves: 6/Prep Time: 4 hours 10 mins

Ingredients

- 1 pound raw chicken tenders
- ½ teaspoon dried basil
- 24 ounces whole white button mushrooms
- 3 garlic cloves
- ½ teaspoon dried oregano
- 2 bay leaves
- Salt and black pepper, to taste
- ¼ cup heavy whipping cream
- ¼ cup fresh parsley, chopped
- ¼ teaspoon dried thyme
- 1 cup chicken broth
- 2 tablespoons butter
- 8 slices bacon, cooked and chopped

Directions

1. Put the garlic, mushrooms, chicken, oregano, basil, thyme, chicken broth and bay leaves into the slow cooker.
2. Cook, covered for about 4 hours on LOW.
3. Stir in butter and heavy whipping cream.
4. Top with crumbled bacon and parsley to serve.

Nutrition Calories: 369 Carbs: 5.6g Fats: 22.2g Proteins: 36.4g Sodium: 828mg Sugar: 0.2g

West African Chicken and Peanut Stew with Chiles, Ginger, And Green Onions

Serves: 6/Prep Time: 30 mins

Ingredients

- ¼ cup red onion, finely diced
- 2 teaspoons jalapeno, finely minced
- 2 tablespoons olive oil
- 1 tablespoon ginger root, finely minced
- Salt and black pepper, to taste
- 1 cup chicken stock

- 2 tablespoons tomato paste
- 3 cups chicken, cooked and diced
- 3 green onions, thinly sliced
- 1 teaspoon chili powder
- ½ cup chunky peanut butter
- 1 tablespoon cider vinegar

Directions
1. Heat olive oil in a heavy pan and add ginger, red onions and jalapenos.
2. Season with salt and chili powder and sauté for about 2 minutes.
3. Stir in peanut butter, chicken stock, tomato paste, apple cider vinegar and tomato paste.
4. Bring to a boil and add chicken.
5. Simmer for about 15 minutes and dish out.
6. Garnish with green onions and serve.

Nutrition Calories: 285 Carbs: 7.2g Fats: 17.7g Proteins: 26.1g Sodium: 287mg Sugar: 3g

Hearty Crock Pot Chicken Stew

Serves: 9/Prep Time: 6 hours 10 mins
Ingredients
- 1 medium green pepper
- 1½ cups tomato sauce
- 3 pounds chicken thighs, boneless and skinless
- 3 cups mushrooms
- ½ cup tomatoes, sliced
- 1/3 cup hot wing sauce
- 2 teaspoons ranch seasoning
- 2 teaspoons paprika
- 1 teaspoon oregano
- 3 tablespoons butter
- 2 teaspoons garlic, minced
- 1 teaspoon red pepper flakes

Directions
1. Mix together garlic, chicken thighs, tomatoes, peppers, mushrooms, tomato sauce, hot sauce and spices.
2. Add into the crock pot and cook on LOW for about 5 hours.
3. Add butter and cook for 1 more hour.
4. Dish out and serve hot.

Nutrition Calories: 346 Carbs: 4.7g Fats: 15.3g Proteins: 45.4g Sodium: 441mg Sugar: 2.8g

Beef Chuck Roast Stew

Serves: 8/Prep Time: 2 hours 45 mins
Ingredients
- 8 ounces whole mushrooms, quartered
- 4 ounces onions, trimmed and peeled
- 30 ounces carrots, roll-cut
- 2 tablespoons tomato paste
- 1 large bay leaf
- Salt and black pepper, to taste
- 1¼ pounds beef chuck roast, cubed into 1 inch pieces
- 6 ounces celery root, peeled and cubed into ¾ inch pieces
- 2 celery sticks, sliced
- 2 garlic cloves, sliced
- 2 tablespoons olive oil
- 5 cups beef broth
- ½ teaspoon dried thyme

Directions
1. Heat 1 tablespoon of oil in a heavy bottomed pot over medium heat and add mushrooms.
2. Sauté for about 2 minutes and mix in a bowl with other vegetables.
3. Heat 1 tablespoon of oil in the pot and brown the beef in batches.

5. Stir in the tomato paste, bay leaf and thyme and cook for about 2 minutes.
6. Add broth and reduce the heat to low.
7. Simmer gently for about 1½ hours and add the vegetables.
8. Simmer for about 1 hour and season with salt and pepper.

Nutrition Calories: 343 Carbs: 7.4g Fats: 24.3g Proteins: 23.4g Sodium: 565mg Sugar: 3g

Easy Crockpot Chicken Stew

Serves: 6/Prep Time: 2 hours 5mins
Ingredients

- 2 cups chicken stock
- ½ cup carrots, peeled and finely diced
- 2 celery sticks, diced
- ½ onion, diced
- 28 ounces skinless and deboned chicken thighs, diced into 1" pieces
- ½ teaspoon dried rosemary
- 3 garlic cloves, minced
- ¼ teaspoon dried thyme
- ½ teaspoon dried oregano
- 1 cup fresh spinach
- ½ cup heavy cream
- Salt and black pepper, to taste
- ½ teaspoon xanthan gum

Directions

1. Place the onions, chicken thighs, carrots, chicken stock, celery, garlic, rosemary, oregano and thyme into a crockpot.
2. Cook on LOW for about 4 hours and season with salt and pepper.
3. Stir in the heavy cream, spinach and xanthan gum.
4. Cook for another 10 minutes, while stirring continuously.
5. Dish out and serve hot.

Nutrition Calories: 239 Carbs: 4.6g Fats: 15.6g Proteins: 23.2g Sodium: 401mg Sugar: 1.3g

Coffee and Wine Beef Stew

Serves: 9/Prep Time: 10 mins
Ingredients

- 3 cups coffee
- 1½ cups baby bella mushrooms, sliced
- 3 tablespoons coconut oil
- 2½ pounds stew meat, cubed
- 1 cup beef stock
- 2/3 cup red wine
- 1 medium onion, sliced
- 2 tablespoons capers
- 1 teaspoon salt
- 2 teaspoons garlic
- 1 teaspoon black pepper

Directions

1. Season beef with salt and black pepper.
2. Heat coconut oil in a pan and add garlic, onions and mushrooms.
3. Sauté for about 3 minutes and add seasoned beef.
4. Brown the beef on all sides and add beef stock, red wine, capers and coffee.
5. Bring to a boil and reduce heat to low.
6. Cook, covered for about 3 hours and dish out to serve.

Nutrition Calories: 383 Carbs: 2.8g Fats: 21.2g Proteins: 40.2g Sodium: 497mg Sugar: 0.9g

Beef Vegetables Keto Stew

Serves: 6/Prep Time: 10 mins
Ingredients
- 2cupsbeef broth
- 100gramonions
- 100gramradishes
- 1poundbeef short rib
- 4cloves garlic, minced
- 100gramcarrots
- ¼ teaspoon pink salt
- ½ teaspoon xanthan gum
- 1tablespooncoconut oil
- ¼ teaspoon pepper
- 1tablespoonbutter

Directions
1. Heat coconut oil on medium-high heat in a large saucepan and add beef short rib.
2. Cook for about 4 minutes until brown on all sides and add onions, garlic and butter.
3. Cook for about 3 minutes and add the broth and xanthan gum.
4. Bring to a boil and simmer for about 30 minutes.
5. Add the carrots and radishes and cook for 30 more minutes, stirring repeatedly.
6. Dish out and serve hot.

Nutrition Calories: 224 Carbs: 5.8g Fats: 11.5g Proteins: 24.1g Sodium: 366mg Sugar: 2.1g

Spicy Crockpot Double Beef Stew

Serves: 6/Prep Time: 6 hours 10 mins
Ingredients
- 1(14.5 oz) can chili-ready diced tomatoes
- 1½ pounds Stew beef
- 1 tablespoon chili mix
- 2 teaspoons hot sauce
- Salt, to taste
- 1 cup beef broth
- 1 tablespoon Worcestershire sauce

Directions
1. Put all the ingredients in crockpot and mix well.
2. Cook for about 6 hours on HIGH and break up meat with a fork.
3. Season with more salt if needed and cook for about 2 hours on LOW.
4. Dish out and serve hot.

Nutrition Calories: 197 Carbs: 5.6g Fats: 7.1g Proteins: 26.5g Sodium: 425mg Sugar: 4.2g

Beef Stew with Herby Dumplings

Serves: 8/Prep Time: 4 hours
Ingredients
- 1 carrot
- 1 red onion, chopped
- 3 bay leaves
- 2 tablespoons olive oil
- 2 pounds stew beef
- 100 g pumpkin
- 2 cloves garlic, minced
- ½ cup dry red wine
- 3 sprigs of fresh rosemary
- ¼ teaspoon black pepper
- ¾ teaspoon sea salt
- 2 tablespoons tomato puree
- 2 cups beef stock

Dumplings:
- 1 cup water, boiling
- ¾ cup almond flour

- 1½ teaspoons gluten-free baking powder
- 1 teaspoon fresh lemon zest
- 1 large egg
- 3 large egg whites
- ¼ cup coconut flour
- 1 tablespoon chopped rosemary
- 1/3 cup sesame seed flour
- ¼ teaspoon sea salt
- 1 pinch black pepper
- Fresh parsley, for topping
- 1 tablespoon psyllium husk powder
- 1 tablespoon fresh thyme

Directions
1. Preheat the oven to 320 °F.
2. Heat 1 tablespoon of olive oil in a pan and add meat.
3. Cook for about 5 minutes on a medium heat until brown.
4. Heat 1 tablespoon of olive oil in a pan and add vegetables.
5. Cook for about 10 minutes on a medium heat and add rosemary, beef, bay leaves, garlic and tomato puree.
6. Sauté for about 2 minutes and add the red wine.
7. Reduce the heat to low and simmer for about 5 minutes.
8. Add the stock and season with salt and black pepper.
9. Bring to a boil and transfer into a casserole dish.
10. Place in the oven and roast for about 3 hours.
11. Dish out and change the temperature to about 350 °F.
12. Mix together all the ingredients for dumplings and make dumplings shape out of this mixture.
13. Grease cupcake tins with olive oil and place dumplings in the cupcake holes.
14. Transfer in the oven and bake for about 25 minutes.
15. Flip with a spoon and place back in the oven to cook for another 5 minutes.
16. Add the dumplings to the stew and serve.

Nutrition Calories: 333 Carbs: 9.9g Fats: 17.1g Proteins: 31.6g Sodium: 612mg Sugar: 1.6g

Beef Stew with Bone Marrow

Serves: 15/Prep Time: 3 hours 30 mins
Ingredients
- 3medium carrots
- 5poundsbeef shank
- 8Campari tomatoes
- 8 garliccloves
- 1quartchicken broth
- ¼ cup tomato sauce
- 2medium onions
- 2cupswater
- 2tablespoonsapple cider vinegar

Spices
- 3teaspoonscrushed red pepper
- 2teaspoonsbasil
- 4teaspoonssalt
- 3whole bay leaves
- 2teaspoons parsley
- 2teaspoonsgarlic powder
- 1teaspooncayenne
- 2teaspoonsonion powder
- 2teaspoonsblack pepper

Directions
1. Heat oil in a soup pot and add onions, garlic and carrots.
2. Sauté for about 3 minutes and add beef shanks.
3. Brown on all sides and add chicken broth, water and apple cider vinegar.

5. Cook for about 5 minutes and add tomatoes, tomato sauce and spices.
6. Stir well and reduce heat to low.
7. Simmer for about 3 hours so that the bone marrow turns grey and mixed in the stew.
8. Remove bay leaves and dish out to serve hot.

Nutrition Calories: 314 Carbs: 5.4g Fats: 9.9g Proteins: 48g Sodium: 957mg Sugar: 2.1g

Keto Chicken Curry Stew

Serves: 8/Prep Time: 10 mins
Ingredients
- 2 tables poonscurry powder
- ¼ cup coconut oil
- 1green bell pepper
- 1.5 pounds boneless chicken thighs
- 2 teaspoons garlic powder
- 1 pound cauliflower
- 14 oz.coconut milk
- ¼ cup fresh cilantro
- Salt and black pepper, to taste

Directions
1. Heat coconut oil in a wok pan and add curry powder and garlic powder.
2. Sauté for about 1 minute and add chicken, salt and black pepper.
3. Sauté for about 5 minutes and dish out the chicken mixture.
4. Add cauliflowers and bell peppers to the same wok pan and cook for about 3 minutes.
5. Add coconut milk and simmer for about 10 minutes.
6. Season with salt and black pepper and add fried chicken to the stew.
7. Garnish with fresh cilantro and serve hot.

Nutrition Calories: 314 Carbs: 8.4g Fats: 23.9g Proteins: 19.5g Sodium: 99mg Sugar: 4g
Per serving

Low Carb Lamb Stew

Serves: 3/Prep Time: 6 hours 15 mins
Ingredients
- 8ozturnips,peeled and chopped
- 14ozcan of beef broth
- 1teaspoongarlic paste
- 1poundboneless lamb stewing meat
- 8ozmushrooms,sliced or quartered
- 1teaspoononion powder
- Salt and black pepper, to taste
- ¼ cup fresh flat-leaf parsley, chopped

Directions
1. Put turnips, mushrooms, lamb, beef broth, garlic paste, onion powder, salt and black pepper in a slow cooker.
2. Cook on LOW for about 6 hours and dish out.
3. Garnish with fresh flat-leaf parsley and serve.

Nutrition Calories: 360 Carbs: 8.7g Fats: 20.7g Proteins: 33g Sodium: 597mg Sugar: 4.5g

Leftover Turkey Stew

Serves: 12/Prep Time: 35 mins
Ingredients
- 2 cups turkey, cooked and cubed
- 3 tablespoons butter
- 15 ounce can mixed vegetables
- 14 ounce can chicken broth

Directions

1. Put all the ingredients in a large sauce pan and bring to a boil.
2. Reduce heat to low and simmer for about 25 minutes.
3. Dish out and serve hot.

Nutrition Calories: 143 Carbs: 3.5g Fats: 6.8g Proteins: 16.2g Sodium: 134mg Sugar: 0.9g

Spicy Pork Stew with Spinach

Serves: 4/Prep Time: 45 mins

Ingredients

- 4garlic cloves
- 1largeonion
- 1teaspoondried thyme
- 1poundpork butt meat,cut into 2 inch chunks
- 4cups baby spinach, chopped
- 2teaspoons Cajun seasoning blend
- ½ cup heavy whipping cream

Directions

1. Blend together onions and garlic and put into the pressure cooker.
2. Add Cajun Seasoning blend and pork and lock the lid.
3. Cook for about 20 minutes at high pressure.
4. Release the pressure naturally for about 10 minutes and add baby spinach and cream.
5. Select "Sauté" and cook for about 5 minutes.
6. Dish out and serve hot.

Nutrition Calories: 376 Carbs: 6.2g Fats: 24.7g Proteins: 31.5g Sodium: 140mg Sugar: 1.8g

Desserts Recipes

Chocolate Hazelnut Cookies

Serves: 2/Prep Time: 10 mins

Ingredients

- ¾ cup chocolate hazelnut
- ¼ cup coconut flour
- ¼ cup monk fruit
- 1 tablespoon cream
- 1/3 cup hazelnuts, crushed

Directions

1. Mix together all the ingredients in a large mixing bowl except hazelnuts until a dough is formed.
2. Make small balls out of this mixture and keep aside.
3. Put hazelnuts in another bowl and roll the balls in it.
4. Press each ball into a cookie shape and refrigerate until set to serve.

Nutrition Calories: 214 Carbs: 13.2g Fats: 13g Proteins: 5.4g Sodium: 2mg Sugar: 1g

Keto Mug Cake

Serves: 2/Prep Time: 25 mins

Ingredients

- 2 tablespoons + 4 teaspoons cocoa powder
- 12 tablespoons almond flour
- 2 tablespoons stevia
- ½ teaspoon baking powder
- ½ teaspoon pure vanilla extract
- ¼ teaspoon salt
- 6 tablespoons almond milk

Directions

1. Preheat the oven to 350 degrees F and grease 2 ramekins.
2. Mix together all the ingredients and pour into ramekins.
3. Transfer the ramekins in the oven and bake for about 10 minutes.
4. Remove from the oven and serve.

Nutrition Calories: 372 Carbs: 15.1g Fats: 31.4g Proteins: 11.1g Sodium: 315mg Sugar: 1.7g

Peppermint Hemp Fat Fudge

Serves: 2/Prep Time: 30 mins

Ingredients

- ¼ cup stevia-sweetened dark chocolate chips, melted
- ¼ cup coconut oil, melted
- 1/8 cup Manitoba Harvest Hemp Hearts, soaked overnight, strained and rinsed
- 4 drops vanilla extract
- ¼ teaspoon peppermint extract
- 1 pinch salt

Directions

1. Place a silicone mould with rectangular cavities on a baking sheet and keep aside.
2. Put all the ingredients in the blender and blend until smooth.
3. Transfer the mixture into prepared mould and refrigerate for about 20 minutes.
4. Dish out and serve.

Nutrition Calories: 387 Carbs: 12.1g Fats: 35.6g Proteins: 4.3g Sodium: 78mg Sugar: 9.1g

Chocolate Coconut Crack Bars

Serves: 2/Prep Time: 25 mins

Ingredients

- ¼ cup coconut oil, melted
- ¾ cup unsweetened coconut flakes, shredded
- 1/8 cup monk fruit sweetened maple syrup
- ½ cup chocolate chips

Directions

1. Line a loaf pan with parchment paper and keep aside.
2. Mix together all the ingredients except chocolate chips in a large mixing bowl and transfer into the loaf pan.
3. Refrigerate for about 1 hour until firm and remove to cut into bars.
4. Melt chocolate chips and dip each coconut bar in the melted chocolate until evenly coated.
5. Refrigerate for 1 more hour and serve chilled.

Nutrition Calories: 540 Carbs: 14g Fats: 52.3g Proteins: 5.5g Sodium: 10mg Sugar: 0g

Keto Ice Cream

Serves: 2/Prep Time: 25 mins

Ingredients
- 2 tablespoons erythritol
- 1 cup full-fat coconut milk
- 2 pinches salt
- ¾ teaspoon pure vanilla extract

Directions
1. Mix together the milk, erythritol, salt and vanilla extract in a bowl.
2. Transfer the mixture in ice cube trays and blend the frozen cubes in a high-speed blender.
3. Freeze for an hour and serve.

Nutrition Calories: 245 Carbs: 19.2g Fats: 24g Proteins: 2g Sodium: 185mg Sugar: 17.2g

Air Fryer Breakfast Recipes

Ham, Spinach & Egg in a Cup

Serves: 8/Prep Time: 35 mins

Ingredients
- 2 tablespoons olive oil
- 2 tablespoons unsalted butter, melted
- 2 pounds fresh baby spinach
- 8 eggs
- 8 teaspoons milk
- 14-ounce ham, sliced
- Salt and black pepper, to taste

Directions
1. Preheat the Airfryer to 360 degrees F and grease 8 ramekins with butter.
2. Heat oil in a skillet on medium heat and add spinach.
3. Cook for about 3 minutes and drain the liquid completely from the spinach.
4. Divide the spinach into prepared ramekins and layer with ham slices.
5. Crack 1 egg over ham slices into each ramekin and drizzle evenly with milk.
6. Sprinkle with salt and black pepper and bake for about 20 minutes.

Nutrition: Calories: 228 Carbs: 6.6g Fats: 15.6g Proteins: 17.2g Sodium: 821mg Sugar: 1.1g

Eggs with Sausage & Bacon

Serves: 2/Prep Time: 25 mins

Ingredients
- 4 chicken sausages
- 4 bacon slices
- 2 eggs
- Salt and freshly ground black pepper, to taste

Directions
1. Preheat the Airfryer to 330 degrees F and place sausages and bacon slices in an Airfryer basket.
2. Cook for about 10 minutes and lightly grease 2 ramekins.
3. Crack 1 egg in each prepared ramekin and season with salt and black pepper.
4. Cook for about 10 minutes and divide sausages and bacon slices in serving plates.

Nutrition Calories: 245 Carbs: 5.7g Fats: 15.8g Proteins: 17.8g Sodium: 480mg Sugar: 0.7g

Tropical Almond Pancakes

Serves: 8/Prep Time: 15 mins
Ingredients
- 2 cups creamy milk
- 3½ cups almond flour
- 1 teaspoon baking soda
- ½ teaspoon salt
- 1 teaspoon allspice
- 2 tablespoons vanilla
- 1 teaspoon cinnamon
- 1 teaspoon baking powder
- ½ cup club soda

Directions
1. Preheat the Air fryer at 290 degrees F and grease the cooking basket of the air fryer.
2. Whisk together salt, almond flour, baking soda, allspice and cinnamon in a large bowl.
3. Mix together the vanilla, baking powder and club soda and add to the flour mixture.
4. Stir the mixture thoroughly and pour the mixture into the cooking basket.
5. Cook for about 10 minutes and dish out in a serving platter.

Nutrition: Calories: 324 Carbs: 12.8g Fats: 24.5g Proteins: 11.4g Sodium: 342mg Sugar: 1.6g

Bacon & Hot Dogs Omelet

Serves: 4/Prep Time: 15 mins
Ingredients
- 4 hot dogs, chopped
- 8 eggs
- 2 bacon slices, chopped
- 4 small onions, chopped

Directions
1. Preheat the Airfryer to 325 degrees F.
2. Crack the eggs in an Airfryer baking pan and beat well.
3. Stir in the remaining ingredients and cook for about 10 minutes until completely done.

Nutrition Calories: 298 Carbs: 9g Fats: 21.8g Proteins: 16.9g Sodium: 628mg Sugar: 5.1g

Toasted Bagels

Serves: 6/Prep Time: 10 mins
Ingredients
- 6 teaspoons butter
- 3 bagels, halved

Directions
1. Preheat the Airfryer to 375 degrees F and arrange the bagels into an Airfryer basket.
2. Cook for about 3 minutes and remove the bagels from Airfryer.
3. Spread butter evenly over bagels and cook for about 3 more minutes.

Nutrition Calories: 169 Carbs: 26.5g Fats: 4.7g Proteins: 5.3g Sodium: 262mg Sugar: 2.7g

Eggless Spinach & Bacon Quiche

Serves: 8/Prep Time: 20 mins

Ingredients

- 1 cup fresh spinach, chopped
- 4 slices of bacon, cooked and chopped
- ½ cup mozzarella cheese, shredded
- 4 tablespoons milk
- 4 dashes Tabasco sauce
- 1 cup Parmesan cheese, shredded
- Salt and freshly ground black pepper, to taste

Directions

1. Preheat the Airfryer to 325 degrees F and grease a baking dish.
2. Put all the ingredients in a bowl and mix well.
3. Transfer the mixture into prepared baking dish and cook for about 8 minutes.
4. Dish out and serve.

Nutrition Calories: 72 Carbs: 0.9g Fats: 5.2g Proteins: 5.5g Sodium: 271mg Sugar: 0.4g

Ham Casserole

Serves: 4/Prep Time: 25 mins

Ingredients

- 4-ounce ham, sliced thinly
- 4 teaspoons unsalted butter, softened
- 8 large eggs, divided
- 4 tablespoons heavy cream
- ¼ teaspoon smoked paprika
- 4 teaspoons fresh chives, minced
- Salt and freshly ground black pepper, to taste
- 6 tablespoons Parmesan cheese, grated finely

Directions

1. Preheat the Airfryer to 325 degrees F and spread butter in the pie pan.
2. Place ham slices in the bottom of the pie pan.
3. Whisk together 2 eggs, cream, salt and black pepper until smooth.
4. Place the egg mixture evenly over the ham slices and crack the remaining eggs on top.
5. Season with paprika, salt and black pepper.
6. Top evenly with chives and cheese and place the pie pan in an Airfryer.
7. Cook for about 12 minutes and serve with toasted bread slices.

Nutrition: Calories: 410 Carbs: 3.9g Fats: 30.8g Proteins: 31.2g Sodium: 933mg Sugar: 0.8g

Sausage & Bacon with Beans

Serves: 12/Prep Time: 30 mins

Ingredients

- 12 medium sausages
- 12 bacon slices
- 8 eggs
- 2 cans baked beans
- 12 bread slices, toasted

Directions

1. Preheat the Airfryer at 325 degrees F and place sausages and bacon in a fryer basket.
2. Cook for about 10 minutes and place the baked beans in a ramekin.
3. Place eggs in another ramekin and the Airfryer to 395 degrees F.
4. Cook for about 10 more minutes and divide the sausage mixture, beans and eggs in serving plates
5. Serve with bread slices.

Nutrition Calories: 276 Carbs: 14.1g Fats: 17g Proteins: 16.3g Sodium: 817mg Sugar: 0.6g

French Toasts

Serves: 4/Prep Time: 15 mins
Ingredients
- ½ cup evaporated milk
- 4 eggs
- 6 tablespoons sugar
- ¼ teaspoon vanilla extract
- 8 bread slices
- 4 teaspoons olive oil

Directions
1. Preheat the Airfryer to 395 degrees F and grease a pan.
2. Put all the ingredients in a large shallow dish except the bread slices.
3. Beat till well combined and dip each bread slice in egg mixture from both sides.
4. Arrange the bread slices in the prepared pan and cook for about 3 minutes per side.

Nutrition Calories: 261 Carbs: 30.6g Fats: 12g Proteins: 9.1g Sodium: 218mg Sugar: 22.3g

Veggie Hash

Serves: 8/Prep Time: 55 mins
Ingredients
- 2 medium onions, chopped
- 2 teaspoons dried thyme, crushed
- 4 teaspoons butter
- 1 green bell pepper, seeded and chopped
- 3 pounds russet potatoes, peeled and cubed
- Salt and freshly ground black pepper, to taste
- 10 eggs

Directions
1. Preheat the Airfryer to 395 degrees F and grease the Airfryer pan with butter.
2. Add bell peppers and onions and cook for about 5 minutes.
3. Add the herbs, potatoes, salt and black pepper and cook for about 30 minutes.
4. Heat a greased skillet on medium heat and add beaten eggs.
5. Cook for about 1 minute on each side and remove from the skillet.
6. Cut it into small pieces and add egg pieces into Airfryer pan.
7. Cook for about 5 more minutes and dish out.

Nutrition Calories: 229 Carbs: 31g Fats: 7.6g Proteins: 10.3g Sodium: 102mg Sugar: 4.3g

Parmesan Garlic Rolls

Serves: 4/Prep Time: 15 mins
Ingredients
- 1 cup Parmesan cheese, grated
- 4 dinner rolls
- 4 tablespoons unsalted butter, melted
- 1 tablespoon garlic bread seasoning mix

Directions
1. Preheat the Airfryer at 360 degrees F and cut the dinner rolls into cross style.
2. Stuff the slits evenly with the cheese and coat the tops of each roll with butter.
3. Sprinkle with the seasoning mix and cook for about 5 minutes until cheese is fully melted.

Nutrition Calories: 391 Carbs: 45g Fats: 18.6g Proteins: 11.7g Sodium: 608mg Sugar: 4.8g

Pickled Toasts

Serves: 4/Prep Time: 25 mins
Ingredients
- 4 tablespoons unsalted butter, softened
- 8 bread slices, toasted
- 4 tablespoons Branston pickle
- ½ cup Parmesan cheese, grated

Directions
1. Preheat the Airfryer to 385 degrees F and place the bread slice in a fryer basket.
2. Cook for about 5 minutes and spread butter evenly over bread slices.
3. Layer with Branston pickle and top evenly with cheese.
4. Cook for about 5 minutes until cheese is fully melted.

Nutrition Calories: 186 Carbs: 16.3g Fats: 12.9g Proteins: 2.6g Sodium: 397mg Sugar: 6.8g

Potato Rosti

Serves: 4/Prep Time: 15 mins
Ingredients
- ½ pound russet potatoes, peeled and grated roughly
- Salt and freshly ground black pepper, to taste
- 3.5 ounces smoked salmon, cut into slices
- 1 teaspoon olive oil
- 1 tablespoon chives, chopped finely
- 2 tablespoons sour cream

Directions
1. Preheat the Airfryer to 360 degrees F and grease a pizza pan with the olive oil.
2. Add chives, potatoes, salt and black pepper in a large bowl and mix until well combined.
3. Place the potato mixture into the prepared pizza pan and transfer the pizza pan in an Airfryer basket.
4. Cook for about 15 minutes and cut the potato rosti into wedges.
5. Top with the smoked salmon slices and sour cream and serve.

Nutrition Calories: 91 Carbs: 9.2g Fats: 3.6g Proteins: 5.7g Sodium: 503mg Sugar: 0.7g

Pumpkin Pancakes

Serves: 8/Prep Time: 20 mins
Ingredients
- 2 squares puff pastry
- 6 tablespoons pumpkin filling
- 2 small eggs, beaten
- ¼ teaspoon cinnamon

Directions
1. Preheat the Airfryer to 360 degrees F and roll out a square of puff pastry.
2. Layer it with pumpkin pie filling, leaving about ¼-inch space around the edges.
3. Cut it up into equal sized square pieces and cover the gaps with beaten egg.
4. Arrange the squares into a baking dish and cook for about 12 minutes.
5. Sprinkle some cinnamon and serve.

Nutrition Calories: 51 Carbs: 5g Fats: 2.5g Proteins: 2.4g Sodium: 48mg Sugar: 0.5g

Simple Cheese Sandwiches

Serves: 4/Prep Time: 10 mins

Ingredients
- 8 American cheese slices
- 8 bread slices
- 8 teaspoons butter

Directions
1. Preheat the Air fryer to 365 degrees F and arrange cheese slices between bread slices.
2. Spread butter over outer sides of sandwich and repeat with the remaining butter, slices and cheese.
3. Arrange the sandwiches in an Air fryer basket and cook for about 8 minutes, flipping once in the middle way.

Nutrition Calories: 254 Carbs: 12.4g Fats: 18.8g Proteins: 9.2g Sodium: 708mg Sugar: 3.9g

Air Fryer Poultry Recipes

Sweet & Sour Chicken Wings

Serves: 4/Prep Time: 20 mins

Ingredients

For Wings Marinade:
- 2 tablespoons fresh lemon juice
- 2 teaspoons garlic, chopped finely
- 2 tablespoons soy sauce
- Salt and black pepper, to taste
- 1 teaspoon dried oregano, crushed
- 16 chicken wings

For Sauce:
- 4 teaspoons scallions, chopped finely
- 2 tablespoons tomato ketchup
- 2 tablespoons chili sauce
- 2 teaspoons brown sugar
- 2 tablespoons vinegar

For Sprinkling:
- 4 tablespoons all-purpose flour

Directions
1. Preheat the air fryer to 355 degrees F and grease Airfryer tray.
2. For marinade: Mix together all ingredients in a large bowl except wings.
3. Add wings and coat generously with marinade.
4. Cover and refrigerate for about 2 hours.
5. Remove the chicken wings from marinade and sprinkle evenly with flour.
6. Place wings in an Airfryer tray and cook for about 6 minutes, flipping once after 3 minutes.
7. Add all sauce ingredients in a bowl and mix until well combined.
8. Remove chicken wings from Air fryer tray and coat generously with sauce.
9. Return the wings in Airfryer and cook for about 3 more minutes.

Nutrition Calories: 120 Carbs: 11.1g Fats: 2.8g Proteins: 11.8g Sodium: 758mg Sugar: 3.7

Breaded Chicken

Serves: 8/Prep Time: 25 mins

Ingredients

- 4 tablespoons vegetable oil
- 2 eggs, beaten
- 1 cup breadcrumbs
- 16 skinless, boneless chicken tenderloins

Directions

1. Preheat the air fryer to 360 degrees F.
2. Beat the eggs in a shallow dish and in another shallow dish, add breadcrumbs and oil.
3. Mix until a crumbly mixture is formed and dip the chicken tenderloins in egg.
4. Coat in the breadcrumbs mixture and marinate for about 2 hours.
5. Place the chicken tenderloins in the Airfryer and cook for about 12 minutes.

Nutrition Calories: 409 Carbs: 9.8g Fats: 16.6g Proteins: 53.2g Sodium: 194mg Sugar: 0.9g

Herbed Duck Legs

Serves: 4/Prep Time: 40 mins

Ingredients

- 1 tablespoon fresh thyme, chopped
- 2 garlic cloves, minced
- 1 tablespoon fresh parsley, chopped
- 2 teaspoons five spice powder
- 4 duck legs
- Salt and freshly ground black pepper, to taste

Directions

1. Preheat the Airfryer to 345 degrees F.
2. Mix together herbs, garlic, five spice powder, salt and black pepper in a bowl.
3. Rub the duck legs generously with garlic mixture.
4. Cook the duck legs in Airfryer for about 25 minutes.
5. Reset the Airfryer to 390 degrees F and cook for about 5 more minutes.

Nutrition Calories: 138 Carbs: 1g Fats: 4.5g Proteins: 22g Sodium: 82mg Sugar: 0g

Whole Spring Chicken

Serves: 8/Prep Time: 45 mins

Ingredients

- 4 teaspoons oyster sauce
- 4 teaspoons dried rosemary, crushed
- Salt and freshly ground black pepper, to taste
- 4 bay leaves
- 2 tablespoons olive oil
- 2 (1½-pounds) spring chicken
- 8 bell peppers, seeded and cut into chunks

Directions

1. Preheat the Airfryer to 355 degrees F and grease an Airfryer grill pan.
2. Mix together oyster sauce, rosemary, salt and black pepper in a bowl.
3. Rub the chicken evenly with rosemary mixture and stuff the chicken cavity with bay leaves.
4. Place the potatoes into an Airfryer grill pan and cook for about 15 minutes.
5. Coat the bell pepper pieces with oil and remove grill pan from Airfryer.
6. Transfer the chicken onto a plate and line the grill pan with bell pepper pieces.
7. Arrange chicken over bell pepper pieces and cook for 15 more minutes.

Nutrition Calories: 394 Carbs: 9.7g Fats: 16.5g Proteins: 50.5g Sodium: 168mg Sugar: 6g

Chicken Wings with Prawn Paste

Serves: 6/Prep Time: 20 mins
Ingredients

- 2 tablespoons prawn paste
- 4 tablespoons olive oil
- 1½ teaspoons sugar
- 2 teaspoons sesame oil
- 1 teaspoon Shaoxing wine
- Corn flour, as required
- 2 teaspoons fresh ginger juice
- 2 pounds mid-joint chicken wings

Directions

1. Mix together all the ingredients in a bowl except wings and corn flour.
2. Add chicken wings and coat generously with marinade.
3. Refrigerate overnight and coat the chicken wings evenly with corn flour.
4. Shake off the excess flour and preheat the air fryer to 360 degrees F.
5. Coat the wings with a little extra oil and arrange the chicken wings in Airfryer basket.
6. Cook for about 8 minutes and dish out.

Nutrition: Calories: 416 Carbs: 11.2g Fats: 31.5g Proteins: 24.4g Sodium: 661mg Sugar: 1.6g

Spicy Green Crusted Chicken

Serves: 6/Prep Time: 40 mins
Ingredients

- 6 teaspoons oregano
- 6 eggs, beaten
- 6 teaspoons parsley
- 4 teaspoons thyme
- Salt and freshly ground black pepper, to taste
- 4 teaspoons paprika
- 1 pound chicken pieces

Directions

1. Preheat the air fryer to 360 degrees F and grease Air fryer basket.
2. Place eggs in a bowl and mix together remaining ingredients in another bowl except chicken pieces.
3. Dip the chicken in eggs and then coat with the dry mixture.
4. Arrange half of the chicken pieces in Air fryer basket and cook for about 20 minutes.
5. Repeat with the remaining mixture and serve.

Nutrition Calories: 218 Carbs: 2.6g Fats: 10.4g Proteins: 27.9g Sodium: 128mg Sugar: 0.6g

Glazed Chicken Tenders

Serves: 4/Prep Time: 10 mins
Ingredients

- 1 cup brown sugar
- 4 skinless, boneless chicken tenders
- 2 cups ketchup
- 4 tablespoons honey

Directions

1. Preheat the air fryer to 355 degrees F.
2. Mix together all ingredients in a bowl except chicken tenders.

4. Add chicken tenders and coat generously with glazed mixture.
5. Arrange the chicken tenderloins in Airfryer basket and cook for about 10 minutes.

Nutrition Calories: 458 Carbs: 83g Fats: 4.4g Proteins: 27.2g Sodium: 1388mg Sugar: 79.7g

Mongolian Chicken

Serves: 2/Prep Time: 20 mins

Ingredients

- ½ pound boneless chicken, cubed
- ¼ tablespoon corn starch
- 1 egg
- ½ medium yellow onion, sliced thinly
- 1½ teaspoons garlic, minced
- 2 curry leaves
- ¼ teaspoon curry powder
- ½ teaspoon sugar
- Pinch of black pepper
- ½ tablespoon light soy sauce
- 1 tablespoon olive oil
- 1 green chili, chopped
- ½ teaspoon fresh ginger, grated
- ½ tablespoon chili sauce
- ¼ teaspoon salt
- ¼ cup evaporated milk

Directions

1. Mix together egg, chicken, corn starch and soy sauce in a bowl.
2. Cover for about 1 hour and then pat with paper towels to dry.
3. Preheat the Airfryer to 390 degrees F and grease an Airfryer basket.
4. Place the chicken in an Airfryer basket and cook for about 10 minutes.
5. Heat oil in a skillet on medium heat and add green chili, onions, garlic and ginger.
6. Sauté for about 2 minutes and add chicken, chili sauce, curry powder, sugar, salt and black pepper.
7. Mix until well combined and add evaporated milk.
8. Cook for about 4 minutes and dish out.

Nutrition Calories: 387 Carbs: 15g Fats: 20.3g Proteins: 39.3g Sodium: 1785mg Sugar: 8.4g

Creamy Chicken Tenders

Serves: 8/Prep Time: 20 mins

Ingredients

- 2 pounds chicken tenders
- 4 tablespoons olive oil
- 1 cup cream
- Salt and freshly ground black pepper, to taste
- 1 cup feta cheese

Directions

1. Season chicken tenders with salt and black pepper in a bowl.
2. Preheat the air fryer to 340 degrees F.
3. Put the chicken tenderloins and oil in Air fryer basket.
4. Top with feta cheese and cream and cook for about 15 minutes.
5. Reset the Air fryer to 390 degrees F and cook for about 5 more minutes.

Nutrition Calories: 344 Carbs: 1.7g Fats: 21.1g Proteins: 35.7g Sodium: 317mg Sugar: 1.4g

Mirin Coated Chicken Kebabs

Serves: 8/Prep Time: 15 mins
Ingredients
- 2 tablespoons mirin
- ½ cup light soy sauce
- 2 teaspoons garlic salt
- 8 (4-ounce) skinless, boneless chicken thighs, cubed into 1-inch size
- 2 teaspoons sugar
- 10 scallions, cut into 1-inch pieces lengthwise

Directions
1. Mix together mirin, soy sauce, garlic salt and sugar in a large baking dish.
2. Thread green onions and chicken onto pre-soaked wooden skewers.
3. Place the skewers into the baking dish and coat with marinade generously.
4. Cover and refrigerate for about 1 hour.
5. Preheat the air fryer to 355 degrees F and place the skewers in a fryer basket.
6. Cook for about 12 minutes and dish out.

Nutrition: Calories: 161 Carbs: 5.6g Fats: 4.1g Proteins: 26g Sodium: 370mg Sugar: 3.2g

Mexican Style Chicken

Serves: 8/Prep Time: 45 mins
Ingredients
- 2 pounds skinless, boneless chicken breasts
- 4 bay leaves
- 2 small yellow onions, chopped
- 6 garlic cloves, chopped
- 1 poblano pepper
- 2 (14½-ounce) cans diced tomatoes
- 2 (10-ounce) cans rotel tomatoes
- Salt, to taste
- 20 corn tortillas, cut into diamond slices
- 2 tablespoons olive oil
- 8 tablespoons feta cheese, crumbled
- ½ cup sour cream
- 4 red onions, sliced

Directions
1. Put the bay leaves and chicken in a pan of water and cook for about 20 minutes.
2. Dish out the chicken breasts in a bowl and keep aside to cool.
3. Shred the chicken with 2 forks.
4. Put the onions, garlic, poblano pepper and tomatoes in a food processor and pulse until smooth.
5. Transfer the sauce into a skillet on medium-high heat and bring to a boil.
6. Reduce the heat to medium-low and cook for about 10 minutes.
7. Season with salt and keep aside.
8. Preheat the Airfryer to 400 degrees F.
9. Put half of oil, half of tortilla slices and salt in a bowl and toss to coat well.
10. Place the tortilla slices in an Airfryer basket and cook for about 10 minutes.
11. Repeat with the remaining tortillas and transfer the tortillas into the serving bowl.
12. Stir in cheese, sauce and sour cream and top with the red onion and chicken.

Nutrition Calories: 472 Carbs: 52.9g Fats: 15.4g Proteins: 35.9g Sodium: 490mg Sugar: 15.1g

Honey Glazed Chicken Drumsticks

Serves: 8/Prep Time: 22 mins

Ingredients

- 2 tablespoons honey
- 2 tablespoons fresh thyme, minced
- 8 chicken drumsticks
- ½ cup Dijon mustard
- 4 tablespoons olive oil
- 1 tablespoon fresh rosemary, minced
- Salt and freshly ground black pepper, to taste

Directions

1. Put all the ingredients in a bowl except the drumsticks and mix well.
2. Add drumsticks and coat generously with the mixture.
3. Cover and refrigerate to marinate for overnight.
4. Preheat the Airfryer at 325 degrees F and place the drumsticks in air fryer basket.
5. Cook for about 12 minutes and reset the air fryer to 355 degrees F.
6. Cook for about 10 minutes and serve.

Nutrition Calories: 301 Carbs: 6g Fats: 19.7g Proteins: 4.5g Sodium: 316mg Sugar: 4.5g

Chicken Thighs with Chili Sauce

Serves: 4/Prep Time: 15 mins

Ingredients

For Chicken:

- 2 garlic cloves, minced
- 1 tablespoon rice vinegar
- Freshly ground black pepper, to taste
- 2 scallions, finely chopped
- 1 tablespoon soy sauce
- 1 teaspoon sugar
- 4 chicken thighs, deboned
- Potato flour, as required

For Chili Sauce:

- 2 shallots, sliced thinly
- 4 bird's eye chilies, chopped
- 3 tablespoons Thai chili sauce
- 2 tablespoons fresh lime juice
- 2 tablespoons sugar
- Salt, to taste

Directions

1. For chicken: Mix together all the ingredients in a bowl except chicken and potato flour.
2. Add chicken thighs and coat generously with marinade.
3. Remove chicken thighs from marinade and coat with corn flour.
4. Preheat the Airfryer to 395 degrees F and arrange the chicken thighs in the Airfryer pan, with skin side down.
5. Cook for about 10 minutes and reset the Airfryer to 355 degrees F.
6. Cook for about 10 minutes and meanwhile, mix together all ingredients in a bowl for chili sauce.
7. Remove chicken thighs from the Airfryer and top with the sauce immediately to serve.

Nutrition Calories: 241 Carbs: 16.7g Fats: 6.9g Proteins: 26.6g Sodium: 745mg Sugar: 9.5g

Asian Style Chicken

Serves: 4/Prep Time: 35 mins

Ingredients

- 2 teaspoons ginger,minced
- 1 tablespoon olive oil
- 6 tablespoons brown sugar
- 1½ pounds chickenpieces

- 2 tablespoons soy sauce
- 2 tablespoons fresh rosemary,chopped
- 2 tablespoons oyster sauce
- 2 lemons, cut into wedges

Directions

1. Mix together chicken, soy sauce, ginger and olive oil in a bowl.
2. Cover and refrigerate for about 30 minutes.
3. Preheat the Airfryer to 385 degrees F and place the chicken in an Airfryer pan.
4. Cook for about 6 minutes and meanwhile, mix together the remaining ingredients in a small bowl.
5. Dish out chicken from the Airfryer and drizzle the sauce mixture over it.

Nutrition Calories: 427 Carbs: 18.5g Fats: 16.5g Proteins: 50.2g Sodium: 657mg Sugar: 14g

Chicken Thighs with Apple

Serves: 4/Prep Time: 20 mins

Ingredients

- 2 shallots, thinly sliced
- 2 tablespoons fresh ginger, finely grated
- 2 teaspoons fresh thyme, minced
- 1 cup apple cider
- 4 tablespoons maple syrup
- Salt and freshly ground black pepper, to taste
- 4 skinless, boneless chicken thighs, cut into chunks
- 2 large apples, cored and cubed

Directions

1. Mix together all the ingredients in a large bowl except chicken and apple.
2. Add chicken pieces and coat generously with marinade.
3. Refrigerate to marinate for about 8 hours.
4. Preheat the Airfryer to 390 degrees F and place the chicken pieces and cubed apple in Airfryer basket.
5. Cook for about 20 minutes, flipping once in the middle way.

Nutrition Calories: 294 Carbs: 39.1g Fats: 4.5g Proteins: 25.8g Sodium: 46mg Sugar: 30.4g

Air Fryer Meat Recipes

Honey Mustard Cheesy Meatballs

Serves: 8/Prep Time: 15 mins

Ingredients

- 2 onions, chopped
- 1 pound ground beef
- 2 teaspoons garlic paste
- 4 tablespoons fresh basil, chopped
- 2 teaspoons honey
- Salt and freshly ground black pepper, to taste
- 2 teaspoons mustard
- 2 tablespoons cheddar cheese, grated

Directions

1. Preheat the Airfryer to 385 degrees F.
2. Put all the ingredients in a bowl and mix until well combined.
3. Make equal-sized balls from the mixture and arrange the balls in an Airfryer basket.
4. Cook for about 15 minutes and serve with fresh greens.

Nutrition Calories: 134 Carbs: 4.6g Fats: 4.4g Proteins: 18.2g Sodium: 50mg Sugar: 2.7

Spicy Lamb Kebabs

Serves: 6/Prep Time: 30 mins
Ingredients

- 4 eggs, beaten
- 1 cup pistachios, chopped
- 2 teaspoons chiliflakes
- 1 pound ground lamb
- 4 garlic cloves, minced
- 2 tablespoons fresh lemon juice
- 4 tablespoons plain flour
- 2 teaspoons cumin seeds
- 1 teaspoon fennel seeds
- 2 teaspoons dried mint
- 2 teaspoons salt
- Olive oil
- 1 teaspoon coriander seeds
- 4 tablespoons chopped flat-leaf parsley
- 1 teaspoon freshly ground black pepper

Directions

1. Mix together lamb, pistachios, eggs, lemon juice, chili flakes, flour, cumin seeds, fennel seeds, coriander seeds, mint, parsley, salt and pepper in a bowl.
2. Mold handfuls of the lamb mixture to form sausages around skewers.
3. Grease lamb skewers with olive oil.
4. Preheat the air fryer to 355 degrees F and place the lamb skewer in airfryer basket.
5. Cook for about 8 minutes on each side and dish out.

Nutrition Calories: 284 Carbs: 8.4g Fats: 15.8g Proteins: 27.9g Sodium: 932mg Sugar: 1.1g

Simple Beef Burgers

Serves: 6/Prep Time: 25 mins
Ingredients

- 2 pounds ground beef
- 12 cheddar cheese slices
- 6 tablespoons tomato ketchup
- Salt and freshly ground black pepper, to taste
- 12 dinner rolls

Directions

1. Preheat the Airfryer to 390 degrees F and grease an Airfryer pan.
2. Mix together beef, salt and black pepper in a bowl and make small patties from mixture.
3. Place half of patties onto the prepared pan and cook for about 12 minutes.
4. Top each patty with 1 cheese slice and arrange patties between rolls.
5. Top with ketchup and repeat with the remaining batch.

Nutrition Calories: 537 Carbs: 7.6g Fats: 28.3g Proteins: 60.6g Sodium: 636mg Sugar: 4.2g

Lamb with Potatoes

Serves: 2/Prep Time: 40 mins
Ingredients

- 1 garlic clove, crushed
- ½ pound lamb meat
- ½ tablespoon dried rosemary, crushed
- 2 small potatoes, peeled and halved
- 1 teaspoon olive oil
- ½ small onion, peeled and halved
- ¼ cup frozen sweet potato fries

Directions

1. Preheat the Airfryer to 355 degrees F and rub the lamb evenly with garlic.
2. Sprinkle with rosemary and arrange a divider in Airfryer.
3. Place the lamb on one side of Airfryer divider and cook for about 20 minutes.
4. Meanwhile, place the potatoes in a microwave safe bowl and microwave for about 4 minutes.
5. Drain the water from the potatoes and dish out in a large bowl along with onions and oil.
6. Toss to coat well and transfer in Airfryer divider after 20 minutes.
7. Set the Airfryer to 390 degrees F and change the side of lamb ramp.
8. Top with potato and onion halves.
9. Place the sweet potato fries in another part of Airfryer divider.
10. Cook for about 15 minutes, flipping the vegetables once after 10 minutes.

Nutrition Calories: 399 Carbs: 32.3g Fats: 18.5g Proteins: 24.5g Sodium: 104mg Sugar: 3.8g

Herbed Pork Burgers

Serves: 8/Prep Time: 45 mins

Ingredients

- 2 small onions, chopped
- 2 teaspoons mustard
- 21-ounce ground pork
- 2 teaspoons garlic puree
- 2 teaspoons tomato puree
- 2 teaspoons fresh basil, chopped
- Salt and freshly ground black pepper, to taste
- 8 burger buns
- 2 teaspoons dried mixed herbs, crushed
- ½ cup cheddar cheese, grated

Directions

1. Mix together all the ingredients in a bowl except cheese and buns.
2. Make 8 medium sized patties from the mixture.
3. Preheat the Airfryer to 395 degrees F and grease the Airfryer pan with olive oil.
4. Place patties onto the prepared pan and cook for about 45 minutes, flipping once after 25 minutes.
5. Arrange the patties in buns with cheese and serve immediately.

Nutrition: Calories: 289 Carbs: 29.2g Fats: 6.5g Proteins: 28.7g Sodium: 384mg Sugar: 4.9g

Garlicky Lamb Chops

Serves: 8/Prep Time: 45 mins

Ingredients

- 2 bulbs garlic
- 2 tablespoons fresh thyme, chopped
- ½ cup olive oil, divided
- 2 tablespoons fresh oregano, chopped
- Salt and freshly ground black pepper, to taste
- 16 (4-ounce) lamb chops

Directions

1. Preheat the Airfryer to 385 degrees F and coat the garlic bulbs with olive oil.
2. Place the garlic bulb in an Airfryer basket and cook for about 12 minutes.
3. Mix together remaining oil, herbs, salt and black pepper in a large bowl.
4. Coat the chops with about 2 tablespoons of the herb mixture.

6. Place 4 chops in Airfryer basket with 1 garlic bulb.
7. Cook for about 5 minutes and repeat with the remaining lamb chops.
8. Squeeze the garlic bulb in remaining herb mixture and mix until well combined.
9. Serve lamb chops with herb mixture.

Nutrition: Calories: 433 Carbs: 1.9g Fats: 25.2g Proteins: 47.9g Sodium: 130mg Sugar: 0.1g

Chinese Style Pork Meatballs

Serves: 3/Prep Time: 15 mins

Ingredients

- 1 egg, beaten
- 1 teaspoon oyster sauce
- 6-ounce ground pork
- ½ tablespoon light soy sauce
- ½ teaspoon sesame oil
- ¼ teaspoon five spice powder
- ½ tablespoon olive oil
- ¼ teaspoon brown sugar
- ¼ cup cornstarch

Directions

1. Mix together all the ingredients in a large bowl except cornstarch and oil.
2. Make equal sized small balls from the mixture.
3. Place the cornstarch in a shallow dish and roll the meatballs evenly into cornstarch mixture.
4. Place the meatballs in a large tray and keep aside for about 15 minutes.
5. Preheat the Airfryer to 390 degrees F and line the Airfryer basket with foil paper.
6. Arrange the balls into prepared basket and cook for about 10 minutes.
7. Drizzle the meatballs with oil and flip the side.
8. Cook for about 10 more minutes and dish out.

Nutrition Calories: 171 Carbs: 10.8g Fats: 6.6g Proteins: 16.9g Sodium: 254mg Sugar: 0.7g

Lamb Chops with Veggies

Serves: 8/Prep Time: 46 mins

Ingredients

- 4 tablespoons fresh mint leaves, minced
- 6 tablespoons olive oil
- 4 tablespoons fresh rosemary, minced
- 2 garlic cloves, minced
- Salt and freshly ground black pepper, to taste
- 2 purple carrots, peeled and cubed
- 2 parsnips, peeled and cubed
- 8 (6-ounce) lamb chops
- 2 yellow carrots, peeled and cubed
- 2 fennel bulbs, cubed

Directions

1. Mix together herbs, garlic and oil in a large bowl and add chops.
2. Coat generously with mixture and refrigerate to marinate for about 3 hours.
3. Soak the vegetables for about 15 minutes in a large pan of water.
4. Drain the vegetables and preheat the Airfryer to 385 degrees F.
5. Place half of the chops in an Airfryer basket and cook for about 2 minutes.
6. Remove the chops from the Airfryer and place half of the vegetables in the Airfryer basket.

8.   Top with the chops and cook for about 6 minutes.
9.   Repeat with the remaining lamb chops and serve.

Nutrition Calories: 488 Carbs: 17.2g Fats: 24.1g Proteins: 50.2g Sodium: 267mg Sugar: 3.7g

Simple Steak

Serves: 4/Prep Time: 15 mins
Ingredients
- 1 pound quality cut steaks
- Salt and freshly ground black pepper, to taste

Directions
1.   Preheat the Airfryer to 385 degrees F and rub the steaks evenly with salt and pepper.
2.   Place the steak in air fryer basket and cook for about 15 minutes until crispy.

Nutrition Calories: 301 Carbs: 0g Fats: 25.1g Proteins: 19.1g Sodium: 65mg Sugar: 0g

Almonds Crusted Rack of Lamb

Serves: 3/Prep Time: 50 mins
Ingredients
- 1 garlic clove, minced
- 1 pound rack of lamb
- ½ tablespoon olive oil
- Salt and freshly ground black pepper, to taste
- 1 egg
- 3-ounce almonds, finely chopped
- 1 tablespoon breadcrumbs
- ½ tablespoon fresh rosemary, chopped

Directions
1.   Mix together oil, garlic, salt and black pepper in a bowl.
2.   Coat the rack of lamb evenly with oil mixture.
3.   Beat the egg in a shallow dish and mix together breadcrumbs, almonds and rosemary in another shallow dish.
4.   Dip the rack of lamb in egg and coat with almond mixture.
5.   Preheat the Airfryer to 230 degrees F and place the rack of lamb in an Airfryer basket.
6.   Cook for about 30 minutes and reset the Airfryer to 390 degrees F.
7.   Cook for about 5 more minutes and dish out.

Nutrition: Calories: 471 Carbs: 8.5g Fats: 31.6g Proteins: 39g Sodium: 145mg Sugar: 1.5g

Rib Eye Steak

Serves: 3/Prep Time: 15 mins
Ingredients
- 1 pound rib eye steak
- 1 tablespoon steak rub
- 1 tablespoon olive oil

Directions
1.   Drizzle the steak with olive oil and rub generously with steak rub.
2.   Preheat the Airfryer to 400 degrees and place the steak in air fryer basket.
3.   Cook for about 15 minutes until crispy.

Nutrition Calories: 462 Carbs: 1g Fats: 38.1g Proteins: 26.8g Sodium: 307mg Sugar: 0g

Spicy Skirt Steak

Serves: 8/Prep Time: 20 mins

Ingredients

- 2 cups fresh parsley leaves, finely chopped
- 6 tablespoons fresh mint leaves, finely chopped
- 6 garlic cloves, minced
- 6 tablespoons fresh oregano, finely chopped
- 2 tablespoons ground cumin
- 4 teaspoons smoked paprika
- 2 teaspoons red pepper flakes, crushed
- 1½ cups olive oil
- 6 tablespoons red wine vinegar
- 2 teaspoons cayenne pepper
- Salt and freshly ground black pepper, to taste
- 4 (8-ounce) skirt steaks

Directions

1. Mix together all the ingredients in a bowl except the steaks.
2. Add steaks and ¼ cup of the herb mixture in a resealable bag and shake to coat well.
3. Refrigerate for about 24 hours and reserve the remaining herb mixture.
4. Remove steaks from the refrigerator and keep at room temperature for about 30 minutes.
5. Preheat the Airfryer to 390 degrees F and place half of the steaks in an Airfryer basket.
6. Cook for about 10 minutes and repeat with the remaining steaks.
7. Top with remaining herb mixture to serve.

Nutrition Calories: 445 Carbs: 5.8g Fats: 43.1g Proteins: 12.9g Sodium: 46mg Sugar: 0.5g

Leg of Lamb

Serves: 6/Prep Time: 1 hour 15 mins

Ingredients

- 2 tablespoons olive oil
- 2 pounds leg of lamb
- Salt and freshly ground black pepper, to taste
- 3 fresh thyme sprigs
- 3 fresh rosemary sprigs

Directions

1. Preheat the Airfryer to 310 degrees F.
2. Coat the leg of lamb with olive oil and season with salt and black pepper.
3. Cover the leg of lamb with herb sprigs and place the chops in an Airfryer basket.
4. Cook for about 1 hour 15 minutes and dish out.

Nutrition Calories: 325 Carbs: 0.7g Fats: 15.9g Proteins: 42.5g Sodium: 115mg Sugar: 0g

Barbecue Flavored Pork Ribs

Serves: 6/Prep Time: 15 mins

Ingredients

- 1 cup BBQ sauce
- 3 tablespoons tomato ketchup
- ¾ teaspoon garlic powder
- ½ cup honey, divided
- 1½ tablespoons Worcestershire sauce
- 1½ tablespoons soy sauce
- Freshly ground white pepper, to taste
- 2 pounds pork ribs

Directions

1. Mix together half of honey and remaining ingredients except pork ribs in a large bowl.

3. Refrigerate to marinate for about 30 minutes.
4. Preheat the Airfryer to 360 degrees F and place the ribs in an Airfryer basket.
5. Cook for about 15 minutes and remove the ribs from Airfryer.
6. Coat with remaining honey and serve hot.

Nutrition Calories: 576 Carbs: 41.6g Fats: 26.9g Proteins: 40.6g Sodium: 906mg Sugar: 36.7g

Pork Tenderloin with Veggies

Serves: 4/Prep Time: 30 mins
Ingredients
- 12 bacon slices
- 2 tablespoons olive oil
- 8 potatoes
- 1½ pounds frozen green beans
- 4 pork tenderloins

Directions
1. Preheat the Airfryer to 395 degrees F.
2. Pierce the potatoes with a fork and place in the Airfryer.
3. Cook for about 15 minutes and wrap the green beans with bacon slices.
4. Coat the pork tenderloin with some olive oil and keep aside for about 15 minutes.
5. Add pork tenderloins in Airfryer with potatoes and cook for about 5 minutes.
6. Remove the pork tenderloin and place the bean rolls in the basket.
7. Top with the pork tenderloin and cook for about 7 minutes.

Nutrition Calories: 638 Carbs: 79.1g Fats: 19g Proteins: 39.4g Sodium: 263mg Sugar: 7.3g

Air Fryer Seafood Recipes

Buttered Scallops

Serves: 4/Prep Time: 15 mins
Ingredients
- 2 tablespoons butter, melted
- 1½ pounds sea scallops
- 1 tablespoon fresh thyme, minced
- Salt and freshly ground black pepper, to taste

Directions
1. Preheat the Airfryer to 385 degrees F and grease Airfryer basket.
2. Put all the ingredients in a large bowl and toss to coat well.
3. Arrange half of the scallops in an Airfryer basket and cook for about 5 minutes.
4. Repeat with the remaining scallops and serve.

Nutrition Calories: 202 Carbs: 4.4g Fats: 7.1g Proteins: 28.7g Sodium: 315mg Sugar: 0g

Ham Wrapped Prawns

Serves: 2/Prep Time: 20 mins
Ingredients
- 1 tablespoon olive oil
- Salt and freshly ground black pepper, to taste
- 1 garlic clove, minced
- ½ tablespoon paprika

- 4 king prawns, peeled, deveined and chopped
- 2 ham slices, halved

Directions
1. Preheat the air fryer to 430 degrees F and place the bell pepper in a fryer basket
2. Cook for about 10 minutes and transfer the bell pepper into a bowl covering with a foil paper.
3. Keep aside for about 15 minutes and add the bell pepper along with garlic, paprika and oil in a blender.
4. Pulse till a puree forms and keep aside.
5. Wrap each prawn with a slice of ham and arrange in the fryer basket.
6. Cook for about 4 minutes until golden brown and serve with bell pepper dip.

Nutrition: Calories: 553 Carbs: 2.5g Fats: 33.6g Proteins: 5g Sodium: 366mg Sugar: 7.2g

Breaded Shrimp with Sauce

Serves: 2/Prep Time: 45 mins
Ingredients
For Shrimp:
- ¼ cup panko breadcrumbs
- ¼ teaspoon cayenne pepper
- 4 large shrimps, peeled and deveined
- 4 ounces coconut milk
- Salt and freshly ground black pepper, to taste

For Sauce:
- ½ teaspoon mustard
- ¼ cup orange marmalade
- ¼ teaspoon hot sauce
- ½ tablespoon honey

Directions
1. Preheat the air fryer to 345 degrees F.
2. Mix together coconut milk, salt and black pepper in a shallow dish.
3. Combine breadcrumbs, cayenne pepper, salt and black pepper in another shallow dish.
4. Coat the shrimp in coconut milk mixture and then dredge into breadcrumbs mixture.
5. Place the shrimp in the Airfryer and cook for about 20 minutes until desired doneness.
6. Meanwhile, mix together all the sauce ingredients for sauce in a bowl.
7. Serve shrimp with sauce.

Nutrition Calories: 298 Carbs: 42.1g Fats: 14.2g Proteins: 5.2g Sodium: 142mg Sugar: 30.5g

Nacho Chips Crusted Prawns

Serves: 6/Prep Time: 20 mins
Ingredients
- 1 large egg
- 18 prawns, peeled and deveined
- ounce Nacho flavored chips, crushed finely

Directions
1. Beat the egg in a bowl and place nacho chips in another bowl.
2. Dip each prawn into the beaten egg and coat with the crushed nacho chips.
3. Preheat the air fryer to 350 degrees F and place the prawns in the Airfryer.
4. Cook for about 8 minutes and dish out.

Nutrition Calories: 333 Carbs: 30.2g Fats: 14.3g Proteins: 19.9g Sodium: 463mg Sugar: 1.9g

Spicy Shrimp

Serves: 4/Prep Time: 15 mins
Ingredients
- 2 tablespoons olive oil
- 1 pound tiger shrimp
- 1 teaspoon old bay seasoning
- ½ teaspoon cayenne pepper
- ½ teaspoon smoked paprika
- Salt, to taste

Directions
1. Preheat the Airfryer to 390 degrees F and grease an Airfryer basket.
2. Put all the ingredients in a large bowl and mix until well combined.
3. Place the shrimp in an Airfryer basket and cook for about 5 minutes.

Nutrition Calories: 174 Carbs: 0.3g Fats: 8.3g Proteins: 23.8g Sodium: 414mg Sugar: 0.1g

Lemony Tuna

Serves: 8/Prep Time: 20 mins
Ingredients
- 4 teaspoons Dijon mustard
- 4 tablespoons fresh parsley, chopped
- 4 (6-ounce) cans water packed plain tuna
- 1 cup breadcrumbs
- 2 tablespoons fresh lime juice
- 2 eggs
- 6 tablespoons canola oil
- Dash of hot sauce
- Salt and freshly ground black pepper, to taste

Directions
1. Mix together tuna fish, crumbs, mustard, parsley, hot sauce and citrus juice in a bowl.
2. Add oil, eggs and salt and make the patties from tuna mixture.
3. Refrigerate the tuna patties for about 3 hours and transfer to Airfryer basket.
4. Preheat the air fryer to 360 degrees F and place Airfryer basket.
5. Cook for about 12 minutes and serve.

Nutrition: Calories: 388 Carbs: 31.7g Fats: 21.8g Proteins: 14.2g Sodium: 680mg Sugar: 1.2g

Bacon Wrapped Shrimp

Serves: 8/Prep Time: 20 mins
Ingredients
- 2 pounds bacon
- 2½ pounds tiger shrimp, peeled and deveined

Directions
1. Wrap each shrimp with a slice of bacon and refrigerate for about 20 minutes.
2. Preheat the Airfryer to 385 degrees F and arrange half of the shrimps in Airfryer basket.
3. Cook for about 7 minutes and repeat with the remaining shrimps.

Nutrition Calories: 492 Carbs: 7.2g Fats: 35g Proteins: 41.8g Sodium: 1979mg Sugar: 0g

Lemony & Spicy Coconut Crusted Prawns

Serves: 8/Prep Time: 20 mins

Ingredients

- 1 cup flour
- 1 cup breadcrumbs
- Salt and freshly ground black pepper, to taste
- 2 pounds prawns, peeled and de-veined
- 4 egg whites
- 1 cup unsweetened coconut, shredded
- ½ teaspoon lemon zest
- ½ teaspoon cayenne pepper
- Vegetable oil, as required
- ½ teaspoon red pepper flakes, crushed

Directions

1. Mix together the flour, salt and pepper in a shallow dish.
2. Beat the eggs in another shallow dish.
3. Combine the breadcrumbs, lime zest, coconut, salt and cayenne pepper in a third shallow dish.
4. Preheat the Airfryer to 395 degrees F.
5. Dredge each shrimp in the flour mixture, then dip in the egg and roll evenly into the breadcrumbs mixture.
6. Place half the shrimps in the Airfryer basket and drizzle with vegetable oil.
7. Cook for about 7 minutes and repeat with the remaining mixture.

Nutrition: Calories: 305 Carbs: 25.1g Fats: 7.9g Proteins: 31.4g Sodium: 394mg Sugar: 1.6g

Tuna Stuffed Potatoes

Serves: 2/Prep Time: 45 mins

Ingredients

- ¼ tablespoon olive oil
- 2 starchy potatoes, soaked for 30 minutes
- ½ (6-ounce) can tuna, drained
- 1 tablespoon plain Greek yogurt
- Salt and freshly ground black pepper, to taste
- ½ tablespoon capers
- ½ teaspoon red chili powder
- ½ scallion, chopped and divided

Directions

1. Preheat the air fryer to 355 degrees F and place the potatoes in a fryer basket.
2. Cook for about 30 minutes and remove onto a smooth surface.
3. Meanwhile, add yogurt, tuna, red chili powder, half of scallion, salt and black pepper in a bowl and mash the mixture completely with a potato masher.
4. Cut each potato from top side lengthwise and press the open side of potato halves slightly.
5. Stuff the potato evenly with tuna mixture and sprinkle with the capers and remaining scallion.
6. Dish out and serve immediately.

Nutrition: Calories: 222 Carbs: 28.1g Fats: 5.7g Proteins: 15.4g Sodium: 105mg Sugar: 2.1g

Cod Burgers with Salsa

Serves: 3/Prep Time: 20 mins

Ingredients

For Mango Salsa:
- 1½ cups mango, peeled, pitted and cubed
- ½ tablespoon fresh parsley, chopped
- ½ teaspoon fresh lime zest, finely grated
- ¼ teaspoon red chili paste
- ½ tablespoon fresh lime juice

For Cod Cakes:
- ½ teaspoon fresh lime zest, finely grated
- Salt, to taste
- ¼ cup coconut, grated and divided
- ½ pound cod fillets
- 1 egg
- ½ teaspoon red chili paste
- ½ tablespoon fresh lime juice
- ½ scallion, finely chopped
- 1 tablespoon fresh parsley, chopped

Directions
1. For salsa: Mix together all ingredients in a bowl and refrigerate until serving.
2. For cod cakes: Put cod filets, egg, lime zest, chili paste, lime juice and salt in a food processor and pulse until smooth.
3. Transfer the cod mixture into a bowl and mix together scallion, parsley and 1 tablespoon coconut.
4. Make equal sized round cakes from the mixture and place the remaining coconut in a shallow dish.
5. Coat the cod cakes evenly in coconut and preheat the air fryer to 375 degrees F.
6. Arrange half cakes in an Airfryer basket and cook for about 7 minutes.
7. Repeat with the remaining cod cakes and serve with mango salsa.

Nutrition Calories: 164 Carbs: 15.1g Fats: 5g Proteins: 16.5g Sodium: 91mg Sugar: 12.5g

Cajun Spiced Salmon

Serves: 4/Prep Time: 15 mins
Ingredients
- 4 tablespoons Cajun seasoning
- 4 salmon steaks

Directions
1. Rub the salmon evenly with the Cajun seasoning and keep aside for about 10 minutes.
2. Preheat the Airfryer to 385 degrees F and arrange the salmon steaks on the grill pan.
3. Cook for about 8 minutes, flipping once in the middle way.

Nutrition Calories: 225 Carbs: 0g Fats: 10.5g Proteins: 33.1g Sodium: 225mg Sugar: 0g

Tangy Salmon

Serves: 4/Prep Time: 15 mins
Ingredients
- 2 tablespoons Cajun seasoning
- 4 (7-ounce) (¾-inch thick) salmon fillets
- 2 tablespoons fresh lemon juice

Directions
1. Preheat the air fryer to 360 degrees F and season evenly with Cajun seasoning.
2. Place the fish in an Airfryer, grill pan, skin-side up and cook for about 7 minutes.
3. Drizzle with lemon juice and serve

Nutrition Calories: 264 Carbs: 0.2g Fats: 12.3g Proteins: 38.6g Sodium: 164mg Sugar: 0.2g

Haddock with Cheese Sauce

Serves: 4/Prep Time: 15 mins

Ingredients

- 2 tablespoons olive oil
- 4 (6-ounce) haddock fillets
- Salt and freshly ground black pepper, to taste
- 6 tablespoons fresh basil, chopped
- 4 tablespoons pine nuts
- 2 tablespoons Parmesan cheese, grated

Directions

1. Preheat the Airfryer at 360 degrees F.
2. Coat the haddock fillets evenly with oil and season with salt and black pepper.
3. Place the fish fillets in an Airfryer basket and cook for about 8 minutes.
4. Meanwhile, add remaining ingredients in a food processor and pulse until smooth.
5. Transfer the fish fillets in serving plates and top with cheese sauce to serve.

Nutrition Calories: 354 Carbs: 1.7g Fats: 17.5g Proteins: 47g Sodium: 278mg Sugar: 0.3g

Sesame Seeds Coated Fish

Serves: 14/Prep Time: 20 mins

Ingredients

- 3 eggs
- ¾ cup breadcrumbs
- Pinch of black pepper
- 4 tablespoons plain flour
- ¾ cup sesame seeds, toasted
- ¼ teaspoon dried rosemary, crushed
- Pinch of salt
- 4 tablespoons olive oil
- 7 frozen fish fillets (white fish of your choice)

Directions

1. Place flour in a shallow dish and beat the eggs in a second shallow dish.
2. Mix together the remaining ingredients except fish fillets in a third shallow dish.
3. Coat the fillets with flour and dip the fillets in egg.
4. Dredge the fillets generously with sesame seeds mixture.
5. Preheat the Airfryer to 390 degrees F and line an Airfryer basket with a piece of foil.
6. Arrange the fillets into prepared basket and cook for about 14 minutes, flipping once in the middle way.

Nutrition: Calories: 223 Carbs: 19.8g Fats: 12.1g Proteins: 9.1g Sodium: 283mg Sugar: 1g

Crumbed Cod

Serves: 4/Prep Time: 20 mins

Ingredients

- 1 cup flour
- 4 garlic cloves, minced
- 4 (4-ounce) skinless cod fish fillets, cut into rectangular pieces
- 6 eggs
- 2 green chilies, finely chopped
- 6 scallions, finely chopped
- Salt and freshly ground black pepper, to taste
- 2 teaspoons soy sauce

Directions

2. Place the flour in a shallow dish and mix together remaining ingredients except cod in another shallow dish.
3. Coat each cod fillet into the flour and then dip in egg mixture.
4. Preheat the Airfryer to 375 degrees F and place cod fillets in an Airfryer basket.
5. Cook for about 7 minutes and dish out.

Nutrition Calories: 462 Carbs: 51.3g Fats: 16.9g Proteins: 24.4g Sodium: 646mg Sugar: 3.3g

Air Fryer Snacks Recipes

Apple Chips

Serves: 4/Prep Time: 15 mins
Ingredients
- 2 tablespoons sugar
- 2 apples, peeled, cored and thinly sliced
- 1 teaspoon ground cinnamon
- ½ teaspoon salt
- ½ teaspoon ground ginger

Directions
1. Preheat the Airfryer to 390 degrees F.
2. Put all the ingredients in a bowl and toss to coat well.
3. Place the apple slices in an Airfryer basket.
4. Cook for about 8 minutes, flipping once in the middle way.

Nutrition Calories: 83 Carbs: 22g Fats: 0.2g Proteins: 0.3g Sodium: 292mg Sugar: 17.6g

Roasted Cashews

Serves: 4/Prep Time: 15 mins
Ingredients
- ½ teaspoon butter, melted
- 1 cup raw cashew nuts
- Salt and freshly ground black pepper, to taste

Directions
1. Preheat the Airfryer to 360 degrees F.
2. Put all the ingredients in a bowl and toss to coat well.
3. Place the cashews in an Airfryer basket and cook for about 5 minutes.

Nutrition Calories: 201 Carbs: 11.2g Fats: 16.4g Proteins: 5.3g Sodium: 9mg Sugar: 1.7g

Buttered Corn

Serves: 4/Prep Time: 30 mins
Ingredients
- 4 corns on the cob
- 4 tablespoons butter, softened and divided
- Salt and freshly ground pepper, to taste

Directions
1. Preheat the Airfryer to 325 degrees F.
2. Season the cobs evenly with salt and black pepper.
3. Rub with 1 tablespoon butter and wrap the cobs in foil paper.
4. Place in the Airfryer basket and cook for about 20 minutes.

6. Top with remaining butter and serve.
Nutrition Calories: 257 Carbs: 31.9g Fats: 14.9g Proteins: 4.6g Sodium: 111mg Sugar: 0g

Polenta Sticks

Serves: 8/Prep Time: 15 mins
Ingredients
- 5 cups cooked polenta
- 2 tablespoons oil
- Salt, to taste
- ½ cup Parmesan cheese

Directions
1. Preheat the air fryer at 360 degrees F and grease the baking dish with oil.
2. Place the polenta in a baking dish and refrigerate for about 1 hour.
3. Remove from the refrigerator and cut into desired sized slices.
4. Place the polenta sticks into the Airfryer and season with salt.
5. Cook for about 6 minutes and serve.

Nutrition Calories: 382 Carbs: 76.1g Fats: 4.6g Proteins: 7.8g Sodium: 20mg Sugar: 1g

Zucchini Fries

Serves: 8/Prep Time: 30 mins
Ingredients
- 2 pounds zucchinis, sliced into 2 ½-inch sticks
- 4 tablespoons olive oil
- Salt, to taste
- 1½ cups panko bread crumbs

Directions
1. Place the zucchini in a colander and season with salt.
2. Keep aside for about 10 minutes and preheat the Airfryer to 395 degrees F.
3. Pat dry the zucchini fries with the paper towels.
4. Place the bread crumbs in a shallow dish and coat zucchini fries evenly.
5. Place the zucchini in a fryer basket in batches and cook for about 10 minutes.

Nutrition Calories: 158 Carbs: 18.4g Fats: 8.3g Proteins: 4.1g Sodium: 160mg Sugar: 3.2g

Eggplant Slices

Serves: 8/Prep Time: 30 mins
Ingredients
- ½ cup olive oil
- 2 medium eggplants, peeled and cut into ½-inch round slices
- 1 cup all-purpose flour
- 2 cups Italian-style breadcrumbs
- 4 eggs, beaten
- Salt, to taste

Directions
1. Place the eggplant slices in a colander and season with salt.
2. Keep aside for about 45 minutes and drain excess water with paper towels.
3. Preheat the Airfryer to 385 degrees F.
4. Place the flour in a shallow dish and beat the eggs in a second shallow dish.
5. Mix together oil and breadcrumbs in a third shallow dish.

7. Coat the eggplant slices in flour mixture, then dip in the beaten eggs and dredge in the breadcrumbs.
8. Place half of the eggplant slices in the Airfryer and cook for about 5 minutes.

Nutrition: Calories: 335 Carbs: 38.8g Fats: 16.7g Proteins: 9.5g Sodium: 483mg Sugar: 5.7g

Broccoli Poppers

Serves: 4/Prep Time: 20 mins
Ingredients

- 1 teaspoon red chili powder
- 4 tablespoons plain yogurt
- ½ teaspoon ground cumin
- Salt, to taste
- 2 pounds broccoli, cut into small florets
- ½ teaspoon ground turmeric
- 4 tablespoons chickpea flour

Directions
1. Mix together yogurt and spices in a bowl and add broccoli.
2. Coat with the marinade and refrigerate for about 20 minutes.
3. Preheat the Airfryer to 395 degrees F and season the broccoli florets with chickpea flour.
4. Place the broccoli in the Airfryer basket and cook
5. Cook for about 10 minutes, tossing once in the middle way.

Nutrition Calories: 138 Carbs: 24.4g Fats: 1.9g Proteins: 9.8g Sodium: 96mg Sugar: 6.4g

Risotto Bites

Serves: 8/Prep Time: 30 mins
Ingredients

- ½ cup Parmesan cheese, grated
- 6 cups cooked risotto
- 2 eggs, beaten
- 1½ cups bread crumbs
- ounce mozzarella cheese, cubed

Directions
1. Mix together risotto, Parmesan cheese and egg in a bowl.
2. Make equal-sized balls from the mixture and insert a mozzarella cube in the center of each ball.
3. Smooth the risotto mixture with your fingers to cover the ball.
4. Place the bread crumbs in a shallow dish and coat the balls evenly with bread crumbs.
5. Preheat the Airfryer to 390 degrees F and place the balls in an Airfryer basket in batches.
6. Cook for about 10 minutes until golden brown.

Nutrition Calories: 487 Carbs: 82.1g Fats: 9.2g Proteins: 20.1g Sodium: 703mg Sugar: 4.7g

Salmon Croquettes

Serves: 8/Prep Time: 25 mins
Ingredients

- 1 egg, lightly beaten
- Salt and freshly ground black pepper, to taste
- ½ large can red salmon, drained
- 1 tablespoon fresh parsley, chopped
- ¼ cup vegetable oil
- ½ cup bread crumbs

Directions

1. Preheat the Airfryer to 385 degrees F.
2. Add salmon and mash completely in a bowl.
3. Add parsley, egg, salt and black pepper and mix until well combined.
4. Make equal-sized croquettes from the mixture.
5. Mix together oil and breadcrumbs in a shallow dish.
6. Coat croquettes in breadcrumbs mixture and place the croquettes in an Airfryer basket in batches.
7. Cook for about 7 minutes.

Nutrition Calories: 105 Carbs: 4.9g Fats: 8.2g Proteins: 3.1g Sodium: 82mg Sugar: 0.5g

Cod Nuggets

Serves: 8/Prep Time: 25 mins

Ingredients

- 2 cups all-purpose flour
- 4 eggs
- 1½ cups breadcrumbs
- ½ teaspoon salt
- 4 tablespoons olive oil
- 2 pounds cod, cut into 1x2½-inch strips

Directions

1. Preheat the Airfryer to 385 degrees F.
2. Place the flour in a shallow dish and beat the eggs in another shallow dish.
3. Combine breadcrumbs, salt and oil in a third shallow dish.
4. Coat the cod strips evenly in flour.
5. Dip in eggs and roll evenly into breadcrumbs mixture.
6. Arrange the croquettes in an Airfryer basket and cook for about 10 minutes.

Nutrition Calories: 404 Carbs: 38.6g Fats: 11.6g Proteins: 34.6g Sodium: 415mg Sugar: 1.5g

Air Fryer Desserts Recipes

Fudge Brownies Muffins

Serves: 6/Prep Time: 20 mins

Ingredients

- 1/8 cup walnuts, chopped
- ½ package Betty Crocker fudge brownie mix
- 1 egg
- 1 teaspoon water
- ¼ cup vegetable oil

Directions

1. Preheat the Airfryer to 300 degrees F and grease 6 muffin molds.
2. Mix together all the ingredients in a bowl and transfer the mixture into prepared muffin molds.
3. Cook for about 10 minutes and remove the muffin molds from Airfryer.
4. Keep on wire rack to cool for about 10 minutes.

Nutrition Calories: 115 Carbs: 2.2g Fats: 11.4g Proteins: 1.6g Sodium: 18mg Sugar: 1.3g

Chocolaty Squares

Serves: 4/Prep Time: 35 mins

Ingredients
- 1¼-ounce brown sugar
- 2-ounce cold butter
- 3-ounce self-rising flour
- 1/8 cup honey
- ½ tablespoon milk
- ounce chocolate, chopped

Directions
1. Preheat the Airfryer at 320 degrees F.
2. Put the butter in a large bowl and beat until soft.
3. Add brown sugar, flour and honey and beat till smooth.
4. Stir in milk and chocolate and place the mixture into a tin.
5. Arrange the tin in a baking sheet and place in an Airfryer basket.
6. Cook for about 20 minutes and remove from Airfryer.
7. Keep aside to cool slightly and cut into desired squares and serve.

Nutrition Calories: 322 Carbs: 42.2g Fats: 15.9g Proteins: 3.5g Sodium: 97mg Sugar: 24.8g

Lemon Biscuits

Serves: 5/Prep Time: 20 mins
Ingredients
- 2-ounce caster sugar
- 5-ounce self-rising flour
- 2-ounce cold butter
- ½ teaspoon fresh lemon zest, grated finely
- ½ teaspoon vanilla extract
- ½ small egg
- 1 tablespoon fresh lemon juice

Directions
1. Mix together flour and sugar in a large bowl.
2. Cut cold butter with a pastry cutter and mix until a coarse crumb forms.
3. Add lemon zest, egg and lemon juice and mix until a soft dough forms.
4. Place the dough onto a floured surface and roll the dough.
5. Cut the dough into medium-sized biscuits and arrange the biscuits in a baking sheet in a single layer.
6. Preheat the Airfryer at 360 degrees F and cook for about 5 minutes.

Nutrition: Calories: 234 Carbs: 33.2g Fats: 9.9g Proteins: 3.5g Sodium: 72mg Sugar: 11.6g

Buttered Cookies

Serves: 8/Prep Time: 25 mins
Ingredients
- 2½-ounce icing sugar
- ounce unsalted butter, softened
- 2 cups all-purpose flour
- ½ teaspoon baking powder

Directions
1. Preheat the Airfryer to 345 degrees F.
2. Add butter in a large bowl and beat until soft.
3. Add icing sugar and beat until smooth.
4. Add baking powder and flour and beat until a sticky dough forms.
5. Place the dough into a piping bag fitted with a fluted nozzle.
6. Pipe the dough onto a baking sheet in a single layer.

8. Place the baking sheet in an Airfryer basket and cook for about 10 minutes.

Nutrition Calories: 352 Carbs: 32.8g Fats: 23.3g Proteins: 3.5g Sodium: 164mg Sugar: 8.8g

Stuffed Pear Pouch

Serves: 8/Prep Time: 25 mins

Ingredients

- 4 cups vanilla custard
- 2 eggs, beaten lightly
- 4 small pears, peeled, cored and halved
- 8 puff pastry sheets
- 4 tablespoons sugar
- Pinch of ground cinnamon
- 4 tablespoons whipped cream

Directions

1. Put a spoonful of vanilla custard in the center of each pastry sheet and top with a pear half.
2. Mix together sugar and cinnamon in a bowl and sprinkle this mixture over pear halves evenly.
3. Pinch the corners to shape into a pouch and preheat the Airfryer at 335 degrees F.
4. Place the pear pouches in an Airfryer basket and cook for about 15 minutes.
5. Top with whipped cream and serve with remaining custard

Nutrition: Calories: 308 Carbs: 37.6g Fats: 15.5g Proteins: 5.9g Sodium: 139mg Sugar: 20g

Nutty Banana Split

Serves: 4/Prep Time: 20 mins

Ingredients

- ½ cup panko bread crumbs
- 1½ tablespoons coconut oil
- 2 bananas, peeled and halved lengthwise
- ¼ cup corn flour
- 1½ tablespoons sugar
- 1 tablespoon walnuts, chopped
- 1 egg
- 1/8 teaspoon ground cinnamon

Directions

1. Heat oil in a skillet on medium heat and add bread crumbs.
2. Cook for 4 minutes until golden brown and transfer into a bowl.
3. Keep aside to cool and put the flour in a shallow dish.
4. Beat egg in another shallow dish and coat banana slices evenly with flour.
5. Dip in the egg and coat with bread crumbs evenly.
6. Mix together sugar and cinnamon in a small bowl.
7. Preheat the air fryer at 285 degrees F and place banana slices in an Airfryer basket.
8. Sprinkle with cinnamon sugar and cook for about 10 minutes.
9. Sprinkle with walnuts and serve.

Nutrition: Calories: 221 Carbs: 33.7g Fats: 8.5g Proteins: 4.8g Sodium: 115mg Sugar: 12.7g

Cherry Pie

Serves: 4/Prep Time: 35 mins

Ingredients

- ½ (21-ounce) can cherry pie filling
- 1 refrigerated pre-made pie crust
- ½ tablespoon milk
- 1 egg yolk

Directions

1. Preheat the Airfryer to 325 degrees F and press pie crust into a pie pan.
2. Poke the holes all over dough with a fork.
3. Place the pie pan into Airfryer basket and cook for about 5 minutes.
4. Remove pie pan from Airfryer basket and pour cherry pie filling into pie crust.
5. Roll out the remaining pie crust and cut into ¾-inch strips.
6. Place strips in a criss-cross manner.
7. Add milk and egg in a small bowl and beat well.
8. Brush the top of pie with egg wash and place the pie pan into Airfryer basket.
9. Cook for about 15 minutes and serve.

Nutrition: Calories: 307 Carbs: 70g Fats: 1.4g Proteins: 1g Sodium: 130mg Sugar: 57.9g

Apple Crumble

Serves: 8/Prep Time: 40 mins

Ingredients

- ½ cup butter, softened
- 2 (14-ounce) cans apple pie
- 18 tablespoons self-rising flour
- ¼ teaspoon salt
- 14 tablespoons caster sugar

Directions

1. Preheat the Airfryer at 320 degrees F and lightly grease a baking dish.
2. Place the apple pie evenly in the prepared baking dish.
3. Add remaining ingredients in a bowl and mix until a crumbly mixture forms.
4. Spread the mixture over apple pie evenly and arange the baking dish in an Airfryer basket.
5. Cook for about 25 minutes and serve.

Nutrition Calories: 425 Carbs: 66.5g Fats: 16.7g Proteins: 3.4g Sodium: 401mg Sugar: 33.6g

Marshmallow Pastries

Serves: 8/Prep Time: 20 mins

Ingredients

- 4-ounce butter, melted
- 8 phyllo pastry sheets, thawed
- ½ cup chunky peanut butter
- Pinch of salt
- 8 teaspoons marshmallow fluff

Directions

1. Brush 1 filo pastry sheet with butter and place a second sheet of filo on top of first one.
2. Brush it with butter and repeat till all sheets are used.
3. Cut the phyllo layers in 8 strips and put 1 teaspoon of marshmallow fluff and 1 tablespoon of peanut butter on the underside of a filo strip.
4. Fold the tip of the sheet over the filling to form a triangle.
5. Fold repeatedly in a zigzag manner until the filling is fully covered.
6. Preheat air fryer 360 degrees F and place the pastries into cooking basket.
7. Cook for about 5 minutes and season with a pinch of salt before serving.

Nutrition: Calories: 283 Carbs: 20.2g Fats: 20.6g Proteins: 6g Sodium: 320mg Sugar: 3.4g

Fruity Tacos

Serves: 4/Prep Time: 15 mins

Ingredients
- 8 tablespoons strawberryjelly
- 4 soft shell tortillas
- ½ cup blueberries
- 4 tablespoons powdered sugar
- ½ cup raspberries

Directions
1. Preheat the air fryer at 300 degrees F.
2. Spread strawberryjelly over each tortilla and top with blueberries and raspberries.
3. Sprinkle with powdered sugar and place the tortillas in an Airfryer basket.
4. Cook for about 5 minutes until crispy.

Nutrition Calories: 310 Carbs: 64.4g Fats: 4.7g Proteins: 3.3g Sodium: 370mg Sugar: 35.3g

Main Dish - Beef Recipes

Beef and Broccoli

Serves: 4

Ingredients:

- 2 tbsp. olive oil
- 3 crowns broccoli florets
- 1 ½ lbs. flank steak, cut into thin slices
- 1 tbsp. minced garlic
- ¾ cup beef broth
- 2 tbsp. sesame oil
- ½ tsp. onion powder
- ½ cup coconut aminos
- ¼ tsp. red pepper flakes
- ¼ tsp. salt
- 1/8 tsp. pepper
- 2 tsp. arrowroot flour
- Chopped green onions
- Sesame seeds

Directions:

1. Fill a microwave-safe dish with water and add the broccoli florets. Heat in the microwave until slightly steamed, for about 3 minutes. Drain and set aside.

2. Set the pot to Sauté and add olive oil. Working in batches, sear the beef slices for about 1 minute per side. Place cooked beef on a plate.

3. In the same pot, sauté garlic for 1 minute or until fragrant. Stir in beef broth, sesame oil, onion powder, coconut aminos, salt, pepper, and red pepper flakes. Add beef and any juices from the plate. Secure the lid and cook for 10 minutes on Manual function.

4. Quick-release pressure and remove the lid. Switch back to Sauté.

6. Slowly stir in arrowroot flour, whisking with a fork as you do so. Add the broccoli florets and continue stirring to thicken sauce. Spoon out the beef and florets and arrange in a serving dish.

7. Let the remaining sauce simmer and thicken up. Once it's bubbling and thick, pour it over the beef and broccoli in the dish. Garnish with extra red pepper flakes, green onions, and sesame seeds.

Pot Roast

Serves: 8

Ingredients:

- 3 lbs. grass-fed beef roast, cut into 4 chunks
- 1 tbsp. avocado oil
- 1 tbsp. garlic oil
- 1 tsp. salt
- 1 cup water
- 1 bunch fresh thyme
- 2 tbsp. fresh rosemary, chopped
- 2 cups diced potatoes
- 2 cups diced carrots
- ½ cup diced green onions
- 2 tbsp. cassava flour

Directions:

1. Select Sauté and add the oils. Place the roast in the bottom of the pot and season with salt. Cook until browned on all sides, about 5 minutes.

2. Press Cancel and stir in water and fresh herbs. Secure the lid, select the Manual function, and cook for 40 minutes.

3. Meanwhile, combine the chopped vegetables in a bowl. Set aside.

4. When timer goes off, release pressure naturally for 15 minutes and quick-release any remaining steam. Remove the lid and add in the vegetable mix. Cover the veggies with as much liquid as possible. Secure the lid.

5. Set to Manual function and cook again for additional 10 minutes. Hit Cancel and release pressure. Take the beef and vegetables out into a large serving platter.

6. Stir the cassava flour into the liquid that is left in the pot. Stir well until completely incorporated. Set to Sauté and stir continuously until the sauce thickens.

7. Pour the sauce over the beef and veggies in the platter and serve hot!

Beef and Plantain Curry

Serves: 5 - 6

Ingredients:

For the marinade

- 2 tsp. coconut oil
- 1 tsp. sea salt
- 1 tsp. turmeric powder

- 1 tsp. ginger powder
- 1 tsp. garlic powder

For the curry

- 2 lbs. bottom-blade pot roast, sliced into 1.5-inch cubes
- 3 tsp. coconut oil
- 2 small onions, thinly sliced
- 1 cup coconut milk
- 1 cinnamon stick

- 4 kaffir lime leaves
- 1 ripe plantain, cut lengthwise and sliced into 1-inch chunks
- 1 tsp. sea salt
- 1 tbsp. chopped coriander leaves

Directions:

1. Combine all the ingredients for the marinade in a small mixing bowl. Marinate the beef in this mixture for at least an hour.

2. Select Sauté and add coconut oil. Cook the onions until translucent and set aside.

3. Cook the marinated beef in the pot until browned on all sides. Add extra oil as needed. Set aside.

4. Add coconut milk to the pot, stirring and scraping off any browned bits at the bottom. Add in the cooked onions, seared beef, cinnamon stick, and kaffir lime leaves. Secure the lid, turn to Manual function, and cook for 35 minutes.

5. Once done, release pressure naturally. Switch to Sauté and stir in the plantain. Stir gently to combine. Season with salt and let simmer until the gravy is thickened and the plantain is cooked, about 5 minutes.

6. Remove the kaffir lime leaves and cinnamon stick. Garnish with chopped coriander before serving.

Corned Beef with Cabbage

Serves: 4 - 6

Ingredients:

- 2-3 lbs. corned beef brisket

- 3 cups beef broth

- ½ tsp. mustard seeds
- 1 tsp. whole white or black peppercorns
- 4 whole cloves
- 4 bay leaves
- 2 drops liquid smoke
- Purified water
- 4 Yukon gold potatoes, skinned and sliced into bitesize pieces
- 4 carrots, sliced into bitesize pieces
- 1 head cabbage, sliced into large chunks

Directions:

1. Place the brisket in the Instant Pot, along with beef broth, mustard seeds, peppercorns, cloves, bay leaves, and liquid smoke. Add water until the brisket is covered. Secure the lid. Select the Meat/Stew function and cook for 55 minutes on high pressure.

2. Once done, release pressure naturally for about 15 minutes and open the lid. Pour the liquid through a sieve and into a stockpot, catching the cloves, bay leaves, and peppercorns. Turn off the Instant Pot and keep the brisket covered.

3. Add the potatoes and carrots to the stockpot and put to a boil over medium-high heat. Once it starts boiling, stir in the cabbage and lower the heat. Cover and simmer for 20 minutes or until the veggies are soft. Add salt as needed.

4. Cut up the brisket and serve hot with the broth and vegetables.

Saucy Meatballs

Serves: 4

Ingredients:

For the meatballs

- 1 ½ lbs. grass-fed ground beef
- ½ tsp. sea salt

For the sauce

- 1 cup tomato sauce
- 4 heirloom tomatoes, roughly chopped
- 1 medium onion, roughly chopped
- 4 cloves garlic, crushed
- 10 mini bell peppers, halved and seeded

- ¼ tsp. black pepper
- 2 tsp. adobo spice

- 1 tsp. garlic powder
- 1 tsp. sea salt
- ½ tsp. red pepper flakes
- ¼ tsp. black pepper

Directions:

1. Season ground beef with sea salt, black pepper, and adobo spice. Form into meatballs using your hands. Set the Instant Pot to Sauté and cook the meatballs until browned on all sides. Remove and set aside.

3. Switch to Stew/Meat function. Add all the ingredients for the sauce to the pot and place the seared meatballs on top. Secure the lid and cook for 35 minutes.

4. When cooking time is up, spoon the meatballs out and place on a serving dish.

5. Using an immersion blender, puree the veggies that remain in the pot until the consistency becomes saucy or soup-like. Pour this sauce all over the meatballs and serve.

Mexican Beef

Serves: 6

Ingredients:

- 2 ½ lbs. beef brisket, cut into 1.5-inch cubes
- 1 ½ tsp. kosher salt
- 1 tbsp. chili powder
- 1 tbsp. ghee
- 1 medium onion, thinly sliced
- 6 cloves garlic, crushed
- 1 tbsp. tomato paste
- ½ tsp. fish sauce
- ½ cup bone broth
- ½ cup roasted tomato salsa
- Ground black pepper
- 2 radishes, thinly sliced
- ½ cup chopped cilantro

Directions:

1. Mix together cubed beef, salt and chili powder in a large bowl.

2. Select the Sauté function on the Instant Pot. Melt the ghee and sauté the onions until translucent. Add garlic and tomato paste and cook until fragrant, about 30 seconds.

3. Stir in seasoned beef, along with fish sauce, bone broth, and tomato salsa. Secure the lid and turn to Manual setting. Cook for 35 minutes on high pressure.

4. Once cooking time is up, release pressure naturally for 15 minutes and open the lid. Season beef with salt and pepper. Top with radishes and cilantro and serve hot.

Braised Cubed Steak

Serves: 8

Ingredients:

- 8 pcs. cubed steak (about 28 oz.)
- 1 ¾ tsp. adobo seasoning
- black pepper
- ½ medium onion, thinly sliced
- 1 small red bell pepper, thinly sliced
- 1 cup water
- 1 (8 oz.) can tomato sauce
- 1/3 cup pitted green olives

- 2 tbsp. brine (liquid from the olives jar)

Directions:

1. Season the cubed steak with adobo seasoning and black pepper. Place in the Instant Pot and top with bell peppers and onions. Pour water and tomato sauce all over, then add the green olives and brine.

2. Secure the lid and cook for 25 minutes on high pressure. Once done, release pressure naturally and serve hot.

Beef Barbacoa

Serves: 8 - 10

Ingredients:

- 3 lbs. grass-fed chuck roast, trimmed of fat and sliced into large chunks
- 6 cloves garlic, crushed
- 1 large onion, chopped
- 2 (4 oz.) cans green chilies
- 1 tsp. salt
- 1 tsp. pepper
- 1 tbsp. cumin

- 1 tbsp. oregano
- Juice of 3 fresh limes
- 3 dried chipotle peppers, stemmed and broken
- 3 tbsp. coconut vinegar
- ½ cup water
- Chopped fresh chives

Directions:

1. Place all the ingredients in the Instant Pot. Stir to combine. Secure the lid, select Manual function, and cook for 60 minutes.

2. Release pressure naturally once done. Open the lid. Shred the beef using a fork and turn to Sauté function. Stir continuously until some the liquid is reduced. This can take up to 20-30 minutes.

3. Garnish with fresh chives and serve.

Ground Beef Tacos

Serves: 4

Ingredients:

- 2 lbs. grass-fed ground beef
- 3 tbsp. avocado oil
- ½ cup white onion, chopped

- 5 tbsp. tomato paste
- ¼ cup apple cider vinegar
- ¾ cup chicken broth

Spices:

- ¼ tsp. cayenne pepper
- 1 tsp. chipotle powder
- 1 tsp. salt
- 1 tsp. oregano
- 2 tsp. minced garlic
- 2 tsp. ground coriander
- 2 tsp. paprika
- 3 tsp. cumin
- 1 tbsp. chili powder

Directions:

1. Select the Sauté function. Add avocado oil and sauté onions for 2-3 minutes. Add ground beef and cook for another 2-3 minutes. Hit Cancel.

2. Combine all the spices in a bowl and toss it into the pot. Stir in tomato paste, apple cider vinegar, and broth. Close the lid, select Manual setting, and set cooking time to 7 minutes. Once done, quick-release pressure.

3. Serve in a salad or over taco shells.

Beef Stroganoff

Serves: 6

Ingredients:

- 1 tbsp. avocado oil
- 1 small white onion, diced
- 3 cloves garlic, minced
- 1 ½ lbs. sirloin steak tips, cut into small chunks
- ½ tsp. garlic powder
- ½ tsp. onion powder
- ¼ cup red wine vinegar
- ¼ cup coconut aminos
- 1 ¼ cups beef broth
- 1 ¼ cups sliced mushrooms
- ½ cup coconut milk
- 2 tbsp. water
- 3 tbsp. arrowroot starch
- Salt and pepper

Directions:

1. Turn to Sauté setting and add avocado oil. Sauté onions for 2 minutes. Add garlic and sauté for another 2 minutes. Press Cancel.

2. Season beef with onion and garlic powder and a tad of salt and pepper. Set the beef on top of the onion-garlic mix in the pot.

3. In a small mixing bowl, stir together red wine vinegar, coconut aminos, and beef broth, and pour over the beef. Toss in the sliced mushrooms.

5. Secure the lid and cook for 15 minutes on high pressure. Release pressure naturally when cooked and remove lid carefully. Stir in coconut milk. Turn to Sauté function and cook until the milk dissolves. Combine water and arrowroot starch and pour into the pot to thicken sauce.

6. Serve over zoodles or cauliflower rice.

Main Dish - Chicken Recipes

Greek Chicken

Serves: 6

Ingredients:

- 2 lbs. boneless, skinless chicken thighs
- ½ tsp. sea salt
- ¼ tsp. ground black pepper
- 2 tbsp. olive oil
- 3 cloves garlic, crushed
- 1 cup kalamata olives
- 1 (8 oz.) jar artichoke hearts (marinated), drained
- 1 (12 oz.) jar roasted red peppers (marinated), drained and chopped
- 1 small red onion, sliced
- ¼ cup red wine vinegar
- 2/3 cup chicken broth
- ½ fresh lemon, juiced
- 1 tsp. dried thyme
- 1 tsp. dried oregano
- 2 tbsp. arrowroot starch
- Chopped fresh basil, for garnish
- ½ cup feta cheese, crumbled (optional), for garnish

Directions:

1. Season both sides of the chicken breasts with salt and pepper.

2. Set the pot to Sauté. Heat olive oil and sauté garlic for 1 minute. Add the chicken breasts and sear for about 2 minutes per side.

3. Place the kalamata olives, artichoke hearts, and red peppers in the bottom of the pot so that they fill in the gaps in between the chicken breasts. Place some on top. Add the sliced onions over the mixture.

4. In a large bowl, combine red wine vinegar, chicken broth, lemon, thyme, and oregano. Stir well. Pour this mixture over the chicken mixture in the pot. Close and secure lid.

5. Select the Manual setting and cook for 7 minutes on high pressure. Once done, quick-release pressure to release all the steam.

6. Open the lid and spoon some of the juice out into a small bowl. Add the arrowroot starch to the bowl and whisk well to combine. Add the mixture back to the pot. Leave the sauce to thicken up for a few minutes.

8. Serve over cauliflower rice or potatoes. Season with salt and pepper and garnish with basil and feta cheese (if using) before serving.

Chicken Tikka Masala

Serves: 4

Ingredients:

- 2 tbsp. olive oil
- 3 cloves garlic, minced
- 1 small onion, diced
- 1 1-inch piece fresh ginger, skinned and chopped
- ¼ tsp. cayenne pepper
- 1 tsp. ground coriander
- 1 tsp. ground turmeric
- 1 tsp. garam masala
- 2 tsp. paprika
- 2 tsp. cumin
- 1 (14 oz.) can diced tomatoes, undrained
- 1 ½ lbs. skinless, boneless chicken breasts
- ½ cup chicken broth
- ½ cup coconut milk
- 1 tbsp. arrowroot starch
- Juice of 1 fresh lemon
- Fresh basil, chopped

Directions:

1. Set the Instant Pot to Sauté. Heat olive oil and cook garlic, onion, and ginger for 3-4 minutes. Hit Cancel then stir in all the spices. Scrape the bottom of the pot to create a paste.

2. Mix in diced tomatoes, then place the chicken breast on top. Add the broth then secure the lid. Set to Manual function and cook for 7 minutes on high pressure.

3. When cooking time is up, quick-release pressure and carefully open the lid. Place the chicken on a plate or chopping board and chop with a knife or fork (the meat will be tender so a fork will do as well). Return the chicken to the pot.

4. Select the Sauté function and simmer for 4-5 minutes. Add coconut milk. Combine lemon juice and arrowroot starch in a bowl and pour it into the pot to thicken the mixture. Sprinkle with salt to taste.

5. Once the sauce is thick, ladle the dish into separate bowls and garnish with fresh basil. Serve immediately.

Braised Chicken Drumsticks

Serves: 6

Ingredients:

- 6 chicken drumsticks, skin removed
- 1 tsp. kosher salt
- 1/8 tsp. ground black pepper
- 1 tsp. dried oregano
- 1 tbsp. cider vinegar
- 1 tsp. olive oil
- 1 ½ cups tomatillo sauce (in jar)
- 1 jalapeno, cut in half and seeded
- ¼ cup chopped leaves, divided

Directions:

1. Season drumsticks with salt, pepper, oregano, and cider vinegar. Marinate for a few hours.

2. Select the Sauté function on your Instant Pot. Heat olive oil and cook the marinated chicken until browned, about 4 minutes per side.

3. Stir in tomatillo sauce, jalapeno, and 2 tablespoons cilantro. Secure the lid and cook for 20 minutes on high pressure. Quick-release pressure.

4. Transfer to a serving bowl and garnish with the remaining cilantro leaves before serving.

Chicken Mushroom Stroganoff

Serves: 6

Ingredients:

- 1 ½ lbs. chicken breast, sliced into 1/5-inch chunks
- 2-3 tbsp. arrowroot starch
- 2 tbsp. olive oil
- 4 large portobello mushrooms, sliced
- 3 cloves garlic, minced
- ¾ cup chicken broth
- 1 tbsp. apple cider vinegar
- 2 tbsp. coconut aminos
- ½ cup full-fat coconut milk
- Salt to taste

Directions:

1. Place chicken breast chunks into a Ziploc bag or Tupperware. Add the arrowroot starch and toss to completely cover the chicken.

2. Set Instant Pot to Sauté function. Heat oil and add the coated chicken. Cook until slightly brown on both sides, about 1-2 minutes per side. Toss in garlic and mushrooms. Hit Cancel.

3. In a small mixing bowl, combine chicken broth, apple cider vinegar, and coconut aminos. Pour this mixture over the chicken in the pot. Secure lid. Set to Manual and cook for 7 minutes on high pressure.

5. Once done, release pressure naturally for 15 minutes. Quick-release any remaining steam and remove the lid.

6. If the mixture is too thin, add another tablespoon of arrowroot starch to the coconut milk, otherwise pour in the coconut milk alone. Mix until everything is well incorporated. Hit Cancel.

7. Select the Sauté function and cook again for additional 10 minutes until the sauce becomes creamy. Press Cancel and serve immediately.

Sweet Potato Chicken Curry

Serves: 4 - 5

Ingredients:

- 2 tsp. coconut oil
- 3 cloves garlic, minced
- 1 small yellow onion, chopped
- 1 lb. chicken breast, cut into 1-inch cubed
- 2/3 cup chicken broth
- 1 sweet potato, diced
- 2 cups green beans, trimmed
- 1 red pepper, diced
- ½ tsp. sea salt
- ½ tsp. cayenne
- 1 tsp. ground turmeric
- 1 tsp. cumin
- 3 tbsp. curry powder
- 1 (14 oz.) can full-fat coconut milk
- Fresh cilantro, for serving
- Cashew nuts, for serving
- Tapioca or arrowroot starch, to thicken sauce (optional)

Directions:

1. Select the Sauté function. Add coconut oil, garlic, and onion, and sauté until the onion is translucent.

2. Switch to Manual function. Add in the chicken breast, chicken broth, sweet potatoes, green beans, red pepper, sea salt, cayenne, turmeric, cumin, and curry powder. Secure the lid and cook for 12 minutes on high pressure.

3. When timer goes off, quick-release pressure and remove lid. Turn to Sauté function. Stir in coconut milk and allow to cook until heated through, about 2-3 minutes. To thicken sauce, whisk starch with 2 tablespoons of water. Pour into the curry.

4. Garnish with fresh cilantro and cashews, and serve over cauliflower rice, if desired.

Chicken Cacciatore

Serves: 6

Ingredients:

- 2 tsp. olive oil
- 1 green bell pepper, seeded and chopped
- 3 shallots, chopped
- ½ cup chicken broth
- 4 cloves garlic, crushed
- 1 (8-10 oz.) pack mushrooms, sliced
- 6 skinless, boneless chicken breasts
- 2 cans crushed tomatoes
- 2 tbsp. tomato paste
- 1 can black olives, pit removed
- ½ tsp. red pepper flakes
- Fresh parsley
- Sea salt and black pepper

Directions:

1. Select the Sauté function and add olive oil, bell pepper, and shallots. Cook until the shallots are slightly soft, about 2 minutes.

2. Stir in chicken broth and let simmer for 2-3 minutes. Add in garlic and mushrooms and place the chicken breasts on top. Add the crushed tomatoes over the chicken, do not stir. Top with tomato paste, making sure the tomatoes and tomato paste are covering the chicken breasts. Secure the lid. Cook for 8 minutes on high pressure.

3. When time is up, release pressure naturally. Open the lid and stir in black olives, red pepper, parsley, sea salt and black pepper. Stir.

4. Serve hot over noodles or shredded cabbage.

Chicken Tacos

Serves: 4

Ingredients:

- 1 ¼ lbs. chicken thighs or breasts
- ¼ cup water
- ½ cup homemade or organic salsa
- 1/8 tsp. cayenne pepper
- ¼ tsp. sea salt
- ¼ tsp. ground black pepper
- ½ tsp. ground coriander
- ½ tsp. garlic powder
- 1 tsp. chili powder
- 1 tsp. ground cumin
- Fresh cilantro
- Salad greens
- Toppings: avocado, olives, lime wedge, fresh salsa, your choice of chopped veggies

Directions:

1. Add all ingredients, save salad greens and toppings, to the bottom of your Instant Pot. Secure the lid and seal the valve. Select Manual or Poultry setting and cook for 17-19 minutes.

3. Once done, release pressure naturally for 10-15 minutes. Quick-release any remaining steam and carefully open the lid. Using two forks, shred the chicken into the pot. If the meat is watery, turn to Sauté function and cook until the fluid is reduced, about 5-8 minutes.

4. Serve chicken over a layer of salad greens and top with fresh cilantro. Add all or any of the suggested toppings.

Creamy Southwest Chicken

Serves: 5

Ingredients:

- ½ tsp. cayenne pepper
- 1 tsp. sea salt
- 1 tsp. garlic powder
- 1 tsp. ground coriander
- 1 tsp. ground cumin
- 2 tsp. paprika
- 1 tbsp. chili powder
- 2 tsp. olive oil
- 1 ½ lbs. boneless chicken breasts or thighs
- ¼ cup freshly squeezed lime juice
- 1 cup chicken broth
- 2 red bell peppers, sliced
- 1 tbsp. water
- 1 tbsp. arrowroot starch
- ½ cup full-fat coconut milk
- Salt and pepper
- Fresh cilantro

Directions:

1. Combine all the spices in a small mixing bowl and rub the mixture into the chicken. Set aside any remaining spices.

2. Set the Instant Pot to Sauté. Grease the bottom of the pot with olive oil. Cook the spiced chicken for 1-2 minutes per side to seal in the flavors. Hit Cancel.

3. Add lime juice, chicken broth, bell peppers, and leftover spices over the chicken. Close the lid. Select Manual function and cook for 7 minutes on high pressure.

4. Once cooking time is up, quick-release pressure and let out all the steam. Carefully remove the lid and pour in the coconut milk. Combine arrowroot starch and water and pour it into the pot to thicken the mixture. Feel free to add another tablespoon of arrowroot until desired thickness is reached.

5. Season with salt and pepper and garnish with fresh cilantro. Serve over vegetable noodles or cauliflower rice.

Buffalo Chicken Meatballs

Serves: 6

Ingredients:

- 1 ½ lbs. ground chicken
- 2 cloves garlic, minced
- ¾ cup almond meal
- 2 green onions, finely sliced
- 1 tsp. sea salt
- 2 tbsp. ghee
- 4 tbsp. butter
- 6 tbsp. hot sauce
- Chopped green onions

Directions:

1. Using your hands, combine ground chicken, garlic, almond meal, green onions, and sea salt in a large mixing bowl. Be sure not to overdo it.

2. Grease your palms with coconut oil and form the meat batter into balls about 1-2 inches wide.

3. Select the Sauté function on your Instant Pot. Add ghee and place some of the chicken meatballs in the bottom of the pot. Work in batches so as not to overcrowd the pot. Cook until all sides of the meatballs are brown, flipping once every minute.

4. Meanwhile, make the buffalo sauce by combining butter and hot sauce in an oven-proof bowl. Heat in the microwave until the butter has completely melted. Stir the sauce with a spoon.

5. Pour the sauce evenly over the chicken meatballs. Secure the lid and valve. Select Poultry function and cook for 15-20 minutes. Once done, quick-release pressure.

6. Serve hot on its own or over zoodles or cauliflower rice.

Whole Roasted Chicken

Serves: 8 - 10

Ingredients:

- 1 (3-6 lbs.) whole chicken
- 1 ½ tbsp. olive oil
- 1 tbsp. fresh rosemary, chopped
- 4-6 cloves garlic, crushed
- 1 tsp. kosher salt
- ¼ tsp. black pepper
- ½ tsp. paprika
- Zest from 1 fresh lemon
- 1 cup chicken broth
- 1 onion, sliced into 4 wedges

Directions:

1. Remove any stuffing inside the chicken. Rinse chicken with cold water and pat dry with some paper towels. Lay it on a platter or baking pan and set aside.

2. In a small mixing bowl, mix together olive oil, rosemary, garlic, salt, pepper, paprika, and lemon zest. Cut the zested lemon in half and place inside the chicken. Massage the spice mixture onto the sides of the chicken.

3. Select the Sauté function. Add olive oil and cook the chicken until golden brown, about 3-4 minutes. Flip the chicken to cook the other side for another 3-4 minutes.

4. Remove chicken from the pot and back onto the platter. Add chicken broth to the pot and scrape any browned bits off using a spatula. Place the onion wedges in the bottom of the pot and place the chicken, breast-side up, on top of the wedges.

5. Secure the lid and cook for 20-30 minutes on high pressure. Once done, release pressure naturally for 10 minutes, then quick-release any residual steam.

6. Tent a cutting board with aluminum foil and place the chicken over it. Let rest for about 5 minutes before cutting up. You may separate the juices in the pot and use it to make gravy.

Main Dish - Pork Recipes

Pulled Pork w/ BBQ Sauce

Serves: 8

Ingredients:

- 4 lbs. organic pork shoulder, bone-in
- 1 tbsp. onion powder
- 1 tbsp. garlic powder
- 1 tbsp. chili powder
For the sauce
- 2 tsp. chili powder
- 2 tsp. garlic powder
- 4-6 dates, soaked in warm water for 10-15 minutes

- 1 tbsp. ground pepper
- 1 tbsp. sea salt
- 1 tbsp. smoked paprika
- 2 cups bone broth

- ¼ cup tomato paste
- ½ cup coconut aminos

Directions:

1. Mix together onion, garlic, and chili powder, ground pepper, sea salt, and smoked paprika. Rub this spice mixture into the pork roast. Place it in the Instant Pot, skin-side up, then pour in the bone broth. Secure the lid, turn to Manual function, and cook for 90 minutes.

3. Meanwhile, make the BBQ sauce. Add all the ingredients for the sauce in a food processor or blender. Blend until smooth. Set aside until the roast is cooked.

4. When timer goes off, release pressure naturally for 10-15 minutes. Transfer the pork onto a cutting board and shred using tongs or two forks. Place shredded pork in a platter or bowl, pour the BBQ sauce all over, and serve.

90-Minute Kalua Pork

Serves: 8 - 10

Ingredients:

- 4-5 lbs. pork shoulder, bone-in
- 1 tsp. sea salt
- ½ cup water
- 1 tbsp. liquid smoke
- 1 tsp. fish sauce
- ½ cup chopped pineapple

Directions:

1. Season pork with sea salt and place in the Instant Pot. Add water, liquid smoke, fish sauce, and pineapples. Secure the lid and cook for 90 minutes on high pressure.

2. Release pressure naturally for about 10-15 minutes. Transfer pork into a platter and shred, removing excess fat, if any. Pour the liquid that remains in the pot into a jar and wait until fat rises. Remove fat and discard.

3. Pour some of the liquid back onto the pork and serve.

Jamaican Jerk Pork Roast

Serves: 12

Ingredients:

- 4 lbs. pork shoulder
- 1 tbsp. olive oil
- ¼ cup sugar-free, MSG-free Jamaican Jerk spice blend
- ½ cup beef broth

Directions:

1. Rub olive oil into the roast and coat with the spice blend.

2. Select Sauté function and sear the meat until browned on all sides. Pour in the beef broth. Secure the lid and cook for 45 minutes on high pressure.

3. Release pressure naturally. Shred the pork and serve.

Pork Carnitas

Serves: 4 - 6

Ingredients:

- 3 lbs. boneless pork shoulder, sliced into 2-inch chunks
- ¾ tsp. sea salt
- Ground black pepper
- 1 tbsp. Mexican seasoning
- Juice of 1 fresh lime
- Juice of 2 fresh oranges
- 1 tbsp. ghee

Directions:

1. Add pork to the Instant Pot and season with salt, a bit of ground pepper, and Mexican seasoning.

2. Mix together the citrus juices in a measuring cup and add water until you reach the one-cup line. Pour this into the pot. Secure the lid, set to Manual function, and cook for 50 minutes.

3. Release pressure naturally and remove lid. Turn to Sauté setting. Shred the pork using two forks and continue to cook, stirring occasionally, until the liquid in the pot is almost gone. This can take up to 30 minutes.

4. Mix in the ghee and cook for 5 more minutes until the meat is browned in some spots. Serve hot over cauliflower rice, with avocado and lime slices on the side.

Baby Back Ribs

Serves: 4

Ingredients:

- 3 lbs. baby back ribs, sliced into 3 equal parts

Spices:

- ¼ tsp. cumin
- ¼ tsp. black pepper
- ½ tsp. sea salt
- ½ tsp. smoked paprika
- 1 cup broth or water
- Whole30-compliant barbecue sauce
- ½ tsp. onion powder
- ½ tsp. chili powder
- 1 tsp. garlic powder

Directions:

1. Combine all the spices and rub it into the ribs.

2. Place the wire rack in the pot and add broth or water. Stack the ribs upon the rack. Secure the lid, select Manual function, and cook for 30 minutes.

3. Meanwhile, preheat broiler to med-high heat.

5. Once cooking time is up, quick-release pressure and open the lid. Remove the ribs and place on a baking sheet. Brush with BBQ sauce on all sides and broil until the sauce is slightly caramelized and bubbly.

6. Slice up the ribs and serve hot.

Crispy Mojo Pork

Serves: 4

Ingredients:

- ¼ cup lime juice
- ¼ cup orange juice
- 1 tsp. salt
- ½ tsp. ground cumin
- 5 cloves garlic, minced
- 3 lbs. boneless chuck roast, sliced into 2-inch cubes
- Chopped cilantro

Directions:

1. Add lime juice, orange juice, salt, cumin, and garlic to the Instant Pot. Add the cubed pork and toss to evenly coat with the flavors. Close the lid and cook for 45 minutes on high pressure.

2. Release pressure naturally for about 10 minutes, then quick-release any remaining steam. Meanwhile, preheat your broiler.

3. Remove the pork and place on a baking sheet. Turn the pot to Sauté and let the liquid reduce or thicken up for 10-15 minutes, then pour it into a heatproof bowl. Skim off any fat that rises to the top.

4. Broil the pork until browned and crispy, about 3-5 minutes each side.

5. Pour the sauce over the pork and serve.

Pork Sirloin Tip Roast

Serves: 6 - 8

Ingredients:

- 3 lbs. pork sirloin tip roast
- ¼ tsp. chili powder
- ½ tsp. garlic powder
- ½ tsp. onion powder
- ½ tsp. sea salt
- ½ tsp. coarse black pepper
- 1 tbsp. vegetable oil
- ½ cup apple juice
- 1 cup water

Directions:

2. Combine all the spices and rub it into the pork roast.

3. Select Browning. Add oil to the pot and brown the pork on all sides. Pour in apple juice and water. Secure the lid and cook for 25 minutes on high pressure.

4. When timer goes off, release pressure naturally for 5 minutes, and quick-release any residual steam. Serve hot with steamed vegetables.

Pork Chops

Serves: 2

Ingredients:

- 2 pork chops, bone-in
- Salt and pepper
- 1 tbsp. vegetable oil
- 1 cup water
- 2 tbsp. chili paste

Directions:

1. Season pork with salt and pepper. Set the Instant Pot on Sauté function and add the oil. Cook the pork chops until browned, about 2 minutes per side, then transfer to a plate.

2. Add water to the pot and scrape off any browned bits at the bottom. Set the trivet inside the pot and place the pork chops on it. Add chili paste over the pork chops. Secure the lid and select Manual function.

3. Once done, release pressure naturally for about 10 minutes, then quick-release any remaining steam. Serve with sweet potatoes or salad.

Sausage and Peppers

Serves: 5

Ingredients:

- 10 Italian sausages
- 1 (15 oz.) can tomato sauce
- 1 (28 oz.) can diced tomatoes
- 4 cloves garlic, minced
- 4 large green bell peppers, seed and core removed, cut into ½-inch strips
- 1 tbsp. basil
- 1 cup water
- 1 tbsp. Italian seasoning

Directions:

1. Mix together tomato sauce, diced tomatoes, garlic, basil, water, and Italian seasoning in the Instant Pot. Add the sausages and place the bell peppers on top. Do not mix.

3. Secure the lid and cook for 25 minutes on high pressure. Once done, quick release pressure and remove lid. Serve hot and enjoy!

Teriyaki Pork Loin

Serves: 4

Ingredients:

- 1 ½ lbs. pork tenderloin
- 1 tbsp. coconut oil
- 1 tbsp. sesame oil
- 2/3 cup pineapple juice
- 1 ½ tsp. apple cider vinegar
- ½ cup coconut aminos
- 1 tsp. ginger powder
- 1 tbsp. arrowroot powder
- 1 tbsp. water

Directions:

1. Select the Sauté function. Heat coconut oil and cook the tenderloin for about 2 minutes per side, making sure the entire pork is seared.

2. Stir in sesame oil, pineapple juice, apple cider vinegar, coconut aminos, and ginger powder. Secure the lid, select Manual function, and cook for 8 minutes.

3. Once cooked, wait for 3-4 minutes before releasing the pressure. Remove the pork and let rest for a few minutes or until internal temperature reaches 145 degrees.

4. Meanwhile, combine water and arrowroot powder and pour it into the liquid in the pot. Whisk vigorously to thicken the sauce.

5. Pour the sauce over the tenderloin and serve with steamed vegetables or cauliflower rice.

Main Dish - Seafood Recipes

Seafood Gumbo

Serves: 8

Ingredients:

- 1 ½ lbs. sea bass fillets, cut into 2-inch chunks
- 3 tbsp. avocado oil
- 3 tbsp. Cajun seasoning
- 2 bell peppers, chopped
- 2 yellow onions, chopped
- 4 celery ribs, chopped
- ¼ cup tomato paste
- 3 ½ cups diced tomatoes
- 1 ½ cups bone broth
- 3 bay leaves

- 2 lbs. medium raw shrimp, deveined
- Sea salt and black pepper

Directions:

1. Season fillets with a tad of salt and pepper and half of the Cajun seasoning and stir to evenly coat the fish.

2. Add avocado oil to the Instant Pot and select Sauté function. Cook the fish for about 4 minutes or until cooked through on both sides. Transfer to a large platter.

3. Combine bell peppers, onions, celery, and the remaining Cajun seasoning in the pot and cook until fragrant, about 2 minutes. Press Cancel. Add the cooked fillets, tomato paste, diced tomatoes, bone broth, and bay leaves. Stir to combine. Secure the lid and cook for 5 minutes on Manual.

4. Once done, quick-release pressure and carefully open the lid. Switch back to Sauté and add in the shrimps. Cook until the shrimps become opaque, about 3-4 minutes. Season with salt and pepper.

5. Top with chives and serve with cauliflower rice.

Shrimp Boil

Serves: 4

Ingredients:

- 1 lb. white potatoes, sliced into small cubes
- 2 cups chicken broth
- 2 tbsp. Old Bay seasoning
- 1 pack mushrooms, stemmed
- 1 pack no-sugar kielbasa sausage, sliced
- 1 tbsp. minced garlic
- ½ tbsp. onion powder
- ½ tbsp. garlic powder
- ½ tbsp. salt
- 1 tbsp. pepper
- 1 ½ lbs. shrimps
- 1 cup water

Directions:

1. Add potato cubes, chicken broth, old bay seasoning, and a dash of salt to the Instant Pot. Close the lid, set on Beans/Chili function, and cook for 3 minutes at high pressure.

2. Quick-release pressure and add in mushrooms, sausages, shrimps, water, and all the spices. Stir well. Secure the lid and cook again on Beans/Chili function for 4 minutes on high pressure.

3. Release pressure and serve.

Lemon Garlic Salmon

Serves: 4

Ingredients:

- 1 ½ lbs. salmon fillets
- 1 tbsp. avocado oil
- ¾ cup water
- ¼ cup lemon juice
- A few sprigs of fresh basil, dill, parsley, tarragon, or a combo
- ¼ tsp. garlic powder
- ¼ tsp. sea salt
- 1/8 tsp. black pepper
- 1 lemon, thinly sliced

Directions:

1. Pour lemon juice and water to the Instant Pot. Add the fresh herbs and place the steamer rack in the pot.

2. Drizzle salmon fillets with avocado oil and sprinkle with salt, pepper, and garlic powder. Place the fillets in a single layer in the steamer rack. Top with a layer of lemon slices.

3. Secure the lid, set on Manual, and cook for 7 minutes on high pressure. Quick-release pressure once done. Serve warm with roasted veggies or salad.

Coconut Fish Curry

Serves: 4

Ingredients:

- A swirl of olive oil
- 6 curry leaves
- 2 cloves garlic, crushed
- 1 tbsp. freshly grated ginger
- 2 medium onions, cut into thin strips
- ½ tsp. ground fenugreek
- ½ tsp. ground turmeric
- 1 tsp. chili powder
- 2 tsp. ground cumin
- 1 tbsp. ground coriander
- 2 cups unsweetened coconut milk
- 1 ½ lbs. fish steaks, sliced into bitesize pieces
- 2 green chiles, cut into thin strips
- 1 tomato, chopped
- Juice of ½ lemon
- 2 tsp. salt

Directions:

1. Set to Sauté and add olive oil. Fry the curry leaves for about 1 minute, until slightly browned around the edges. Add garlic, ginger, and onion, and cook until the onions are soft. Toss in the 5 spices and sauté together for about 2 minutes.

3. Pour in coconut milk and scrape off any bits stuck at the bottom of the pot. Stir to incorporate all the flavors. Add the fish steaks, green chiles, and tomatoes, stir well. Secure the lid and cook for 5 minutes on low pressure.

4. Release pressure and open the lid. Season with salt and add a squeeze of lemon juice before serving.

Shrimp and Sausage Gumbo

Serves: 4

Ingredients:

- 2 tbsp. olive oil
- 12 oz. andouille sausage, cut into half-inch rounds
- 1 yellow onion, chopped
- 1 red bell pepper, chopped
- 2 celery ribs, chopped
- 2 tbsp. Cajun seasoning
- 2/3 cup chicken stock
- 1 (14.5 oz.) can diced tomatoes, drained
- 2 bay leaves
- 1 lb. shrimps
- Sea salt and ground black pepper
- Fresh chives

Directions:

1. Select Sauté and heat olive oil in the pot. Cook the sausage until browned, about 2-3 minutes each side. Transfer to a plate.

2. Stir together onions, bell pepper, celery, and Cajun seasoning in the pot and cook until fragrant, about 1-2 minutes. Hit Cancel. Add the cooked sausage, chicken stock, diced tomatoes, and bay leaves, and stir together. Secure the lid, select Manual, and cook for 5 minutes.

3. Release pressure naturally and remove the lid. Select Sauté and add in the shrimps. Cook until the shrimps are opaque, about 3-4 minutes. Season with salt and pepper.

4. Top with fresh chives and serve over cauliflower rice, if desired.

Vegetable Recipes

Cauliflower Rice

Serves: 4

Ingredients:

- 1 large cauliflower head, leaves removed, chopped
- 1 cup water
- 2 tbsp. olive oil

- ½ tsp. dried parsley
- ¼ tsp. salt
- ¼ tsp. paprika
- ¼ tsp. turmeric
- ¼ tsp. cumin
- Lime wedges
- Fresh cilantro

Directions:

1. Place the cauliflower in the steamer insert in the Instant Pot. Pour water into the pot. Secure the lid and select Manual function. Cook for 1 minute on high pressure.

2. Quick-release pressure and transfer cauliflower to a plate. Remove water from the pot and set the pot on Sauté function. Add olive oil and then return the cauliflower. Break up the pieces using a potato masher.

3. Add salt, dried parsley, and all the spices while heating and stirring. Top with fresh cilantro and spritz with lime juice. Serve with any main dish.

Butternut Squash

Serves: 6

Ingredients:

- 2 lbs. chopped butternut squash
- 1 cup broth or water
- 1 tsp. chili powder
- 1 tsp. garlic powder
- 1 tbsp. dried oregano
- 1 tbsp. pumpkin pie spice

Directions:

1. Add all the ingredients to the Instant Pot and stir well to combine. Cook for 3 minutes on high pressure.

2. Quick release pressure and serve hot.

Brussels Sprouts with Nuts and Pomegranate

Serves: 4

Ingredients:

- 1 lb. brussels sprouts, trimmed
- ¼ cup toasted pine nuts
- 1 pomegranate
- 1 cup water
- Salt and pepper
- Olive oil

Directions:

1. Pour water into the pot and add the steamer basket. Place the brussels sprouts in the steamer. Secure the lid and cook for 3 minutes on high pressure.

3. Release pressure and transfer the sprouts to a large serving dish. Season with salt and pepper and drizzle with olive oil. Sprinkle with pomegranate seeds and toasted pine nuts. Serve warm.

Beet Borscht

Serves: 4 - 6

Ingredients:

- 8 cups peeled and diced beets
- 2 large carrots, chopped
- 3 stalks celery, chopped
- 2 cloves garlic, chopped
- 1 medium onion, chopped
- 3 cups shredded cabbage
- Bay leaf
- 6 cups vegetable stock
- ½ tbsp. thyme
- 1 tbsp. salt
- ¼ cup chopped dill
- ½ cup sour cream or coconut yogurt

Directions:

1. Add all the ingredients, except dill and sour cream, to the Instant Pot. Select the Soup function and cook for 45 minutes. Once done, release pressure naturally.

2. Ladle into individual bowls. Garnish with chopped dill and add sour cream or coconut yogurt. Serve hot.

Moroccan Spiced Potatoes

Serves: 4

Ingredients:

- 1 lb. yellow potatoes, cut into 1-inch cubes
- 2 tbsp. coconut oil
- 2 tbsp. Moroccan spice mix
- 1 cup water
- ½ lemon

Directions:

1. Pour water to the pot and add the steamer basket. Place the potato cubes in the basket and secure the lid. Set on Manual function and cook for 5 minutes. Release pressure naturally once done.

2. Melt coconut oil in a cast-iron skillet set over medium-high heat. Add the steamed potatoes and sprinkle with Moroccan spice mix. Cook until the potatoes become crispy. Flip to cook the other side.

3. Transfer potatoes to a serving plate and spritz with lemon juice before serving.

Braised Carrots and Kale

Serves: 2

Ingredients:

- 1 tbsp. ghee
- 1 onion, thinly sliced
- 3 carrots, sliced into ½-inch rounds
- 5 cloves garlic, roughly chopped
- 10 oz. kale, roughly chopped (do not remove stems)
- ½ cup vegetable broth
- Kosher salt and freshly ground black pepper
- ¼ tsp. red pepper flakes
- Aged balsamic vinegar

Directions:

1. Select Sauté and melt the ghee. Cook onions and carrots until softened. Toss in garlic and cook until fragrant, about 30 seconds. Add kale, broth, and season with salt and pepper. Secure the lid, select Manual function, and cook for 5 minutes on high pressure.

2. Release pressure naturally for 10-15 minutes. Open the lid and give everything a good stir. Adjust seasoning according to taste. Sprinkle with red pepper flakes and add balsamic vinegar. Serve immediately.

Lemon Basil Ratatouille

Serves: 8

Ingredients:

- 2 medium summer squash, cut into small chunks
- 2 medium zucchini, cut into small chunks
- 1 small eggplant, cut into small chunks
- 1 large white onion, chopped
- 2 cups grape or cherry tomatoes, chopped
- 3 cloves garlic, minced
- 1 cup basil
- Juice of 1 fresh lemon
- 1/3 cup olive oil
- 2 tbsp. white wine vinegar
- 2 tbsp. tomato paste
- 1 tsp. salt

Directions:

1. Add all the chopped vegetables to the bottom of the pot.

2. In a blender or food processor, blend together garlic, basil, lemon juice, olive oil, vinegar, tomato paste, and salt until completely incorporated. Combine this to the vegetables in the pot.

4. Lock the lid and set on Manual function. Cook for 10 minutes on high pressure. Once done, release pressure naturally.

5. Garnish with extra basil and season with salt. Serve hot over vegetable noodles.

Side Dishes

Mashed Potatoes

Serves: 6 - 8

Ingredients:

- 3 lbs. red potatoes, diced
- 2 cups water
- 1 ½ cups bone broth
- ¼ cup ghee
- 1-2 tbsp. almond milk (unflavored, no sweeteners)
- 1 tsp. salt
- ½ tsp. pepper
- Fresh chives or rosemary

Directions:

1. Place potatoes into the bottom of the pot. Add water and broth and stir well. Add ghee and season with salt and pepper. Secure the lid, select Manual function, and cook for 6 minutes on high pressure. Quick-release pressure once done.

2. Spoon the potatoes out into a serving dish and start mashing. Incorporate 1 tablespoon of milk. Add another tablespoon if you want it to be creamier. Sprinkle with more salt and pepper to taste.

3. Top with fresh chives or rosemary and serve with a main dish.

Egg Salad

Serves: 4

Ingredients:

- 8 raw eggs
- 1 cup water
- ¼ cup chopped celery
- 1/3 cup mayonnaise
- 1 tsp. sea salt
- ½ tsp. black pepper

Directions:

1. Lightly coat a casserole or baking dish with cooking spray. (Make sure the dish fits in the Instant Pot). Crack the raw eggs into the dish.

2. Place the metal rack in the pot and pour in water. Set the dish on the rack and secure the lid. Select Manual function and cook for 5 minutes. Release pressure naturally once done.

4. Take the dish out of the pot. Slide the eggs onto a cutting board and chop.

5. In a large mixing bowl, stir together the chopped eggs, celery, mayonnaise, salt and black pepper. Keep in the fridge until ready to serve.

Steamed Asparagus

Serves: 1 - 2

Ingredients:

- Whole artichokes (to fit in a single layer), trimmed
- 1 cup water
- 1 lemon wedge

Directions:

1. Rub the trimmed part of the artichokes with the lemon wedge to avoid browning.

2. Pour water into the pot. Place the steamer basket in the pot and arrange the artichokes in a single layer in the basket. Secure the lid and select the Manual setting. Cook on high pressure for 5-15 minutes, depending on the size of the artichokes.

3. Release steam naturally for 10 minutes and quick-release any remaining pressure. Serve steamed artichokes with your choice of dipping.

Applesauce

Yields 1 quart

Ingredients:

- ½ cup apple juice or water
- 12 medium apples, core removed, diced

Directions:

1. Place the diced apples in the pot. Add water or apple juice. Cut a round parchment paper to cover the apples. Secure the lid, select Manual, and cook for 10 minutes.

2. Release pressure naturally and remove the parchment paper. Using a food mill or a handheld immersion blender, blend the apples until smooth. Store in a glass jar until ready to use.

Tomato and Zucchini Mélange

Serves: 4 - 6

Ingredients:

- 1 tbsp. vegetable oil
- 2 onions, chopped

- 6 medium zucchini, chopped
- 1 lb. cherry tomatoes
- 1 cup water or tomato puree
- 1 tsp. salt

- 1-2 cloves garlic, minced
- Swirls of olive oil
- 1 bunch fresh basil

Directions:

1. Select Sauté and add oil. Cook the onions for about 5 minutes or until soft. Stir in the zucchini, tomatoes, water or tomato puree, and salt. Secure the lid and cook for 5 minutes on high pressure.

2. Release pressure naturally. Add in minced garlic. Remove the vegetables and place in a bowl or dish. Add a few swirls of olive oil and top with fresh basil. Store the liquid in the fridge to be used as soup or stock in other recipes.

Homemade Ghee

Yields 2.5 cups

Ingredients:

- 24 oz. (1 ½ lbs.) grass-fed butter

Directions:

1. Place all the butter in the pot. Select the Slow Cook function and cook at normal temperature for 2 hours. Do not cover.

2. After 2 hours, switch to Sauté mode and stir the milk continuously for 9-10 minutes until it turns golden. Turn off heat and allow the ghee to cool down completely. If the milk solids continue to darken, remove the inner pot.

3. Using a fine mesh strainer, strain the homemade ghee into airtight glass bottles or mason jars. Store in the fridge or in a cabinet at room temperature. Keep away from direct heat or sunlight. Homemade ghee can last for a few months if properly stored.

Creamy Savoy Cabbage

Serves: 4 - 6

Ingredients:

- 1 onion, diced
- 1 cup diced bacon
- 2 cups bone broth
- 1 head (about 2 lbs.) Savoy cabbage, finely chopped

- 1 bay leaf
- 1 cup coconut milk
- ¼ tsp. nutmeg
- 2 tbsp. parsley flakes

- Sea salt

Directions:

1. Select Sauté and fry the onions and bacon until the onions are translucent and the bacon is crispy. Pour in bone broth, followed by cabbage and bay leaf. Scrape off any browned bits stuck at the bottom of the pot.

2. Cut a round parchment paper to cover the mixture in the pot. Secure the lid and cook for 4 minutes on Manual mode. When timer goes off, quick-release pressure, open the lid, and remove the parchment paper.

3. Turn to Sauté and bring the mixture to a boil. Stir in coconut milk and nutmeg. Simmer for about 5 minutes. Mix in parsley flakes before serving.

Steamed Sweet Potatoes

Serves: 4

Ingredients:

- 4 raw sweet potatoes
- 1 ½ cups water

Directions:

1. Add water to the pot. Place the steamer basket in the pot and arrange the potatoes in the basket. Close lid and steam for 18 minutes on Manual mode.

2. Release pressure naturally for 15 minutes. Remove the lid and transfer the potatoes into a bowl. Serve immediately.

The Lectin Free Recipes: Salad Recipes

Roasted Artichoke Salad

Yield: 1 to 2 servings

Ingredients:

For the Seasoning

- 1/8 teaspoon ground paprika
- 1/8 teaspoon ground black pepper
- 1/8 teaspoon Himalayan pink salt
- 1/8 teaspoon ground garlic powder

For the vinaigrette

- 1 tablespoon date nectar

- For the artichokes:
- 1 tablespoon avocado oil (100 percent pure)
- 1 14-ounce can artichoke hearts (drained)
- 1/8 teaspoon black ground pepper

- 1 shallot (finely chopped)
- 1/8 teaspoon Himalayan pink salt
- 2 tablespoons avocado oil (100 percent pure)

For the salad

- 2 to 4 cups mixed salad greens

- 1 tablespoon sesame seeds
- 2 tablespoons apple cider vinegar

Directions:

1. Put all ingredients for the seasoning in a bowl. Mix well and set aside.

2. Chop off the tips of the artichokes and cut into smaller pieces. Put in a different bowl along with avocado oil. Toss to coat. Add the seasoning mix. Gently toss until combined.

3. Arrange the seasoned artichokes in a pan lined with parchment paper. Roast in a preheated oven at 425 degrees for 15 minutes. Toss the pieces and roast for 10 more minutes.

4. Put all ingredients for the vinaigrette in a bowl. Mix until combined. Adjust according to taste.

5. Arrange 2 handfuls of the salad greens in a platter. Add the roasted artichokes on top and drizzle with the vinaigrette.

6. Serve at once.

Salmon Salad with Orange and Cheese

Yield: 1 serving

Ingredients:

- 2 ounces real Feta cheese crumbles
- 2 Navel oranges (peeled and sectioned)
- 1 pound wild salmon flakes

For the Dijon Vinaigrette

- 4 tablespoons extra virgin olive oil
- 1 teaspoon Dijon mustard
- 1 teaspoon honey (optional)
- Salt to taste

- 1/3 cup chopped hazelnuts (toasted)
- 1 small red onion (sliced)
- 5 ounces baby spinach

- 1 tablespoon fresh dill (chopped)
- 3 tablespoons white wine vinegar
- 1 lemon (juiced)

Directions:

1. Toss all ingredients for the salad and arrange on a plate.

2. Put all ingredients for the vinaigrette in a bowl. Whisk until combined.

3. Drizzle salad with the vinaigrette before serving.

Sweet Potato Salad with Vegan Cilantro Pesto

Yield: 2 cups

Ingredients:

For the sweet potatoes

- Himalayan pink salt and ground black pepper to taste

- 2 cups organic sweet potatoes (peeled and cut into cubes)

For the cilantro pesto

- 3 tablespoons apple cider vinegar
- 3 garlic cloves
- 1/3 cup nutritional yeast
- 1/2 cup pine nuts

- 1/2 teaspoon ground black pepper
- 1/2 teaspoon Himalayan pink salt
- 1/2 cup extra virgin olive oil
- 2 cups fresh cilantro

Directions:

1. Arrange the potato cubes on a baking tray lined with parchment paper. Sprinkle with salt and pepper. Bake in a preheated oven at 350 degrees for 35 minutes or until soft.

2. Put all liquid ingredients for the cilantro pesto in a blender. Process until combined. Add the remaining ingredients and process until smooth. Add seasonings according to taste.

3. Transfer the baked potatoes to a bowl. Add the pesto and toss until combined. Cover the bowl and refrigerate for at least 30 minutes before serving.

Kale Salad with Ham

Yield: 1 serving

Ingredients:

- 2 ounces Parmesan cheese (grated)
- 1 sweet onion (sliced)
- 1 bunch Lacinato kale (torn into smaller pieces)

- 1/4 cup pine nuts
- 2 ounces Spanish ham (diced)

For the lemon oil

- 2 tablespoons olive oil

- 1/2 lemon (juiced)

- Salt to taste

Directions:

1. Put all ingredients for the lemon oil in a bowl. Mix well and adjust according to taste.

2. Put all ingredients for the salad on a platter. Drizzle with lemon oil. Gently toss until combined.

Ham and Arugula Salad with Sweet Potato

Yield: 4 servings

Ingredients:

- 1/4 cup fresh tarragon leaves
- 2 ounces real Swiss cheese (shredded)
- 5 ounces baby arugula
- 1 pound sweet potato (peeled and cut into cubes)
- 1/4 cup shredded Parmesan cheese
- 2 ounces Prosciutto di Parma (crumbled)
- 1 tablespoon Dijon mustard
- 1 tablespoon white wine vinegar
- 1/4 cup extra virgin olive oil
- Sea salt and black pepper

Directions:

1. Put the sweet potatoes in a pot. Add enough cold water to cover all potatoes. Bring water to a boil over medium-high flame. Stir in 1 1/2 tablespoons of salt. Turn the heat to low and simmer for about 12 minutes.

2. Drain water from the pot. Rinse potatoes under cold water and dice into thin pieces.

3. Put half a teaspoon of salt, 1/4 teaspoon of pepper, mustard, vinegar, and oil in a bowl. Whisk until combined.

4. Divide the arugula into 4 small plates. Top each plate with sweet potatoes, tarragon, Swiss cheese, and ham. Add sauce and sprinkle with Parmesan cheese.

Steak Salad with Yogurt Dressing

Yield: 1 serving

Ingredients:

- 1 cup shirataki rice (rinsed and drained)
- 2 tablespoons pine nuts (toasted)
- 5 ounces baby spinach
- 1 pound medium-rare cooked grass-fed steak (sliced)

For the Yogurt Dressing

- 1 cup whole goat milk yogurt
- 2 tablespoons red wine vinegar
- 2 teaspoons fresh thyme leaves
- Salt and pepper to taste

Directions:

1. Put all ingredients for the yogurt dressing in a bowl. Whisk until combined.

2. Put all salad ingredients on a platter. Add the dressing. Toss until combined.

Peaches and Berries Salad with Spicy Tahini Dressing

Yield: 4 servings

Ingredients

For the Salad

- 1 cup pecans
- 2 cups blueberries
- 2 cups peaches (peeled and cubed)
- 8 handfuls of spring salad mix

For the Tahini dressing

- 8 to 10 tablespoons purified water
- 1/2 cup date nectar
- 1/2 teaspoon ground ginger
- 1/2 cup tahini

Directions:

1. Put all ingredients for the tahini dressing in a bowl. Whisk until combined. Adjust water and sweetener according to taste.

2. Divide the spring salad mix into 4 bowls. Top each with pecans, peaches, and blueberries. Drizzle salad with the dressing before serving.

Shrimp Salad with Herbed Vinaigrette

Yield: 2 servings

Ingredients:

For the salad

- 1 bunch radishes (quartered)
- 1 head escarole (torn into bite-size pieces)
- 1/2 red onion (thinly sliced)
- 1 pound shrimp (cooked with tail-on)

For the herbed vinaigrette

- 1/4 cup extra virgin olive oil
- 2 tablespoons white wine vinegar
- Salt and pepper to taste
- 1 teaspoon Dijon mustard

- 2 tablespoons fresh chives (chopped)
- 2 tablespoons capers
- 2 garlic cloves (minced)
- 1 small shallot (minced)

Directions:

1. Put all ingredients for the salad in a bowl. Toss to combine.

2. Mix to combine all ingredients for the vinaigrette in a small bowl. Pour this on top of the salad. Toss the salad until combined.

3. Serve at once.

Sweet Potato with Chipotle Salad and Tahini Dressing

Yield: 1 to 2 servings

Ingredients:

- 2 tablespoons red onions (diced)
- 2 handfuls spring salad mix
- 1 avocado (cubed)

For the sweet potatoes

- 1/4 teaspoon Himalayan pink salt
- 1 tablespoon avocado oil (100 percent pure)
- 1/2 teaspoon ground garlic powder
- 2 cups organic sweet potato cubes (peeled and cubed)
- 1 teaspoon ground chipotle powder

For the tahini dressing

- 2 pinches ground black pepper
- 2 tablespoons filtered water
- 1/4 teaspoon Himalayan pink salt
- 3 tablespoons lime juice
- 1/4 teaspoon ground garlic powder
- 1/4 cup organic tahini

Directions:

1. Put the sweet potato cubes in a bowl along with avocado oil. Toss until combined.

2. In another bowl, stir to combine garlic powder, chipotle powder, and Himalayan pink salt.

3. Transfer the sweet potato cubes in a pan lined with parchment paper. Sprinkle with the seasoning mix. Bake in a preheated oven at 350 degrees for 25 minutes.

4. Put all ingredients for the dressing in a bowl. Whisk until combined. Adjust seasonings according to taste.

5. Arrange the spring salad mix in a platter. Top with cubed avocado and diced red onions. Add the baked potatoes and pour dressing all over the salad.

6. Serve while warm.

The Lectin Free Recipes: Vegan Ice Cream

Superfood Ice Cream with Cacao Nibs

Yield: 2 servings

Ingredients:

- 1 teaspoon baobab powder
- 2 teaspoons moringa powder
- 1/2 cup organic granular sweetener
- 1 13.5-ounce can full-fat coconut milk
- 1/2 cup raw cacao nibs (for the mix-in)

Directions:

1. Put all ingredients for the ice cream in a blender. Process until smooth and combined. Adjust sweetener according to taste.

2. Transfer mixture to an ice cream maker. Process according to package directions. Fold in the cacao nibs.

3. You can already enjoy this like a soft-serve ice cream. If you want it firmer, transfer to a container, cover, and freeze for at least an hour.

Chocolatey Avocado Ice Cream

Yield: 2 servings

Ingredients:

For the ice cream

- 1/4 cup Xylitol (non-GMO)
- 1/4 cup raw cacao powder
- 2 avocados (pitted)
- 1 13.5-ounce can full-fat coconut milk

For the swirl

- 1 tablespoon organic date nectar
- 1/2 cup almond butter

Directions:

1. Put all ingredients for the ice cream in a blender. Process until creamy. Adjust the sweetener according to taste. Transfer to an ice cream maker and process according to package directions.

2. Put all ingredients for the swirl in a bowl. Mix until combined. Set this aside.

3. Transfer ice cream to a container. Add a tablespoon of the swirl on top and swirl using the edge of a knife. Cover the container and freeze for at least 2 hours.

Cauli-Banana Ice Cream

Yield: 1 to 2 servings

Ingredients:

For the ice cream

- 1 tablespoon almond butter
- 2 tablespoons raw cacao powder
- 1/4 cup, plus 1 tablespoon homemade almond milk

For the toppings

- 1 to 2 tablespoons raw cacao nibs

- 1 cup cauliflower rice (frozen)
- 1 large banana (frozen)

- 1/2 cup wild blueberries

Directions:

1. Put all ingredients for the ice cream in a blender. Process on a high speed until the consistency is similar to a soft-serve ice cream. Transfer to bowls. Top with blueberries and cacao nibs and serve at once.

Vegan Vanilla Ice Cream

Yield: 2 to 4 servings

Ingredients:

- 2 teaspoons vanilla extract
- 2 13.5-ounce cans full-fat coconut milk
- 1/2 cup Stevia blend (non-GMO)

- 1 pinch Himalayan pink salt
- 1 teaspoon vanilla bean powder

Directions:

1. Put all ingredients in a blender and process until combined. Transfer mixture to an ice cream machine. Process according to package directions.

2. Transfer to a container, cover, and freeze for at least 2 hours before serving. If you don't want to wait, you can enjoy it as a soft serve ice cream directly from the machine.

Strawberry Ice Cream

Yield: 4 servings

Ingredients:

- 2 cups diced strawberries

For the ice cream

- 2 teaspoons organic pure vanilla extract

- 1/2 cup Xylitol (non-GMO)

- 2 13.5-ounce cans organic full-fat coconut milk

Directions:

1. Put all ingredients for the ice cream in a blender and process until smooth. Adjust sweetener according to taste. Transfer to an ice cream machine and process according to package directions.

2. Transfer processed ice cream to a container. Fold in the diced strawberries. Cover the container and freeze for a couple of hours before serving.

Avocado and Raspberry Ice Cream Squares

Yield: 12 small squares

Ingredients:

- 1 cup freeze-dried raspberries for add-ins, plus 1/2 cup for toppings

For the ice cream

- 1/4 teaspoon Himalayan pink salt

- 1/4 teaspoon vanilla bean powder

- 1/4 cup organic date nectar

- 1/2 cup raw cacao powder

- 1 13.5-ounce can full-fat coconut milk

- 2 organic avocados (pitted)

Directions:

1. Freeze the can of coconut milk an hour before making the ice cream. Scoop the hardened fat and put in a blender. Reserve the remaining water from the can for a smoothie or other recipes. Add the rest of the ingredients for the ice cream to the blender and process until smooth. Add a cup of the free-dried raspberries and manually fold them into the mixture.

2. Transfer to an 8 by 5 pan lined with parchment paper. Use a spatula to spread it evenly. Add the toppings and freeze for 3 hours.

3. Once the ice cream is set, slice into squares. Put them in a container and freeze until ready to serve.

The Lectin Free Recipes: Breakfast

Cheesy Breakfast Burritos

Yield: 4 servings

Ingredients:

- 8 cassava flour tortillas (around 6 inches)
- 4 ounces crumbled goat cheese
- 6 eggs (beaten)
- Himalayan sea salt and black pepper to taste
- 2 garlic cloves (sliced)
- 2 ounces chopped spinach
- 2 tablespoons extra virgin olive oil

Directions:

1. Heat oil in a pan over medium flame. Add spinach, 1/4 teaspoon pepper, half a teaspoon of salt, and garlic. Stir until combined. Leave to cook for 3 minutes. Add the eggs all over the spinach. Leave to rest for 30 seconds. Using a spatula, push the eggs around the pan for about 4 minutes or until cooked. Remove from the stove. Put goat cheese on top and leave to soften.

2. Cover 4 tortillas at a time with a moist paper towel and heat in the microwave for 30 seconds.

3. Divide the cooked eggs into the heated tortillas. Fold each piece like a taco and serve while warm.

Flourless Garlic Breadsticks

Yield: 12 breadsticks

Ingredients:

For the garlic topping

- 1/8 teaspoon ground black pepper
- 1/8 teaspoon Himalayan pink salt
- 1 tablespoon dried oregano

For the breadsticks

- 3 flax eggs (combination of 9 tablespoons of filtered water and 3 tablespoons ground flax seeds)
- 1/2 teaspoon Himalayan pink salt
- 1 tablespoon extra virgin olive oil
- 4 garlic cloves (crushed)
- 1 teaspoon ground garlic powder
- 1 teaspoon extra virgin olive oil
- 2 cups mozzarella cheese
- 2 cups almond flour

Directions:

1. Put all ingredients for the breadsticks in a bowl. Mix until combined. Using your hands, shape the mixture into a ball. Put it on a pan lined with parchment paper and flatten out with about half an inch thickness. Bake in a preheated oven at 350 degrees for 20 minutes.

2. Put all ingredients for the garlic topping in a bowl. Mix until combined. Adjust seasonings according to taste. Spread the topping all over the baked bread.

3. Slice the bread into bite-size pieces and immediately serve.

Shirataki Fettuccine Pasta with Artichoke and Basil

Yield: 2 to 4 servings

Ingredients:

- 2 packs Shirataki Fettuccine Pasta
- For the sauce
- 1/2 teaspoon ground black pepper
- 1/2 teaspoon Himalayan pink salt
- 1 tablespoon extra virgin olive oil
- 2 garlic cloves (crushed)
- 2 tablespoons nutritional yeast

- 2 tablespoons freshly squeezed lemon juice
- 3/4 cup homemade almond milk
- 1 1/4 cups pine nuts
- For add-ins
- 1 14-ounce can artichoke hearts (chopped into long strips)
- 8 leaves fresh basil (chopped)

Directions:

1. Cook noodles according to package directions. Set aside.

2. Put all ingredients for the sauce in a blender. Process until combined and smooth. Adjust seasonings according to taste.

3. Put the cooked noodles and add-ins in a bowl. Add the sauce and gently toss until combined. Top with extra chopped basil before serving.

Protein Energy Balls with Dried Blueberries

Yield: 12 balls

Ingredients:

- 1 teaspoon vanilla bean powder
- 1 tablespoon almond butter
- 1 cup Medjool dates (pitted)

- 1 cup dried blueberries
- 2 tablespoons lectin-free protein powder

Directions:

1. Put all ingredients in a food processor. Pulse about 10 times. Get a spoonful of the mixture at a time and form it into a ball using your hands. Arrange the balls on a container. Cover and refrigerate for at least 30 minutes before serving.

Cauliflower Risotto with Mushrooms

Yield: 2 cups

Ingredients:

- 1/2 teaspoon ground sage
- 1 teaspoon ground black pepper
- 1 teaspoon Himalayan pink salt
- 2 tablespoons extra virgin olive oil
- 2 garlic cloves (crushed)
- 1/2 cup red onion (diced)
- 1 1/2 cups baby bella mushrooms (diced)
- For add-ins:
- 4 cups cauliflower rice
- 1 13.5-ounce can full-fat coconut milk

Directions:

1. Refrigerate the can of coconut milk the night before cooking the dish.

2. Put all ingredients in a pan, except the coconut milk and cauliflower rice, over medium-high flame. Saute for 5 minutes.

3. Scoop out the hardened coconut fat from the can. Reserve the liquid for other recipes. Transfer the coconut fat to the pan and add the cauliflower rice. Stir to combine all ingredients. Turn the heat to medium and simmer until the cauliflower rice becomes soft. Adjust seasonings according to taste.

4. Serve while hot.

Tasty Mushroom Soup

Yield: 2 to 4 servings

Ingredients:

- 1 garlic clove (crushed)
- 1 13.5-ounce can full-fat coconut milk
- 1 cup vegetable broth
- 1/2 cup red onions (chopped)
- 1/2 teaspoon dried thyme
- 1/2 teaspoon ground black pepper
- 1/2 teaspoon Himalayan pink salt
- 2 teaspoons avocado oil (100 percent pure)
- 1 tablespoon coconut aminos
- 1 cup baby bella mushrooms (diced)
- 1 cup shitake mushrooms (diced)

Directions:

1. Heat avocado oil in a pan over medium-high flame. Add the onions, garlic, mushrooms, dried thyme, black pepper, and Himalayan salt. Saute for 3 minutes. Add the coconut aminos, coconut milk, and vegetable broth. Stir until combined. Adjust seasonings according to taste. Turn the heat to medium-low and simmer for 15 minutes while stirring occasionally.

2. Top with chopped green onions, sliced mushrooms, and a bit of ground black pepper before serving.

Baked Peach Cobbler Pancakes

Yield: 4 servings

Ingredients:

- 2 ripe peaches (peeled and thinly sliced)
- 1/4 teaspoon baking soda
- 1/2 teaspoon baking powder
- 1/4 teaspoon sea salt
- 1/4 cup cassava flour
- 1/4 cup tapioca flour
- 1/4 cup coconut flour
- 1 tablespoon coconut oil (melted)
- 5 ounces goat milk kefir
- 5 drops liquid stevia
- Cinnamon (for sprinkling)
- 1 teaspoon vanilla extract
- 2 large pastured eggs

Directions:

1. In a bowl, put the eggs, kefir, stevia, and vanilla. Whisk until combined. Continue whisking as you gradually add the coconut oil to make sure that it doesn't solidify.

2. In another bowl, put the baking powder, sea salt, cassava flour, tapioca flour, and coconut flour. Mix until combined. Add this to the wet mixture. Whisk batter until smooth.

3. Transfer batter to a greased pie pan. Add half of the peaches on top and sprinkle with cinnamon. Bake in a preheated oven at 350 degrees for 30 minutes. Leave to cool for a few minutes before adding the remaining peaches on top. Serve while warm.

Cassava Flour Pancakes with Cinnamon

Yield: 4 servings

Ingredients:

- 1/4 cup water
- 3 tablespoons melted butter, plus more for serving
- 2 eggs (room temperature)
- 1/2 teaspoon vanilla extract

- 1 teaspoon cinnamon, plus more for serving
- 1 tablespoon baking powder
- 2 tablespoons monk's fruit sweetener
- 1 1/4 cup goat milk kefir
- 1/8 teaspoon nutmeg
- 1/4 teaspoon sea salt
- 1 cup cassava flour

Directions:

1. In a bowl, whisk to combine the dry ingredients – nutmeg, sea salt, cinnamon, baking powder, sweetener, and flour.

2. Put the wet ingredients in another bowl – eggs, vanilla, water, and kefir. Whisk until combined. Gradually whisk butter into the mixture.

3. Combine the 2 mixtures and whisk unto smooth.

4. Cook 3 pancakes in a nonstick pan over medium-low flame at a time. Transfer to a plate. Add butter and cinnamon on top before serving.

Cream of Asparagus Soup

Yield: 4 cups

Ingredients:

For add-ins

- 1 13.5-ounce can organic full-fat coconut milk
- 1 cup vegetable broth

For the sauteed vegetables

- 2 teaspoons organic extra-virgin olive oil
- 3 garlic cloves (crushed)
- 1 cup onion (diced)
- 12 stalks of asparagus (chopped)
- Himalayan pink salt and ground pepper to taste

Directions:

1. Heat olive oil in a skillet over medium-high flame. Add garlic, onions, asparagus, black pepper, and salt. Saute for 4 to 5 minutes. Adjust the seasonings according to taste.

2. Pour the coconut milk and vegetable broth on a blender. Add the cooked vegetables. Process on a high-speed setting until smooth and creamy. Transfer to a saucepan over medium flame. Simmer until warm.

Cauli Rice with Lime

Yield: 1 1/2 cups

Ingredients:

- 1/4 cup fresh cilantro (chopped)

For the cauliflower rice

- 1/2 teaspoon ground black pepper
- 1 teaspoon Himalayan pink salt
- 1 tablespoon avocado oil (100 percent pure)
- 2 tablespoons lime juice
- 2 cups cauliflower rice

Directions:

1. Put all ingredients for the cauliflower rice in a pan over medium-high flame. Toss until combined. Adjust seasonings according to taste and saute for 5 minutes. Remove from the stove. Stir in the chopped cilantro.

2. Transfer to a platter. Top with extra chopped cilantro before serving.

The Lectin Free Recipes: Main Course

Cheesy Chicken Enchiladas with Adobo Sauce

Yield: 8 enchiladas

Ingredients:

- 4 garlic cloves (peeled)
- 8 ounces crumbled goat cheese
- Sea salt and black pepper to taste
- 2 cups broth (divided)
- 8 ounces cooked pastured chicken (shredded)
- 1 white onion (chopped)
- 8 ounces shiitake mushrooms (chopped)
- 2 tablespoons olive oil
- Hot sauce and chopped fresh cilantro (for serving)
- 8 cassava flour tortillas (warmed in the microwave)
- 1/4 teaspoon paprika
- 1/2 teaspoon dried oregano
- 1/2 teaspoon ground cumin
- 1 teaspoon granular sweetener
- 1 teaspoon coconut aminos
- 3 teaspoons apple cider vinegar

Directions:

1. Heat oil in a pan over medium-high flame. Stir in the onions and mushrooms. Cook for about 8 minutes while constantly stirring. Add 1/4 teaspoon of pepper, half a teaspoon of salt, half a cup of broth, and chicken. Saute for a couple of minutes. Turn the heat to medium. Simmer for 4 minutes while stirring often.

2. Transfer the cooked dish to a bowl and add half of the crumbled goat cheese.

3. Prepare the adobo sauce. Put the remaining broth in a blender. Add coconut aminos, cider vinegar, paprika, oregano, cumin, sweetener, and 2 teaspoons of sea salt. Process for 3 minutes or until smooth. Pour half of the adobo sauce mixture into a glass baking dish.

4. Fill each tortilla with 1/4 cup of the mushroom mixture. Roll up and arrange all filled tortillas in the baking dish with the seam-side facing down. Drizzle the rest of the adobo sauce and goat cheese on top of the tortillas. Bake in a preheated oven at 350 degrees for 15 minutes.

5. Top with hot sauce and cilantro before serving.

Yummy Salmon Cakes

Yield: 4 servings

Ingredients:

- 2 scallions (roughly chopped)
- Sea salt and black pepper
- 2 tablespoons extra virgin olive oil (divided)
- 1/4 cup fresh mint (torn)
- 1/2 cup kalamata olives
- 1 cup millet
- 2 tablespoons Dijon mustard, plus more for serving
- 2 cups vegetable broth
- 1 pound wild Alaskan sockeye salmon (skinned)

Directions:

1. Put broth and millet in a saucepan over medium-high flame. Bring to a boil. Reduce flame to low, cover the pan, and simmer for 20 minutes. Stir in half a teaspoon of salt and pepper, a tablespoon of olive oil, mint, and olives.

2. Put salmon in a paper towel and squeeze out excess liquid. Transfer to a blender and add 1/4 teaspoon of pepper, half a teaspoon of salt, and scallions. Pulse until chopped. Transfer to a bowl. Add mustard and half a cup of the cooked millet. Mix using your hands and form into 8 patties.

3. Heat a tablespoon of oil in a pan over medium flame. Cook the patties until both sides are browned. Transfer to a platter. Add some steamed greens and the remaining millet before serving.

Shirataki Angel Hair Pasta with Avocado Sauce

Yield: 2 servings

Ingredients:

- 2 packs Shirataki Angel Hair Pasta

For the sauce

- 1/2 teaspoon Himalayan pink salt
- 1 teaspoon ground chipotle powder
- 2 tablespoons lime juice

- 1/4 cup extra virgin olive oil
- 2 organic avocados

Directions:

1. Cook the pasta according to package directions.

2. Put all ingredients for the sauce in a blender. Process until smooth and creamy. Adjust the seasonings according to taste.

3. Put the cooked pasta in a bowl, add the sauce, and toss until combined. Top with chopped fresh cilantro and serve while warm.

Chicken Strips with Cilantro Dipping Sauce

Yield: 1 serving

Ingredients:

- 1/4 teaspoon sea salt
- 1/4 cup extra virgin olive oil
- 2 cups cilantro (chopped)

- 1 pastured chicken cutlet (sliced into strips)
- 1 tablespoon avocado oil

Directions:

1. Heat avocado oil in a pan over medium-high flame. Put the meat and sprinkle with salt. Stir for 4 minutes. Transfer to a platter and leave to cool.

2. Put sea salt, olive oil, and cilantro in a blender. Process on a high-speed setting until smooth.

3. Serve warm chicken strips with the dipping sauce on the side.

Cauli Rice with Basil Pesto

Yield: 2 cups

Ingredients:

For the cauliflower rice

- 1/2 teaspoon organic ground black pepper
- 1/2 teaspoon Himalayan pink salt
- 2 cloves organic garlic (freshly crushed)

For the basil pesto

- 1/2 teaspoon Himalayan pink salt
- 2 tablespoons lemon juice
- 1/4 cup extra virgin olive oil
- 1/4 cup nutritional yeast

- 1 tablespoon organic extra-virgin olive oil
- 1/2 cup organic red onions (diced)
- 4 cups organic cauliflower rice

- 1/2 cup walnuts
- 4 cups fresh basil
- 1/4 teaspoon ground black pepper

Directions:

1. Put all ingredients for the basil pesto in a blender. Process until combined and thick. Adjust seasonings according to taste.

2. Put all ingredients for the cauliflower rice in a pan over medium-high flame. Saute until cooked. Stir in the pesto mixture. Season with salt and pepper. Transfer to bowls and serve while warm.

Veggie-Filled Fettuccine Alfredo

Yield: 4 to 6 servings

Ingredients:

- 1/2 teaspoon Italian seasoning
- 1/4 cup Parmesan cheese (grated)
- 1 bunch thin asparagus (trimmed)
- 1/4 cup extra virgin olive oil, plus more for tossing
- Sea salt and black pepper

- 1/2 lemon (zested)
- 1/2 cup basil leaves or fresh Italian parsley (chopped)
- 1 cup mascarpone cheese
- 5 ounces shiitake mushrooms (sliced)
- 4 servings grain-free fettuccine pasta

Directions:

1. Cook pasta. Reserve a cup of the cooking liquid and strain pasta in a colander. Add some extra virgin olive oil and toss.

2. Heat a couple of tablespoons of olive oil in a pan over medium flame. Put the mushrooms, turn the heat to medium-high, and leave for 2 minutes. Stir and cook for 2 more minutes. Add the rest of olive oil, half a teaspoon of salt, and asparagus. Cook for 3 minutes while stirring often. Remove from the stove. Add the cooked noodles and mascarpone cheese. Toss until combined. Gradually add the reserved cooking liquid until you have achieved

the desired consistency for the sauce. Add lemon zest, Italian seasoning, herbs, and pecorino. Gently stir until combined.

3. Transfer to a platter. Season with salt and pepper and serve at once.

Baked Okra Bites

Yield: 2 to 4 servings

Ingredients:

- 2 tablespoons avocado oil (100 percent pure)
- 12 organic okra pods (sliced)

For the bread crumbs:

- 1/4 teaspoon Himalayan pink salt
- 1/4 teaspoon ground cayenne pepper
- 1/4 teaspoon ground garlic powder
- 1/4 cup nutritional yeast
- 1/4 cup almond flour

Directions:

1. Put all ingredients for the bread crumbs in a bowl and mix until combined.

2. Put the okra slices in another bowl along with a tablespoon of avocado oil. Toss until combined. Add half of the bread crumb mixture. Gently toss to coat. Add the rest of the avocado oil and bread crumb mixture. Gently toss to coat.

3. Arrange the coated okra slices in a pan lined with parchment paper. Bake in a preheated oven at 425 degrees for 12 minutes. Flip the okra pieces and bake for 8 more minutes.

4. Serve at once.

Vegan Fudgy Tarts

Yield: 3 tarts

Ingredients:

For the crust

- 1 pinch Himalayan pink salt
- 1 tablespoon organic coconut oil

For the filling

- 1 pinch Himalayan pink salt
- 1/4 cup raw cacao powder

- 1 cup organic medjool dates (pitted)
- 1 cup organic walnuts

- 1/2 cup date nectar
- 1/2 cup coconut oil

- 1/2 cup almond butter

Directions:

1. Put all ingredients for the crust in a food processor. Process until crumbly and wet. Divide the crust mixture into 3 tart molds. Use your finger of the back of a spoon to press the mixture at the bottom and sides of each mold. Set aside.

2. Put all ingredients for the filling in a bowl and whisk until smooth. Scoop filling into the molds. Refrigerate for 2 hours until firm.

3. Remove tarts from the molds and serve immediately.

Baked Sweet Potato Toast

Yield: 4 to 6 slices

Ingredients:

For the toast

- 1 to 2 teaspoons avocado oil (100 percent pure)
- 1 large sweet potato

For the guacamole

- 1/4 teaspoon Himalayan pink salt
- 1 to 2 pinches black ground pepper
- 1 teaspoon freshly squeezed lime juice
- 1 organic jalapeno (diced)

- 2 garlic cloves (crushed)
- 1 tablespoon chopped cilantro
- 1 tablespoon diced red onion
- 2 avocados

Directions:

1. Chop off the ends of the sweet potato. Slice into 1/4-inch thickness and put in a tray lined with parchment paper. Brush the sweet potato slices with a bit of avocado oil. Bake in a preheated oven at 350 degrees for 25 minutes. Flip the potato slices and bake for 20 more minutes.

2. Put all ingredients for the guacamole in a bowl. Mash until combined. Add seasonings according to taste.

3. Put the sweet potato toast on a plate, top with guacamole sauce, and serve.

Walnut Fudge

Yield: 8 bars

Ingredients:

- 1/4 cup date nectar
- 1 teaspoon vanilla bean powder
- 1/4 cup chopped walnuts
- 1/4 cup almond butter
- 1/4 cup raw cacao powder
- 1 cup melted coconut oil

Directions:

1. Put all ingredients in a bowl and mix until smooth. Transfer to a bread pan and spread evenly all over. Freeze for an hour or until ready to serve.

2. Slice and serve.

Tasty Gingerbread in a Mug

Yield: 1 serving

Ingredients:

- 1 egg (lightly beaten)
- 1/2 tablespoon water
- 1/2 teaspoon apple cider vinegar
- 2 teaspoons Erythritol syrup (maple-flavored)
- 1/2 teaspoon baking powder
- 1/4 teaspoon cinnamon
- 1/2 teaspoon ground ginger
- 1 tablespoon cassava flour
- 1 tablespoon coconut flour
- 1 tablespoon butter (room temperature)
- Nutmeg, cloves, and allspice to taste

Directions:

1. Put the flours, butter, baking powder, allspice, cinnamon, and ginger in a heat-proof mug. Mix well. Add egg, cider vinegar, and syrup. Beat until combined. Scrape the sides and bottom of the mug. Continue mixing until the batter is smooth.

2. Microwave for 1 1/2 minutes. Add cinnamon and butter on top before serving.

Ravioli with Basil Pesto

Yield: 10 ravioli

Ingredients:

For serving

- 5 ounces mixed salad greens
- Balsamic vinegar and olive oil

For the ravioli

- 2 large pastured eggs (beaten with a teaspoon of water)

- 5 square coconut wraps

- 1/4 cup Parmesan cheese (grated)

For the basil pesto

- 1/2 cup extra virgin olive oil

- 2 garlic cloves

- 1 ounce crumbled Parmesan cheese

- 1/4 cup mascarpone cheese

- 1 10-ounce package frozen spinach (thawed, squeezed dry, and chopped)

- 4 tablespoons extra virgin olive oil (divided)

- 1/4 cup pine nuts

- 2 cups packed fresh basil

Directions:

1. Heat 2 tablespoons of oil in a pan over medium-high flame. Put the spinach and leave to cook for a couple of minutes. Transfer to a bowl. Add Parmesan cheese and mascarpone cheese. Gently stir until combined.

2. Spread 2 1/2 wraps on a chopping board. Brush them with the egg and water mixture. Put 1 tablespoon of the cheese and spinach mixture in each corner of the wrap. Brush another wrap with the egg mixture, put on top of the filling as you press and seal the ends. Slice to make ravioli squares. Cover with a clean cloth and leave to rest.

3. Put all ingredients for the basil pesto in a blender. Process until smooth.

4. Heat 2 tablespoons of olive oil in a pan over medium flame. Fry the ravioli in batches for around 3 minutes.

5. Arrange salad greens on a platter. Add the fried ravioli and pesto. Drizzle with balsamic vinegar before serving.

The Lectin Free Recipes: Soup and Appetizer

Mint and Berry Soup

Yield: 1 to 2 servings

Ingredients:

For the sweetener

- 1/4 cup Xylitol (non-GMO)

- 1/4 cup filtered water

For the soup

- 8 fresh mint leaves

- 1 teaspoon freshly squeezed lemon juice

- 1/2 cup filtered water

- 1 cup frozen mixed berries (blackberries, blueberries, raspberries)

Directions:

1. Heat water in a pan over low heat. Add sugar and stir until dissolved. Turn off the heat and leave to cool.

2. Pour the sweetener mixture on a blender and add all ingredients for the soup. Process until combined. Strain mixture to remove the seeds. Reserve seeds for a smoothie recipe.

3. Transfer soup to a bowl. Refrigerate for at least 30 minutes before serving.

Spiced Cauliflower Rice Soup

Yield: 4 cups

Ingredients:

- 1 13.5-ounce can full-fat coconut milk
- 1/2 teaspoon ground black pepper
- 1 teaspoon Himalayan pink salt
- 1 teaspoon dried rosemary
- 2 teaspoons pumpkin spice
- 2 tablespoons extra virgin olive oil
- 1 garlic clove (crushed)
- 1/2 cup diced red onion
- 4 cups cauliflower rice

Directions:

1. Heat oil in a pan over medium flame. Add garlic, onions, rosemary, salt, and pepper. Saute for 3 minutes. Add the pumpkin spice, coconut milk, and cauliflower rice. Mix well. Add more seasonings according to taste. Turn the heat to medium-low and simmer until cooked.

2. Transfer to a bowl. Sprinkle with a bit of pepper and dried rosemary and serve while hot.

Swiss Chard Fritters

Yield: 4 servings

Ingredients:

- 1/2 cup cassava flour
- 2 ounces goat cheese (crumbled)
- Sea salt and black pepper to taste
- 1/2 teaspoon ground cumin
- 3 garlic cloves (chopped)
- 1 bunch of Swiss chard (stemmed and torn into bite-size pieces)
- Sour cream (for serving)
- 4 tablespoons extra virgin olive oil (divided)

Directions:

1. Put Swiss chard, cumin, garlic, 1/4 teaspoon of pepper, and half a teaspoon of salt on a blender. Pulse until combined. Transfer mixture to a bowl. Add flour and goat cheese. Mix until combined.

2. Divide the mixture into 4 and form each into a patty with a 1/4-inch thickness.

3. Heat oil in a pan over medium-high flame. Cook the patties until both sides are browned. Transfer to a plate and serve along with a dollop of sour cream.

Crunchy Kale Chips

Yield: 2 to 4 servings

Ingredients:

- 1/2 teaspoon Himalayan pink salt
- 2 tablespoons nutritional yeast
- 1 tablespoon avocado oil (100 percent pure)
- 10 cups organic kale (stemmed and broken into bite-size pieces)

Directions:

1. Put kale and avocado oil in a bowl. Toss until combined. Sprinkle with salt and nutritional yeast. Use your hands to mix. Add more seasonings if preferred. Transfer to a baking sheet lined with parchment paper and spread them all over. Bake in a preheated oven at 350 degrees for 8 minutes. Flip the pieces and continue baking for 8 more minutes.

Vegan Taco Meat

Yield: 1 1/2 cups

Ingredients:

- 1 teaspoon chili powder
- 1 teaspoon chipotle powder
- 1 teaspoon cumin powder
- 1/2 teaspoon Himalayan pink salt
- 10 teaspoons extra-virgin olive oil
- 2 cups walnuts

Directions:

1. Put all ingredients in a food processor and process until chopped. Put more seasonings if preferred.

2. Use the mixture as filling for taco or wrap or as topping for salad.

Baked Artichokes

Yield: 2 to 4 serving

Ingredients:

- 1 tablespoon avocado oil (100 percent pure)

- 1 can artichoke hearts (drained)

For the seasoning

- 1/2 teaspoon Himalayan pink salt
- 1/2 teaspoon ground cayenne pepper
- 1/2 teaspoon ground garlic

- 1/2 cup nutritional yeast
- 1/2 cup almond flour

Directions:

1. Put all ingredients for the seasoning in a bowl. Mix until combined.

2. Chop off the ends of the artichokes and slice each piece into 2. Tear leaves into smaller pieces. Put in a bowl along with avocado oil and half of the seasoning mixture. Toss until combined.

3. Transfer the seasoned artichokes to a pan lined with parchment paper. Spread them all over and sprinkle with the remaining seasoning mixture. Bake in a preheated oven at 425 degrees for 15 minutes.

4. Serve at once.

Tasty Broccoli Bites

Yield: 3 cups

Ingredients:

- 2 tablespoons avocado oil (100 percent pure)
- 3 cups organic broccoli florets

For the seasoning

- 1/4 teaspoon Himalayan pink salt
- 1/4 teaspoon ground cayenne pepper
- 1/4 teaspoon ground garlic powder

- 1/4 cup nutritional yeast
- 1/4 cup almond flour

Directions:

1. Put all ingredients for the seasoning in a bowl. Mix until combined. Add more seasonings according to taste.

2. Put the broccoli florets and avocado oil in a bowl. Toss until combined. Add half of the seasoning mixture and gently toss to coat. Transfer to a pan lined with parchment paper. Bake in a preheated oven at 400 degrees for 10 minutes. Transfer to a bowl and add the remaining seasoning mixture. Toss to coat. Put back to the pan and bake for 25 more minutes.

Baked Rainbow Fries

Yield: 8 servings

Ingredients:

- 3 tablespoons grainy mustard
- 3/4 cup full-fat sour cream
- Black pepper to taste
- 2 teaspoons sea salt
- 2 teaspoons granulated garlic
- 3 tablespoons extra virgin olive oil
- 2 medium sweet potatoes (peeled and sliced into strips)
- 2 medium yuca roots (peeled and sliced into strips)
- 4 purple carrots (peeled and sliced into strips)

Directions:

1. Put sweet potatoes, yucca roots, carrots, black pepper, salt, and granulated garlic in a bowl. Gently toss to coat.

2. Preheat two baking sheets in an oven at 450 degrees. Divide the seasoned rainbow fries into the 2 baking sheets. Place the sheets at the bottom thirds and top of the oven. Bake for 10 minutes. Toss the fries and continue baking for 10 more minutes.

3. In a small bowl, mix to combine the mustard and sour cream. Season with pepper.

4. Transfer fries in a bowl and serve with the dip.

Vegan Pistachio Fudge Mini Cups

Yield: 24 pieces

Ingredients:

- Sea salt as topping

For the fudge

- 1 teaspoon vanilla bean powder
- 1/4 cup almond butter
- 1/4 cup organic date nectar
- 1/4 cup raw cacao powder
- 1 cup melted coconut oil
- 1 cup chopped pistachios

Directions:

1. Put all ingredients for the fudge in a bowl. Mix well until smooth. Scoop batter into 24 mini muffin cups. Arrange cups on a tray and freeze for 10 minutes.

2. Sprinkle each cup with sea salt. Freeze for an hour before serving.

Baked Cheesy Mushrooms

Yield: 1 to 2 servings

Ingredients:

- 1 cup homemade almond milk

- 2 cups baby bella mushrooms (stemmed and sliced)

For the seasoning

- 1/2 teaspoon Himalayan pink salt

- 1/2 teaspoon ground garlic powder

- 1/2 teaspoon ground cayenne pepper

- 1/2 cup nutritional yeast

- 1/2 cup almond flour

Directions:

1. Put all ingredients for the seasoning in a bowl. Mix until combined. Add more salt, garlic, and pepper if preferred. You can use less of the cayenne pepper if you don't want the mixture to be too spicy.

2. Put half of the seasoning mixture in a bowl and almond milk in another bowl.

3. Soak a cup of mushroom in the bowl of milk. Toss until coated. Use a fork to transfer the mushrooms to the bowl of seasoning mixture. Gently toss to coat. Transfer to a baking tray lined with parchment paper and spread all over. Repeat the same sequence to the rest of the mushrooms.

4. Bake in a preheated oven at 425 degrees for 12 minutes. Remove trays from the oven and flip the mushrooms. Continue baking for 8 more minutes.

5. Serve while hot.

Vegan Pumpkin Spice Crackers

Yield: Up to 35 crackers

Ingredients:

- Sea salt for topping

For the crackers

- 1/8 teaspoon ground garlic powder

- 1/4 teaspoon ground black pepper

- 1/2 teaspoon Himalayan pink salt

- 2 teaspoons pumpkin spice

- 1 flax egg (combination of 1 tablespoon of ground flax and 3 tablespoons of filtered water)

- 1 tablespoon avocado oil (100 percent pure)

- 2 cups almond flour

Directions:

1. Put all ingredients for the crackers in a bowl. Mix until combined.

2. Whisk the flax egg mixture before adding to the bowl with the cracker mixture. Mash using a fork until combined and the mixture is moist and crumbly. Use your hand and form the mixture into a compact ball. Transfer to a baking tray lined with parchment paper. Put another sheet of parchment paper on top. Use a rolling pin to flatten it out with a 1/4-inch thickness. Slice into small squares using a knife or a pizza cutter. Discard the crumbs and sprinkle with sea salt all over.

3. Bake in a preheated oven at 350 degrees for 12 minutes. Flip all the pieces and bake for a minute or two.

Garlic Crackers with Thyme

Yield: 60 small crackers

Ingredients:

- 1 flax egg (combination of 3 tablespoons filtered water and 1 tablespoon ground flax)
- 1/2 teaspoon Himalayan pink salt
- 1/2 teaspoon ground black pepper
- 1/2 teaspoon ground garlic powder
- 1 tablespoon avocado oil (100 percent pure)
- 1 tablespoon freshly chopped thyme
- 2 cups almond flour

Directions:

1. Put all ingredients for the crackers in a bowl. Mix until combined.

2. Whisk the flax egg before adding to the cracker mixture. Mix well. Mash the mixture using a fork until moist and crumbly. Use your hands to shape the mixture into a compact ball. Place it on a tray lined with parchment paper. Put another sheet of parchment paper on top and roll using a rolling pin into 1/4-inch thickness. Cut into small squares using a knife or a pizza cutter.

3. Remove the crumbs and bake in a preheated oven at 350 degrees for 12 minutes. Toss the crackers and bake for 2 more minutes.

Avocado Fries

Yield: 2 to 4 servings

Ingredients:

- 1/2 cup homemade almond milk

For the breadcrumbs

- 1/2 teaspoon Himalayan pink salt
- 1/2 teaspoon ground smoked paprika
- 1/2 teaspoon ground garlic powder
- 1/2 cup nutritional yeast

- 2 firm avocados

- 1/2 cup almond flour
- 1/2 teaspoon ground cayenne pepper (optional if you want the breadcrumbs to be spicy)

Directions:

1. Put all ingredients for the breadcrumbs in a bowl. Mix until combined.

2. Slice the avocados, scoop out the meat from the skin, and slice into strips.

3. Put breadcrumbs in a bowl and non-dairy milk in another bowl. Dip the avocado strips in the bowl of milk and coat with the breadcrumb mixture.

4. Arrange the coated avocado strips in a tray lined with parchment paper. Bake in a preheated oven at 420 degrees for 10 minutes. Toss the fries and continue baking for 5 minutes or until golden brown.

5. Serve immediately.

Tasty Apple Chips

Yield: Up to 60 chips

Ingredients:

- 4 small apples (rinse and thinly slice)
- For the cinnamon mixture
- 1 teaspoon ground cinnamon

- 1 tablespoon vanilla bean powder
- 1/4 cup Xylitol (non-GMO)

Directions:

1. Put all ingredients for the cinnamon mixture in a bowl. Mix until combined.

2. Dehydrate the apple chips. Sprinkle cinnamon to both sides of an apple slice you're holding. Put in on the mesh tray of a dehydrator. Repeat the sequence until you're done with all the apple slices. Dehydrate for around 18 hours at 115 degrees.

3. Store chips in an airtight container.

The Lectin Free Recipes: Beverage and Dessert

Mint and Berry Spa Water

Yield: 1 serving

Ingredients:

- 2 fresh mint leaves
- 1/4 cup raspberries
- 1/4 cup blackberries
- 1/4 cup blueberries
- 12 ounces filtered water

Directions:

1. Put all ingredients in a glass container, cover and refrigerate overnight.

Apple and Carrot Juice

Yield: 1 serving

Ingredients:

- 1/2 lemon
- 2 stalks celery
- 1 apple
- 4 carrots

Directions:

1. Rinse and chop the vegetables. Process them in a juicer according to package instructions. Transfer to a glass. Squeeze lemon juice and stir until combined.

Celery Juice with Beet

Yield: 1 serving

Ingredients:

- 1/2 lemon
- 7 celery stalks
- 1 beet

Directions:

1. Put all ingredients in a juicer and process according to package instructions. Transfer to a glass and serve.

Hemp Protein Smoothie with Banana

Yield: 1 serving

Ingredients:

- 3 tablespoons hemp protein powder
- 1 banana
- 1 teaspoon maca powder

- 1 tablespoon spirulina powder
- 1 1/2 cups homemade almond milk

Directions:

1. Put all ingredients in a blender. Process until combined and smooth. Transfer to a glass and serve.

Vanilla Cake in a Mug

Yield: 1 serving

Ingredients:

- 1 large pastured egg (beaten)
- 1 pinch sea salt
- 1/2 teaspoon vanilla
- 1/2 teaspoon baking powder
- 1 tablespoon dark chocolate chips or seasonal fruit (optional)

- 2 teaspoons granular monk fruit sweetener
- 1 tablespoon tigernut flour
- 1 tablespoon coconut flour
- 2 tablespoons extra virgin olive oil

Directions:

1. Put tigernut flour, coconut flour, salt, baking powder, sweetener, vanilla, and oil in a heatproof mug. Mix until combined. Add egg and mix until smooth. Scrape the bottom and sides of the mug as needed. Fold in chocolate chips or chopped fruit. Microwave for a minute and 30 seconds.

2. Leave to cool, unmold, and transfer to a plate. Top with butter and serve.

Almond Balls with Cacao

Yield: 14 balls

Ingredients:

- 1/4 cup raw cacao powder
- 1/2 teaspoon vanilla bean powder
- 1 tablespoon organic date nectar
- 2 tablespoons maca powder

- 2 tablespoons hemp oil
- 1/4 cup almond flour
- 1/2 cup almond butter
- 1 cup raw almonds

Directions:

1. Put all ingredients in a food processor. Process until the consistency becomes similar to a thick paste. Adjust sweetness according to taste.

2. Spoon a mixture into your palm, roll, and shape into a ball. Repeat the process until you're done with the remaining batter. Arrange the balls on a tray. Refrigerate for at least 30 minutes before serving.

Delish Apple Pie Tart

Yield: 4 pie tarts

Ingredients:

For the crust

- 2 pinches Himalayan pink salt
- 1 teaspoon vanilla bean powder
- 4 tablespoons coconut oil

- 1 cup Medjool dates (pitted)
- 1 cup walnuts

For the filling

- 1 pinch Himalayan pink salt
- 1/8 teaspoon vanilla bean powder
- 1/4 teaspoon ground cinnamon
- 1 teaspoon lemon juice

- 2 teaspoons coconut oil
- 1 cup Medjool dates (pitted)
- 4 small red apples

Directions:

1. Put all ingredients for the crust in a food processor. Process until crumbly and sticky. Divide mixture into 4 tart dishes. Use your fingers to press the crust to the sides and bottom parts of the tart dishes.

2. Put all ingredients for the filling in a food processor. Pulse until diced. Spoon filling into each tart dish. Refrigerate for at least 30 minutes before serving.

Strawberry Shortcake

Yield: 8 servings

Ingredients:

For the topping

- 1 quart fresh strawberries (hulled and chopped)
- 1/2 teaspoon vanilla extract

- 1 tablespoon raw honey
- 1 cup grass-fed heavy cream

For the cake

- 3/4 teaspoon baking soda
- 1/2 teaspoon fine sea salt
- 3 tablespoons arrowroot starch
- 3 large pastured eggs
- 1/4 cup golden monk fruit sweetener
- 8 tablespoons unsalted butter (softened)
- 1/3 cup tigernut flour
- 1/3 cup coconut flour
- 1/2 teaspoon vanilla extract
- 1/2 lemon (grated zest)
- 1/2 cup coconut cream (whisked)

Directions:

1. Put butter and sweetener in a bowl. Mix using an electric mixer on a high-speed setting until fluffy. Turn the speed to medium and mix as you add eggs one at a time. Add vanilla, lemon zest, and coconut cream. Scrape the sides of the bowl as needed.

2. In another bowl, sift to combine the baking soda, sea salt, arrowroot starch, tigernut flour, and coconut flour. Gradually add this to the butter and egg mixture as you continue on mixing on a low-speed setting. Mix until smooth.

3. Transfer batter to a greased cake pan. Use a spatula to smoothen the top. Gently tap the pan on the counter to remove excess air. Bake in a preheated oven at 350 degrees for 35 minutes.

4. Leave on a wire rack to cool for half an hour.

5. Put cream, vanilla, and honey in a bowl. Mix using an electric mixer on a high-speed setting. Mix until soft peaks form.

6. Unmold the cake and transfer to a plate. Add the icing and spread all over. Top with sliced strawberries. Slice and serve.

Choco-Creamy Pudding

Yield: 3 cups

Ingredients:

- 1/2 cup organic date nectar
- 1 13.5-ounce can organic full-fat coconut milk
- 1 teaspoon vanilla bean powder
- 1/4 cup raw cacao powder
- 4 avocados (pitted)

Directions:

1. Refrigerate the can of coconut milk the night before you prepare the recipe.

2. Scoop out the coconut fat from the can and reserve the liquid for another recipe. Transfer the coconut fat to a blender. Add the rest of the ingredients and process until smooth.

3. Transfer to a bowl and serve at once.

Pecan Pie Bites

Yield: 8 small bites

Ingredients:

- 1/2 teaspoon vanilla bean powder
- 1 cup pecans
- 8 Medjool dates (pitted)

Directions:

1. Put all ingredients in a food processor. Process until sticky and crumbly.

2. Spoon a mixture into your palm. Squeeze to make it compact and roll into a ball. Repeat the sequence until you're done with the rest of the mixture.

3. Arrange balls on a plate. Refrigerate for at least 15 minutes before serving.

Strawberry Mousse

Yield: 1 to 2 servings

Ingredients:

- 2 tablespoons Xylitol (non-GMO)
- 3 tablespoons freeze-dried strawberries
- 1 13.5-ounce can organic full-fat coconut milk

Directions:

1. Refrigerate the can of coconut milk overnight. Scoop out the hardened fat and put in a bowl. Reserve the liquid part for a smoothie recipe.

2. Add freeze-dried strawberries and Xylitol to the coconut fat. Mix on a high speed until thick and fluffy.

3. Serve at once.

Made in the USA
San Bernardino, CA
18 April 2019